SOA in Practice

Other resources from O'Reilly

Related titles	Beautiful Code	Programming Web Services with Perl
	Packaged Composite Applications	Real World Web Services
	Prefactoring	RESTful Web Services
	Programming .NET Web Services	Security and Usability
		The Art of Project Management

oreilly.com *oreilly.com* is more than a complete catalog of O'Reilly books. You'll also find links to news, events, articles, weblogs, sample chapters, and code examples.

 *oreillynet.com* is the essential portal for developers interested in open and emerging technologies, including new platforms, programming languages, and operating systems.

Conferences O'Reilly brings diverse innovators together to nurture the ideas that spark revolutionary industries. We specialize in documenting the latest tools and systems, translating the innovator's knowledge into useful skills for those in the trenches. Visit *conferences.oreilly.com* for our upcoming events.

 Safari Bookshelf (*safari.oreilly.com*) is the premier online reference library for programmers and IT professionals. Conduct searches across more than 1,000 books. Subscribers can zero in on answers to time-critical questions in a matter of seconds. Read the books on your Bookshelf from cover to cover or simply flip to the page you need. Try it today for free.

SOA in Practice

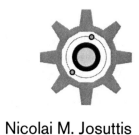

Nicolai M. Josuttis

O'REILLY®

Beijing • Cambridge • Farnham • Köln • Sebastopol • Tokyo

SOA in Practice
by Nicolai M. Josuttis

Copyright © 2007 Nicolai M. Josuttis. All rights reserved. Printed in the United States of America.

Published by O'Reilly Media, Inc. 1005 Gravenstein Highway North, Sebastopol, CA 95472

O'Reilly books may be purchased for educational, business, or sales promotional use. Online editions are also available for most titles (*safari.oreilly.com*). For more information, contact our corporate/institutional sales department: (800) 998-9938 or *corporate@oreilly.com*.

Editor: Simon St.Laurent	**Indexer:** Tolman Creek Design
Production Editor: Sumita Mukherji	**Cover Designer:** Mike Kohnke
Copyeditor: Rachel Head	**Interior Designer:** Marcia Friedman
Proofreader: Nancy Reinhardt	**Illustrator:** Jessamyn Read

Printing History:

      August 2007:   First Edition.

ISBN: 978-0-596-52955-0

[LSI]   [2011-02-25]

CONTENTS

Preface

INEVER PLANNED TO BECOME A **SOA** EXPERT. **I** WAS A TEAM LEADER IN A DEPARTMENT WHICH WAS instructed to use the new service-oriented architecture approach to communicate with the systems of other departments and business units. A cross-departmental SOA team had provided a SOA concept, including thousand of pages of documentation, several frameworks and libraries, and some sketches of corresponding processes. All we, as a business unit—which had its own IT—had to do was use these solutions to establish SOA.

Once we began the project, things turned out to work less smoothly than we had expected. While dealing with the SOA approach, I not only learned what SOA is, but also learned about the differences between theory and practice, which Laurence Peter "Yogi" Berra perfectly describes as follows:

> In theory, theory and practice are the same. In practice, they are not.

In fact, I complained so much about what was provided by the central SOA team that finally I was given the task of cleaning it up. My brief was to ensure that my manager wouldn't hear any more complaints about SOA from the business units.

So, we fixed misconceptions and broken processes, automated manual efforts, influenced strategic decisions, provided support, and (last but not least) taught others about the concepts and ideas behind SOA, and about the reasons and motivations for our specific architectural decisions and policies.

These days, the SOA landscape we built provides support for processes distributed between many local, national, and international systems. With hundreds of services, the systems support millions of service calls each day.

Drawing on this experience, and my observations of SOA approaches and projects at many other companies (in very different stages of expansion), I started to give SOA consultations, reviews, talks, and training sessions. Along the way, I've become well acquainted with the different flavors of SOA, and different ways to deal with it. In addition, I've learned about all the questions that must be answered, and about the best way to teach SOA.

I'm still learning every day, but I believe the knowledge I've gained so far can help you find an appropriate and successful way to establish SOA and deal with its properties in practice.

SOA has become a major paradigm, and it now means different things to different people. I will concentrate on SOA as a strategy to provide and support distributed business processing. In this sense, SOA is a strategy that, although it might be driven by IT, always impacts the business as a whole.

This book will present concepts, but with a focus on their practical application. This is one reason why this book fits perfectly into O'Reilly's "Theory in Practice" series.

What You Should Know Before Reading This Book

As a reader of this book, you should have a common understanding of computer science and programming. Experience with large and distributed systems will help, but it is not required because this book covers all these concepts (from a SOA point of view).

Structure of the Book

The book is designed to be read sequentially, from beginning to end. We'll begin with general SOA concepts, then move on to more advanced topics. Cross-references will help you find explanations and further details contained in other chapters and sections, and the index should help you find information and discussions regarding specific topics and terms.

The first half of the book covers the basics:

Chapter 1, *Motivation*

This chapter explores why you want to use SOA in the context of large distributed systems, explores how SOA emerged, tells the tale of the Magic Bus, and gives a brief overview of SOA.

Chapter 2, *SOA*

This chapter examines and consolidates the different definitions of SOA and its major properties.

Chapter 3, *Services*

This chapter examines and consolidates definitions of the many services involved in SOA.

Chapter 4, *Loose Coupling*

This chapter introduces and discusses loose coupling, a key concept in SOA and building large distributed systems generally.

Chapter 5, *The Enterprise Service Bus*

This chapter takes a look at the enterprise service bus (ESB), the infrastructure foundation for high interoperability in a SOA landscape.

Chapter 6, *Service Classification*

This chapter shows how to categorize services so that you can deal with different service classes, service layers, and stages of SOA expansion.

Chapter 7, *Business Process Management*

This chapter introduces business process management (BPM) as an approach for identifying services as part of business processes. It includes orchestration, Business Process Execution Language (BPEL), portfolio management, and choreography.

Chapter 8, *SOA and the Organization*

This chapter discusses the impacts SOA strategies have on organizations and companies.

Chapter 9, *SOA in Context*

This chapter explores how SOA fits with other architectures and approaches, and how to deal with the various levels of processing at different parts of a business.

The second half of the book discusses specific aspects of introducing and running SOA. Although the topics are presented in a logical order, I have tried to write these chapters in such a way that you can read them in any order, provided you understand the fundamental concepts and terminology:

Chapter 10, *Message Exchange Patterns*

This chapter introduces and discusses message exchange patterns (MEPs). MEPs define the sequence of messages in a service call or operation. One of these patterns will lead to events and event-driven architectures (EDA).

Chapter 11, *Service Lifecycle*

This chapter follows the lifecycle of services, from needs identification to implementation, and from running to withdrawing.

Chapter 12, *Versioning*

This chapter discusses the thorny question of version services, including versioning of associated data types.

Chapter 13, *SOA and Performance*

This chapter discusses how performance, especially running time, affects the design and reusability of services.

Chapter 14, *SOA and Security*

This chapter presents security issues in SOA implementations and how to address them.

Chapter 15, *Technical Details*

This chapter explores some key details of SOA, including statefulness, idempotency, testing and debugging, and fundamental data types.

Chapter 16, *Web Services*

This chapter examines Web Services and their position as a de facto standard for SOA infrastructure. It presents the most important Web Services standards, and what their application means in practice.

Chapter 17, *Service Management*

This chapter discusses using repositories and registries to manage services.

Chapter 18, *Model-Driven Service Development*

This chapter describes the consequences of specifying services as models, and generating code from those models.

Chapter 19, *Establishing SOA and SOA Governance*

This chapter examines how SOA might or should be established in an organization, and explores its governance moving forward.

Chapter 20, *Epilogue*

This conclusion finally discusses some major questions about SOA, including whether it is really new, where its use is appropriate, and whether it increases or reduces complexity.

The book concludes with a bibliography (including all referenced resources you can find on the Internet), a glossary of fundamental SOA terms, and an index.

Conventions Used in This Book

The following typographical conventions are used in this book:

Italic

Used for emphasis, new terms where they are defined, URLs, and email addresses.

Constant width

Indicates commands, code examples, parameters, values, objects, service names, XML tags, the contents of files, or the output from commands.

Constant width bold

Used to highlight portions of code.

Constant width italic

Shows text that should be replaced with user-supplied values.

Additional Information

You can acquire more information about this book and SOA in general from my web site:

http://www.soa-in-practice.com

As a convenience, the references and resources used in this book are listed on the site so that you can directly navigate to these resources, and so that any updates are integrated (web sites are typically much more volatile than books).

In addition, the web site includes a maintained SOA glossary, code examples, and supplementary information about SOA.

The publisher also has a web page for this book, which lists errata, examples, and additional information. You can access this page at:

http://www.oreilly.com/catalog/9780596529550/

Safari® Books Online

When you see a Safari® Books Online icon on the cover of your favorite technology book, that means the book is available online through the O'Reilly Network Safari Bookshelf.

Safari offers a solution that's better than e-books. It's a virtual library that lets you easily search thousands of top tech books, cut and paste code samples, download chapters, and find quick answers when you need the most accurate, current information. Try it for free at *http://safari.oreilly.com*.

Feedback, Comments, and Questions

I welcome your feedback and constructive input—both the negative and the positive. I've tried to prepare the book carefully; however, I'm human, and at some point I had to stop writing, reviewing, and tweaking so that I could "release the product." You might, therefore, find errors, inconsistencies, discussions that could be improved, or even topics that are missing altogether. Your feedback will give me the chance to keep all readers informed through the book's web site, and to improve any subsequent editions.

The best way to reach me is by email. However, due to the spam problem, I don't want to include an email address inside this book (I had to stop using the email address I put in one of my C++ books after I started getting thousands of spam emails per day). Please refer to the book's web site, *http://www.soa-in-practice.com*, to request an actual email address.

Alternatively, you can use the publisher's email address, mentioned below. You can also check the book's web site for currently known errata before submitting reports.

Comments and questions concerning this book can also be addressed directly to the publisher:

O'Reilly Media, Inc.
1005 Gravenstein Highway North
Sebastopol, CA 95472
800-998-9938 (in the United States or Canada)
707-829-0515 (international or local)
707-829-0104 (fax)

To comment or ask technical questions about this book, you can send email to:

bookquestions@oreilly.com

For more information about O'Reilly's books, conferences, Resource Centers, and the O'Reilly Network, see the web site at:

http://www.oreilly.com

Acknowledgments

Writing a book is a process that takes many years and involves many different people. I can't thank them all personally. However, I want to thank some people who deserve special credit for this book.

First, I'd like to thank all the reviewers of this book. They did an incredible job, giving me feedback on early versions of the book that contained errors and were hard to understand. Thanks to Mirko Drobietz, Gudrun Dürr, Thomas George, Jochen Hiller, Gregor Hohpe, Alan Lenton, Christian Möllenberg, Bruce Sams, Steffen Schäfer, Hermann Schlamann, Markus Völter, and Torsten Winterberg.

Second, I want to thank my editors at O'Reilly for giving me the ability to publish this book and for all their support. Thanks to Simon St.Laurent, Mike Hendrickson, Mary O'Brien, Tatiana Apandi, Caitrin McCullough, Nancy Reinhardt, Sumita Mukherji, and Jessamyn Read. A special thanks goes to Rachel Head, who did an incredible job transforming my "German English" into "American English."

Third, I want to thank all the people who helped me learn and understand the subject of SOA in real projects and by the help of books, articles, talks, private conversations, and so on. Whenever some key information is a quote from a certain person, book, or resource, I have mentioned this. Please forgive me if I've forgotten anything or anyone.

In addition, I want to thank my kids, who help me to be well grounded and understand what really matters. Thanks to Lucas, Anica, and Frederic.

Last but not least, I thank Jutta Eckstein for the role she has played regarding this book and in my life. Jutta convinced me to go public with my SOA knowledge, gave me incredible support, and makes my life a lot more worth living day by day.

Enjoy your life.

—*Nicolai M. Josuttis*
Braunschweig, July 2007

CHAPTER ONE

Motivation

WE LIVE IN HARD TIMES. THE SOCIAL MARKET ECONOMY IS BEING REPLACED BY A GLOBAL MARKET economy, and the marketing guys rule the world. As a consequence, you have to be fast and flexible to survive. It's a renaissance of Darwinism:

> It is not the strongest of the species that survive, nor the most intelligent, but the ones most responsive to change.

The key is flexibility. For all major companies and large distributed systems, information technology (IT) flexibility is paramount. In fact, IT has become a key business value enabler.

At the same time, processes and systems are also becoming more and more complex. We have left the stage where automation was primarily a matter of individual systems, and are fast moving toward a world where all those individual systems will become *one* distributed system. The challenge is maintainability.

It turns out that the old ways of dealing with the problems of scalability and distribution don't work anymore. We can no longer harmonize or maintain control. Centralization, the precondition for harmonization and control, does not scale, and we have reached its limits. For this reason, we need a new approach—an approach that accepts heterogeneity and leads to decentralization.

In addition, we have to solve the problem of the business/IT gap. This gap is primarily one of semantics—business people and IT people appear to speak and think in entirely different languages. The new approach must bring business and IT much closer than ever before.

Service-oriented architecture (SOA) is exactly what's needed. It's an approach that helps systems remain scalable and flexible while growing, and that also helps bridge the business/IT gap. The approach consists of three major elements:

- *Services*, which on the one hand represent self-contained business functionalities that can be part of one or more processes, and on the other hand, can be implemented by any technology on any platform.
- A specific *infrastructure*, called the enterprise service bus (ESB), that allows us to combine these services in an easy and flexible manner.
- *Policies and processes* that deal with the fact that large distributed systems are heterogeneous, under maintenance, and have different owners.

SOA accepts that the only way to maintain flexibility in large distributed systems is to support heterogeneity, decentralization, and fault tolerance.

Sounds like a dream, doesn't it?

The problem is that you can't just buy SOA; you have to understand it and live it. SOA is a paradigm. SOA is a way of thinking. SOA is a value system for architecture and design.

This book will explain the paradigm and value system of SOA, drawing on real experiences. SOA is often explained with brief statements and prototypes, which leads to a problem illustrated by the infamous "hockey stick function" (see Figure 1-1).* Up to a certain level of complexity, the amount of effort required is low, and things look fine. But when this level of complexity is exceeded, the amount of effort required suddenly begins to rise faster than the benefit you gain, and finally, things collapse.

Too often, SOA is only partly explained and installed. Just introducing an infrastructure like Web Services might help up to a certain level of complexity, but this is not enough to guarantee scalability. The whole architecture, dealing with services, infrastructure, policies, and processes, must match. Once you understand how to implement SOA, it's not hard, but it takes time and courage. (OK, so it *is* hard.) And a lot of effort is required to help people understand (beginning with yourself). If you're not willing to put in the effort, you will fail.

Before we get into the details, I'd like to provide a foundation for the rest of this book by talking about the context and history of SOA. The following sections will present some of the "tales and mystery" of SOA to help you get familiar with SOA.

---

* Thanks to Gregor Hohpe, who told me about the "hockey stick function" at OOP 2006.

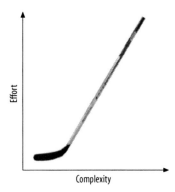

Effort

Complexity

FIGURE 1-1. The hockey stick function

1.1 Characteristics of Large Distributed Systems

SOA is a concept for large distributed systems. To understand SOA, you have to understand the properties of large distributed systems.

First, large systems must deal with *legacies*. You can't introduce SOA by designing everything from scratch. You have to deal with the fact that most of the systems that are in use will remain in use. This also means that establishing SOA is not a project like designing a new system. It involves changing the structure of an existing system, which means you have to deal with old platforms and backward-compatibility issues. In fact, SOA is an approach for the *maintenance* of large system landscapes.

By nature, all large systems are also *heterogeneous*. These systems have different purposes, times of implementation, and ages, and you will find that the system landscapes are accretions of different platforms, programming languages, programming paradigms, and even middleware. In the past, there have been many attempts to solve the problems of scalability by harmonization. And, yes, harmonization helps. Withdrawing old platforms or systems that are no longer maintainable is an important improvement. But chances are that your systems will never be fully harmonized. Right before you remove the last piece of heterogeneity, a company merger, or some other change will open Pandora's box again.

One reason for the heterogeneity is that large systems and their data have an incredibly *long lifetime*. During this lifetime, new functionality that promotes the business is developed by adding new systems and processes. Removing existing systems and data may seem to have no business value, but such changes are investments in the maintainability of your system. Often, these investments come too late, and become incredibly expensive because the systems are out of control, and all the knowledge about them is gone.

By nature, large systems are *complex*. For this reason, finding out the right places for and determining the effects of modifications can be tough. As [Spanyi03] states:

> There is no such thing as a "quick fix…". Organizations are complex business systems, within which a change in any one component is likely to have an impact on other components.

Large distributed systems also have an important additional property: *different owners*. Different teams, departments, divisions, or companies may maintain the systems, and that means different budgets, schedules, views, and interests must be taken into account. Independent from formal structures, you are usually not in a situation where you have enough power and control to command the overall system design and behavior. Negotiation and collaboration are required, which can be problematic due to political intrigue.

Another key characteristic of large systems is *imperfection*. Perfectionism is just too expensive. Or, as Winston Churchill once said:

> Perfectionism spells P-A-R-A-L-Y-S-I-S.

Working systems usually behave a bit sloppily. They may do 99 percent of their work well, but run into trouble with the remaining 1 percent, which usually results in additional manual effort, the need for problem management, or angry customers. Note that the amount of imperfection differs (vitally important systems usually have a higher ratio of perfection, but even for them, there is always a point at which eliminating a risk is not worth the effort).

Similarly, large systems always have a certain amount of *redundancy*. While some redundancy might be accidental, there will also be a significant amount of intentional and "managed" redundancy, because in practice, it is just not possible to have all data normalized so that it is stored in only one place. Eliminating redundancy is difficult, and incurs fundamental runtime penalties. In a simple form of redundancy, at least the master of the data is clear (all redundant data is derived from it). In complex scenarios, there are multiple masters, and/or the master is not clearly defined. Maintaining consistency can thus become very complicated in real-world scenarios.

Finally, for large systems, *bottlenecks are suicide*. That does not mean that they do not exist, but in general, it is a goal to avoid bottlenecks, and to be able to scale. Note that I don't only mean technical bottlenecks. In large systems, bottlenecks also hinder scalability when they are part of a process or the organizational structure.

1.2 The Tale of the Magic Bus

Once upon a time, there was a company that had grown over years and years. Over the course of those years, the system landscape became infected with a disease called "mess." As a consequence, the people lost control over their system, and whenever they tried to improve it, either the effort required proved too high, or they made things even worse.

The company asked several experts, sages, and wizards for help, and they came up with a lot of ideas introducing new patterns, protocols, and system designs. But as a consequence, things only got worse and worse, so the company became desperate.

One day, a prince called Enterprise Integrate came along, and claimed that he had the solution. He told the CEO of the company, "Your problem is your lack of interoperability. When you have such a mess of systems and protocols, it is a problem that you have to create an individual solution for each kind of connection. Even if you only had 10 different platforms and 5 different protocols, if you wanted to enable each platform to communicate with each other platform, you would need over 100 different solutions. And you have many more than 10 platforms." The exact way this number was arrived at was not passed on, but some sketches of the processing led to the conclusion that each possible connection of two platforms was combined with the average number of used protocols.

"Look at my drawing," the prince continued (it's reproduced here in Figure 1-2). "This is how your problem gets solved. We create a *Magic Bus*."

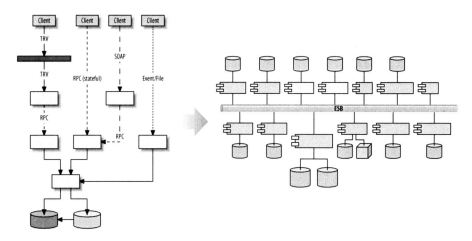

FIGURE 1-2. The original drawing of the Magic Bus

"What's a Magic Bus?" the CEO asked.

The prince answered, "A Magic Bus is a piece of software that reduces the number of connections and interfaces in your system. While your approach might require up to $n \times (n-1)/2$ connections for n systems (and twice as many interfaces), the Magic Bus requires only one connection and interface for each system. That means that for n systems, the number of interfaces is reduced by a factor of $n-1$ (a factor of 9 for 10 systems, 29 for 30 systems, and 49 for 50 systems)."

Convinced by these numbers, the CEO agreed to switch to this new technique. The praise for it was so strong that all over the country, the bards started to write songs about the Magic Bus. The most famous was written by a band called The Who, who praised the bus with the following words (see [MagicBus] for the complete lyrics of the song):

Magic Bus – It's a bus-age wonder

You might expect an "and they lived happily ever after" now, but the tale doesn't end here. After the company had switched to the Magic Bus, it was indeed very easy to connect systems, and suddenly it became very easy to grow again. So the systems grew and grew and grew...until suddenly, it all broke down.

What happened?

It turned out that with the Magic Bus, nobody could understand the dependencies among the systems any longer. In the past, you could see which systems were connected because each connection was unique, but this was no longer possible. Modifying one system could cause problems in other systems, and it was often a surprise that relationships existed between them at all. In fact, each system depended on each other system. When the risk of modifying anything became too high, the company decided to leave the entire system as it was. But slack means death, so one year later, they were out of business.

Of course, they should have known what was coming. Attentive listeners of The Who's song will hear at the end a clear hint about the danger of the "dust" raised by unstructured dependencies created by the Magic Bus:

> Every day you'll see the dust
> As I drive my baby in my Magic Bus

And the competitors lived happily ever after.

1.3   What We Can Learn from the Tale of the Magic Bus

These days, we often praise the "bus-age wonder."* Although the idea of an IT bus is pretty old, recently, there has been a renaissance of this concept. It started with the introduction of the *enterprise application integration bus* (EAI bus), which was later replaced by the *enterprise service bus* (ESB). This has become so important that there has been a public flame war about who invented the ESB (see [ESB Inventor]).

Buses represent high interoperability. The idea behind them is that instead of creating and maintaining individual communication channels between different systems, each system only has to connect to the bus to be able to connect to all other systems. Of course, this does simplify connectivity, but as the preceding tale revealed, this approach has drawbacks. Connectivity scales to chaos unless structures are imposed. That's why we replaced global variables with procedures, and business object models with modules and components. And it will happen again when we start to deal with services in an unstructured way.

---

* For those who may protest that the lyrics do not contain this phrase, please note that there are multiple versions of this song, and listen to the 7-minute live version.

Thus, your first lesson is that in order for large systems to scale, more than just interoperability is required. You need structures provided by technical and organizational rules and patterns. High interoperability must be accompanied by a well-defined architecture, structures, and processes. If you realize this too late, you may be out of the market.

1.4 History of SOA

Surprisingly, it is hard to find out who coined the term SOA. Roy Schulte at Gartner gave me the exact history in a private conversation in 2007:

> Alexander Pasik, a former analyst at Gartner, coined the term SOA for a class on middleware that he was teaching in 1994. Pasik was working before XML or Web Services were invented, but the basic SOA principles have not changed.
>
> Pasik was driven to create the term SOA because "client/server" had lost its classical meaning. Many in the industry had begun to use "client/server" to mean distributed computing involving a PC and another computer. A desktop "client" PC typically ran user-facing presentation logic, and most of the business logic. The backend "server" computer ran the database management system, stored the data, and sometimes ran some business logic. In this usage, "client" and "server" generally referred to the hardware. The software on the frontend PC sometimes related to the server software in the original sense of client/server, but that was largely irrelevant. To avoid confusion between the new and old meanings of client/server, Pasik stressed "server orientation" as he encouraged developers to design SOA business applications.

> **NOTE**
> Gartner analysts Roy W. Schulte and Yefim V. Natis published the first reports about SOA in 1996. See [Gartner96] and [Gartner03] for details.

The real momentum for SOA was created by Web Services, which, initially driven by Microsoft, reached a broader public in 2000 (see Section 16.1.2 for details about the history of Web Services). To quote [Gartner03]:

> Although Web Services do not necessarily translate to SOA, and not all SOA is based on Web Services, the relationship between the two technology directions is important and they are mutually influential: Web Services momentum will bring SOA to mainstream users, and the best-practice architecture of SOA will help make Web Services initiatives successful.

Soon, other companies and vendors jumped in (including major IT vendors such as IBM, Oracle, HP, SAP, and Sun). There was money to be made by explaining the idea, and by selling new concepts and tools (or rebranded concepts and tools). In addition, the time was right because companies were increasingly seeking to integrate their businesses with other systems, departments, and companies (remember the B2B hype).

Later, analysts began to tout SOA as the key concept for future software. For example, in 2005, Gartner stated in [Gartner05]:

> By 2008, SOA will provide the basis for 80 percent of development projects.

Time will show whether this statement is borne out—it may well be a self-fulfilling prophecy.

However, each major movement creates criticism because people hype and misuse the concept as well as the term. Grady Booch, a father of UML and now an IBM fellow, made this comment about SOA in his blog in March 2006 (see [Booch06]):

> My take on the whole SOA scene is a bit edgier than most that I've seen. Too much of the press about SOA makes it look like it's the best thing since punched cards. SOA will apparently not only transform your organization and make you more agile and innovative, but your teenagers will start talking to you and you'll become a better lover. Or a better shot if your name happens to be Dick. Furthermore, if you follow many of these pitches, it appears that you can do so with hardly any pain: just scrape your existing assets, plant services here, there, and younder [sic], wire them together and suddenly you'll be virtualized, automatized, and servicized.
>
> What rubbish.

Booch is right. The important thing is that SOA is a strategy that requires time and effort. You need some experience to understand what SOA really is about, and where and how it helps. Fortunately, it's been around long enough that some of us do have significant experience with SOA (beyond simple prototypes and vague notions of integrating dozens of systems with hundreds of services).

1.5 SOA in Five Slides

The rest of this book will discuss several aspects of SOA in practice. That means we'll go a bit deeper than the usual "five slides" approach, which presents SOA in such a simple way that everybody wonders what's so complicated and/or important about it.

Still, to give you an initial idea about the essence of what you will learn, here are my five slides introducing SOA. Bear in mind that these five slides give an oversimplified impression. The devil is in the details. Nevertheless, this overview might look a bit different from the usual advertisement for SOA.

1.5.1 Slide 1: SOA

Service-oriented architecture (SOA) is a paradigm for the realization and maintenance of business processes that span large distributed systems. It is based on three major technical concepts: services, interoperability through an enterprise service bus, and loose coupling.

- A *service* is a piece of self-contained business functionality. The functionality might be simple (storing or retrieving customer data), or complex (a business process for a customer's order). Because services concentrate on the business value of an interface, they bridge the business/IT gap.

- An *enterprise service bus* (ESB) is the infrastructure that enables high interoperability between distributed systems for services. It makes it easier to distribute business processes over multiple systems using different platforms and technologies.

- *Loose coupling* is the concept of reducing system dependencies. Because business processes are distributed over multiple backends, it is important to minimize the effects of modifications and failures. Otherwise, modifications become too risky, and system failures might break the overall system landscape. Note, however, that there is a price for loose coupling: complexity. Loosely coupled distributed systems are harder to develop, maintain, and debug.

1.5.2 Slide 2: Policies and Processes

Distributed processing is not a technical detail. Distributed processing changes everything in your company. Introducing new functionality is no longer a matter of assigning a specific department a specific task. It is now a combination of multiple tasks for different systems. These systems and the involved teams have to collaborate.

As a consequence, you need clearly defined roles, policies, and processes. The processes include, but are not limited to, defining a service lifecycle and implementing model-driven service development. In addition, you have to set up several processes for distributed software development.

Setting up the appropriate policies and processes usually takes more time than working out the initial technical details. Remember what Fred Brooks said in 1974 (see [Brooks95]):

> A programming system product costs 9 times as much as a simple program.

A factor of three is added because it's a product (with the software being "run, tested, repaired, and extended by anybody"), and another factor of three is added because it's a system component (effort is introduced by integration and integration tests). The factor increases when many components come into play, which is the case with SOA.

1.5.3 Slide 3: Web Services

Web Services are one possible way of realizing the technical aspects of SOA. (Note, however, that there is more to SOA than its technical aspects!)

But Web Services themselves introduce some problems. First, the standards are not yet mature enough to guarantee interoperability. Second, Web Services inherently are insufficient to achieve the right amount of loose coupling.

As a consequence, you should not expect that using Web Services will solve all your technical problems. You should budget enough resources (time and money) to solve the problems that will remain.

Also, you should not fall into the trap of getting too Web Services-specific. Web Services will not be the final standard for system integration. For this reason, let Web Services come into play only when specific infrastructure aspects matter.

1.5.4 Slide 4: SOA in Practice

> In theory, theory and practice are the same. In practice, they are not.
>
> —L. Berra

Of course, this also applies to SOA. General business cases and concepts might not work as well as expected when factors such as performance and security come into play.

In addition, the fact that SOA is a strategy for existing systems under maintenance leads to issues of stability and backward compatibility.

And, in IT, each system is different. As a consequence, you will have to build your specific SOA—you can't buy it. To craft it, you'll need time and an incremental and iterative approach.

Note in addition that whether you introduce SOA is not what's important. The important thing is that the IT solution you introduce is appropriate for your context and requirements.

1.5.5 Slide 5: SOA Governance and Management Support

Probably the most important aspect of SOA is finding the right approach and amount of governance:

- You need a central team that will determine general aspects of your specific SOA. However, the ultimate goal is decentralization (which is key for large systems), so you'll have to find the right balance between centralization and decentralization.

- You need the right people. Large systems are different from small systems, and you need people who have experience with such systems. When concepts don't scale for practical reasons, inexperienced people will try to fight against those practical reasons instead of understanding that they are inherent properties of large systems. In addition, central service teams often tend to become ivory towers. They must be driven by the requirements of the business teams. In fact, they have to understand themselves as service providers for service infrastructures.

- First things first. Don't start with the management of services. You need management when you have many services. Don't start with an approach that first designs all services or first provides the infrastructure. It all must grow together, and while it's growing, you'll have enough to do with solving the current problems to worry about those that will come later.

- Last but not least, you need support from the CEO and CIO. SOA is a strategy that affects the company as a whole. Get them to support the concept, to make appropriate decisions, and to give enough time and money. Note that having a lot of funding in the short term is not the most important thing. You need money for the long run. Cutting SOA budgets when only half of the homework is complete is a recipe for disaster.

CHAPTER TWO

SOA

THE GOAL OF THIS CHAPTER IS TO INTRODUCE **SOA** AS A CONCEPT. **M**Y AIM IS TO OUTLINE THE fundamental aspects of SOA, and to show you the circumstances in which its use is appropriate. The important point is that SOA is a paradigm (or concept, or philosophy) that leads to a value system for large distributed systems with different owners.

I will cite, compare, and discuss definitions from various existing sources, such as the OASIS SOA Reference Model, Wikipedia.org, and some books. I will show how and why these definitions differ, and point out the key aspects of SOA that emerge.

2.1 Definitions of SOA

It is hard to find an exact definition of the term SOA. The problem is not that there aren't any definitions; the problem is that there are many different definitions. To give you an idea of how they are similar and dissimilar, a selection of published definitions are sidebars in this chapter. You'll find some common phrases and attributes as you read them, but you will also find a lot of differences in the context, level of abstraction, and wording.

However, at least all definitions agree that SOA is a paradigm for improved flexibility.

WIKIPEDIA DEFINITION OF SOA (FEB 19, 2006)

In computing, the term "Service-Oriented Architecture" (SOA) expresses a software architectural concept that defines the use of services to support the requirements of software users. In a SOA environment, nodes on a network make resources available to other participants in the network as independent services that the participants access in a standardized way. Most definitions of SOA identify the use of Web services (i.e., using SOAP or REST) in its implementation. However, one can implement SOA using any service-based technology.

…

Unlike traditional point-to-point architectures, SOAs comprise loosely coupled, highly interoperable application services. These services interoperate based on a formal definition independent of the underlying platform and programming language (e.g., WSDL). The interface definition encapsulates (hides) the vendor and language-specific implementation. A SOA is independent of development technology (such as Java and .NET). The software components become very reusable because the interface is defined in a standards-compliant manner.

2.1.1 SOA Is a Paradigm

SOA is not a concrete architecture: it is something that *leads* to a concrete architecture. You might call it a style, paradigm, concept, perspective, philosophy, or representation. That is, SOA is not a concrete tool or framework you can purchase. It is an approach, a way of thinking, a value system that leads to certain concrete decisions when designing a concrete software architecture.

This aspect of SOA has a very important consequence: you can't buy SOA. There is no tool or recipe you can use to make everything work. While applying this paradigm to your concrete situation, you must make specific decisions that are appropriate for your circumstances.

2.1.2 SOA Aims to Improve Flexibility

The key reason for using SOA is that it should help you in your business. For example, you may need IT solutions that store and manage your data, and allow you to automate the usual processes that deal with this data.

A critical factor for business success these days is keeping time to marketshare. As a telecom manager once said (according to Jim Highsmith):

> You can rant and rave all you want about software quality (or lack thereof), but the marketing guys run the world, and they want market share now…period, end of discussion. My job is to deliver on time, on budget, with the "appropriate" quality metrics.

To deliver a quality solution right on time, you need flexibility. But flexibility has a lot to do with clear organization, roles, processes, and so on. Therefore, SOA has to deal with all these aspects.

2.2 SOA Drivers

Of course, flexibility is dealt with very differently on different layers and in different components. So, one important question is which kinds of software systems this paradigm is appropriate for. As it turns out, SOA copes well with many difficult-to-handle characteristics of large systems.

2.2.1 Distributed Systems

As businesses grow, they become more and more complex, and more and more systems and companies become involved. There is constant integration and constant change. SOA is well suited to dealing with complex distributed systems. According to the OASIS SOA Reference Model (see [OasisSoaRM06]), it is a paradigm for "organizing and utilizing distributed capabilities."

> ### NOTE
> A more IT-conforming term for "distributed capabilities" would be "distributed systems," or, as Wikipedia's SOA definitions say, "nodes of a network" or "resources of a network."

SOA allows entities that need certain distributed capabilities to locate and make use of those capabilities. In other words, it facilitates interactions between service providers and service consumers, enabling the realization of business functionalities.

2.2.2 Different Owners

The OASIS SOA Reference Model's definition of SOA continues by stating that those distributed capabilities "may be under the control of different ownership domains." This is a very important point that is often suppressed in SOA definitions. You won't find it in any of the other definitions quoted in this chapter, but it is the key for certain properties of SOA, and a major reason why SOA is not only a technical concept.

SOA includes practices and processes that are based on the fact that networks of distributed systems are not controlled by single owners. Different teams, different departments, or even different companies may manage different systems (see Figure 2-1). Thus, different platforms, schedules, priorities, budgets, and so on must be taken into account. This concept is key to understanding SOA and large distributed systems in general.

FIGURE 2-1. Distributed systems with different owners

The ways you deal with problems and make modifications in environments with different owners and in environments where you control everything will, by necessity, vary. You cannot implement functionality and modify behavior the same way in large systems as in smaller systems. (See Section 1.1 for a discussion of the most important aspects of large systems.) One important consideration is that "politics" come into play: you have to compromise with others, and you have to accept that different priorities and solutions exist. Because you can't control everything, you have to accept that you may not always be able to do things your way.

2.2.3   Heterogeneity

Another very important difference between small and large systems is the lack of harmony. We all know this from experience (although we might not agree about whether it's a natural phenomenon or the result of bad design). Large systems use different platforms, different programming languages (and programming paradigms), and even different middleware. They are a mess of mainframes, SAP hosts, databases, J2EE applications, small rule engines, and so on. In other words, they are heterogeneous.

In the past, a lot of approaches have been proposed to solve the problem of integrating distributed systems by eliminating heterogeneity: "Let's harmonize, and all our problems will be gone," "Let's replace all systems with J2EE applications," "Let's use CORBA everywhere," "Let's use MQ series," and so on. But we all know that these approaches don't work. Large distributed systems with different owners are heterogeneous (see Figure 2-2). This is a fact, and therefore something we must accept when designing large distributed solutions.

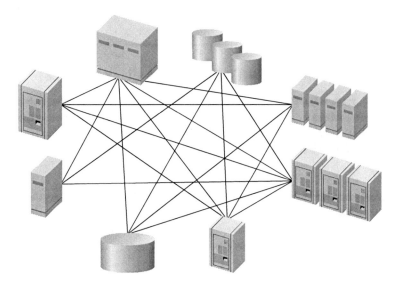

FIGURE 2-2. Distributed systems are heterogeneous

The SOA approach accepts heterogeneity. It deals with large distributed systems by acknowledging and supporting this attribute.

This is one of the key ideas of SOA, and it may give SOA the power to launch a revolution. Similar to "agile" methods of software development, which accept that requirements change instead of trying to fight against those changes, SOA just accepts that there is heterogeneity in large systems. This leads to a very different way of thinking, and suddenly we have a way to deal with large distributed systems that really works.

Please don't misunderstand me: I'm not saying heterogeneity is a goal. If you have a homogeneous system, that's fine. Be happy that a lot of common problems won't trouble you.

However, the majority of large distributed systems are heterogeneous, and the more we integrate, the more heterogeneity we get. SOA is the approach to deal with this situation. It's not concerned with whether heterogeneity is good; its aim is solely to deal with it in an appropriate fashion where it exists.

In the sample SOA definitions quoted in this chapter, the concept of heterogeneity is presented in many ways: you'll see "independent of the underlying platform and programming language," "independent of development technology," "vendor diversity," and "regardless of the operating systems or programming languages." The different wordings all refer to the same concept.

WIKIPEDIA DEFINITION OF SOA (JULY 17, 2006)

In computing, the term Service-Oriented Architecture (SOA) expresses a perspective of software architecture that defines the use of services to support the requirements of software users. In an SOA environment, resources on a network are made available as independent services that can be accessed without knowledge of their underlying platform implementation.

...

SOA is usually based on Web services standards (e.g., using SOAP or REST) that have gained broad industry acceptance. These standards (also referred to as Web service specifications) also provide greater interoperability and some protection from lock-in to proprietary vendor software. However, one can implement SOA using any service-based technology.

...

SOA can also be regarded as a style of Information Systems architecture that enables the creation of applications that are built by combining loosely coupled and interoperable services. These services inter-operate based on a formal definition (or contract, e.g., WSDL) which is independent of the underlying platform and programming language. The interface definition hides the implementation of the language-specific service. SOA-compliant systems can therefore be independent of development technologies and platforms (such as Java, .NET etc.).

...

SOA can support integration and consolidation activities within complex enterprise systems, but SOA does not specify or provide a methodology or framework for documenting capabilities or services.

2.3 SOA Concepts

Here are the key technical concepts of SOA that allow it to cope with the system characteristics just described:

- Services
- Interoperability
- Loose coupling

2.3.1   Services

Software development is the art of abstraction. We have to abstract reality in such a way that only the relevant aspects of a problem are handled. However, we all know that we can abstract from different perspectives. SOA aims to abstract by concentrating on the business aspects of a problem. The fundamental term introduced here is *service*. In essence, a service is an IT representation of some business functionality. The goal of SOA is to structure large distributed systems based on the abstractions of business rules and functions.

This gives a clear structure to the IT systems we design and develop. Although internally they are, of course, technical systems, the external interfaces should be designed in such a way that business people can understand them. Externally, you should not see the technical details. The smart consequence of this approach is that at this level of abstraction, platform-specific details don't matter. Thus, platforms can be heterogeneous.

Besides this broad definition, it is not clear what exactly a service is or can be. There are very different opinions about the exact attributes a service must, can, or should have. I will discuss services in detail in the next chapter (presenting several different existing definitions for services as well). As a rule of thumb, however, you can consider a service to be the IT representation of self-contained business functionality, such as "create a customer," "get a customer's contracts," "transfer money," "turn on the radio," "calculate the best route for my car," and so on.

2.3.2   High Interoperability

With heterogeneous systems, the first goal is to be able to connect those systems easily. This is usually called "high interoperability." High interoperability is not a new idea. Before SOA, we had the concept of *enterprise application integration* (EAI), and regarding interoperability, SOA is nothing new.

However, for SOA, high interoperability is the beginning, not the end. It is the base from which we start to implement business functionality (services) that is spread over multiple distributed systems.

2.3.3   Loose Coupling

As I've already mentioned, we live in a world ruled by marketing guys. We don't always have time to analyze, design, and implement carefully. We need fast times to market, so flexibility is often valued over quality. This leads to several problems.

Consider that at the same time we are integrating more and more systems, and implementing business processes by distributing them over different systems. In principle, data flows in such a way that processes run successfully in all the affected systems: we create a customer in all our systems, transfer money from one system to the other, or process a customer's order by shipping a product and sending a bill.

Multiple systems are involved, but there's no time for robustness. That doesn't sound good. With all that complexity, a minor problem can stop the whole business. This must be avoided. That is, we need fault tolerance. So, here are our goals:

- Flexibility
- Scalability
- Fault tolerance

The key to fulfilling these goals is *loose coupling*. Loose coupling is the concept of minimizing dependencies. When dependencies are minimized, modifications have minimized effects, and the systems still runs when parts of it are broken or down. Minimizing dependencies contributes to fault tolerance and flexibility, which is exactly what we need.

In addition, loose coupling leads to scalability. Large systems tend to challenge limits. Therefore, it is important to avoid bottlenecks; otherwise, growing might become very expensive. Avoiding bottlenecks is important from both a technical and an organizational point of view. All large systems only work if the usual business can be done in as decentralized a manner as possible. One way to introduce loose coupling is to avoid introducing any more centralization than is necessary (unfortunately, you need *some* centralization to establish SOA because you need some common base).

The subject of loose coupling will be revisited many times throughout this book, because in practice there are many ways to realize it. And remember, SOA is only a paradigm, not a recipe. The amount of loose coupling you introduce is up to you. Chapter 4 will discuss loose coupling in detail, and give several examples of ways to decouple SOA systems and processes.

2.4 SOA Ingredients

Having read that the key technical concepts for SOA are services, interoperability, and loose coupling, you might conclude that all you have to do to enable SOA is to introduce services, interoperability, and loose coupling.

But as I stated earlier, you can't buy SOA. What's important is that you introduce these concepts in the appropriate fashion. That is, you have to find the right degree of centralization, you have to set up the corresponding processes, and you have to do your homework. A lack of these "ingredients" is what I most often find as the problem in real SOA projects. To establish SOA successfully, you have to care for your infrastructure, architecture, and processes (including the metaprocess, governance).

2.4.1 Infrastructure

Infrastructure is the technical part of SOA that enables high interoperability. The infrastructure of a SOA landscape is called an enterprise service bus (ESB). This term is taken from enterprise application integration, where it was called the EAI bus or just enterprise bus.

The key feature of the ESB is that it enables you to call services between heterogeneous systems. Its responsibilities include data transformation, (intelligent) routing, dealing with security and reliability, service management, monitoring, and logging.

Chapter 5 will discuss the purpose and properties of an ESB in detail.

2.4.2 Architecture

Architecture is necessary to restrict all the possibilities of SOA in such a way that it leads to a working, maintainable system. SOA concepts, SOA tools, and SOA standards leave room for specific decisions that you must make in order to avoid a mess. You have to classify different types of services, you have to decide on the amount of loose coupling, you have to restrict the data model of service interfaces, you have to define policies, rules, and patterns, you have to clarify roles and responsibilities, you have to decide on the infrastructure technology, you have to decide which (version of) standards to use, and so on.

In this book, I will very often state that you have to decide something according to your concrete situation (requirements and context). By making these decisions, you will build your system architecture (or system of systems of architecture).

2.4.3 Processes

One thing that makes large systems complicated is that many different people and teams are involved in them. As a consequence, it is a long path from an initial business idea or requirement to a solution running in production mode.

Because there is not typically only one person or a few people controlling everything, you will have to set up appropriate processes (these processes may be explicitly defined, or just implicitly evolve). These processes include:

Business process modeling (BPM)
  BPM is the task of breaking business processes into smaller activities and tasks, which are services in this case (see Chapter 7).

Service lifecycles
  Defining a service lifecycle involves defining the different steps a service takes to become reality (see Chapter 11).

Model-driven software development (MDSD)
  MDSD is the process of generating code for dealing with services (see Chapter 18).

2.4.4 Governance

The metaprocess of all processes and a SOA strategy as a whole is *governance*. You have to set up the right process to establish SOA in your organization. This includes finding the right people who are able to combine all the different SOA ingredients to create a result that works and is appropriate. There is usually a central team (sometimes called the SOA competence center) that deals with infrastructure, architecture, and processes. This team is also responsible for establishing a common understanding, and doing the homework right. This requires management support, because in addition to time and resources, courage is required to deal with the organizational impacts of SOA (see Chapter 8). Understanding, governance, management support, and homework are key factors for the success of SOA. See Chapter 19 for details about governance and establishing SOA.

OASIS SOA REFERENCE MODEL DEFINITION OF SOA

See [OasisSoaRM06]

Service Oriented Architecture (SOA) is a paradigm for organizing and utilizing distributed capabilities that may be under the control of different ownership domains.

…

Visibility, interaction, and effect are key concepts for describing the SOA paradigm. Visibility refers to the capacity for those with needs and those with capabilities to be able to see each other. This is typically done by providing descriptions for such aspects as functions and technical requirements, related constraints and policies, and mechanisms for access or response. The descriptions need to be in a form (or can be transformed to a form) in which their syntax and semantics are widely accessible and understandable.

Whereas visibility introduces the possibilities for matching needs to capabilities (and vice versa), interaction is the activity of using a capability. Typically mediated by the exchange of messages, an interaction proceeds through a series of information exchanges and invoked actions. There are many facets of interaction; but they are all grounded in a particular execution context—the set of technical and business elements that form a path between those with needs and those with capabilities. This permits service providers and consumers to interact and provides a decision point for any policies and contracts that may be in force.

The purpose of using a capability is to realize one or more real world effects. At its core, an interaction is "an act" as opposed to "an object" and the result of an interaction is an effect (or a set/series of effects).

…

In most discussions of SOA, the terms "loose coupling" and "coarse-grained" are commonly applied as SOA concepts, but these terms have intentionally not been used in the current discussion because they are subjective trade-offs and without useful metrics. In terms of needs and capabilities, granularity and coarseness are usually relative to detail for the level of the problem being addressed, e.g. one that is more strategic vs. one down to the algorithm level, and defining the optimum level is not amenable to counting the number of interfaces or the number or types of information exchanges connected to an interface.

Note that although SOA is commonly implemented using Web Services, services can be made visible, support interaction, and generate effects through other implementation strategies. Web Service-based architectures and technologies are specific and concrete. While the concepts in the Reference Model apply to such systems, Web Services are too solution specific to be part of a general reference model.

2.5 SOA Is Not a Silver Bullet

SOA has been widely hyped, and is starting to become mainstream. With popular new concepts, there is always a danger that people will try to apply them everywhere. People like to try out cool new things (although, on the other hand, they fear change), and when everyone's saying that you have to use SOA, it's easy to fall into the trap of making everything SOA-like. (If you have a hammer, everything looks like a nail.)

As I wrote earlier, SOA is the ideal solution for very special circumstances: heterogeneous distributed systems with different owners. As you will see throughout this book, though, there's a price to pay for dealing with heterogeneity and different owners, and providing flexibility, scalability, and fault tolerance.

THOMAS ERL'S DEFINITION OF SOA IN "SERVICE-ORIENTED ARCHITECTURE"

See [Erl05] pp. 54-55

Contemporary SOA represents an open, extensible, federated, composable architecture that promotes service-orientation and is comprised of autonomous, QoS-capable, vendor diverse, interoperable, discoverable, and potentially reusable services, implemented as Web services.

SOA can establish an abstraction of business logic and technology, resulting in a loose coupling between these domains.

SOA is an evolution of past platforms, preserving successful characteristics of traditional architectures, and bringing with it distinct principles that foster service-orientation in support of a service-oriented enterprise.

SOA is ideally standardized throughout an enterprise, but achieving this state requires a planned transition and the support of a still evolving technology set.

…

Contemporary SOA supports, fosters, or promotes: vendor diversity, intrinsic interoperability, discoverability, federation, inherent reusability, extensibility, service-oriented business modeling, layers of abstraction, enterprise-wide loose coupling, organizational agility.

For this reason, if you don't have the type of system I've just described, think about not using SOA. If you have everything under control (i.e., a homogenous system and/or no different owners), SOA might be pointlessly expensive for you. For example, SOA is not the right approach just to separate a frontend from a backend. Of course, SOA will help to introduce different horizontal layers, but there are other approaches (such as modules and libraries) that are probably more appropriate. However, even if you fall into this category, the rules, problems, and principles of system abstractions are the same. So, you can still benefit from different topics presented in this book, even if you decide not to use SOA.

Keep in mind that SOA is only the means to an end, which is to find an appropriate solution for your individual needs. Software requirements are too different to lump them together. Use your mind instead of just following rules.

ERIC NEWCOMER AND GREG LOMOW'S DEFINITION OF SOA IN "UNDERSTANDING SOA WITH WEB SERVICES"

See [NewcomerLomow05] p. 54

A Service Oriented Architecture (SOA) is a style of design that guides all aspects of creating and using business services throughout their lifecycle (from conception to retirement), as well as defining and provisioning the IT infrastructure that allows different applications to exchange data and participate in business processes regardless of the operating systems or programming languages underlying those applications.

2.6 SOA Is Not a Specific Technology

Many SOA definitions include the term Web Services, but SOA is not the same as Web Services. SOA is the paradigm; Web Services are one possible way to realize the *infrastructure* by using a specific implementation strategy. This is an important distinction.

Web Services are emerging as the de facto standard for SOA implementations. Most discussions about SOA more or less claim that it should be implemented with Web Services (for example, in his definition Thomas Erl writes: "Contemporary SOA represents an… architecture that…is comprised of…services, implemented as Web services"). The good news is that the evolution of such a standard will lead to more freedom of choice: instead of using proprietary technology or making everything by yourself, you will be able to buy existing solutions at reasonable prices (open source solutions also are available).

This does not mean that building SOA with Web Services will solve all your problems. Web Services might help provide the infrastructure, but you will still have to construct the architecture, and set up all the complicated processes that are necessary for successful

SOA. In addition, the Web Services standard is not as mature as it seems, and Web Services introduce some problems other implementation strategies don't have. I will discuss these issues in detail in Chapter 16.

Note that it is possible to implement SOA with other technologies (CORBA, MQ, Tibco, etc.). I have seen SOA landscapes that use different implementation strategies (see Section 5.2).

2.7   SOA Versus Distributed Objects

There have been many different approaches to dealing with distributed systems. One approach, the initial concept of CORBA, was to use distributed objects. The idea was to enable remote access to objects of external systems. You were able to call methods of objects, including setters and getters, remotely. That is, for each access to an attribute, you were calling a remote function.

This was a very fine-grained kind of interface to remote systems, and, as a consequence, the approach was the base for the idea of having one general business object model spanning distributed systems.

In practice, it turned out that this approach didn't scale. Having one business object model that was used by each connected system was hard to organize, and introduced too much centralization, and too many dependencies.

In fact, SOA is the exact opposite of the concept of distributed objects. With SOA, data is exchanged between different systems, and each system operates on its local (redundant) copy with its own local methods and procedures. Unlike with distributed objects, this approach decouples the systems and lets them scale.

> **NOTE**
> Note that version 2.3 of CORBA introduced value objects, or Objects by Value (OBV), which allow you to copy chunks of data (objects) from one system and operate on them locally. You can implement SOA using this technology (provided you don't use OBV with operations). This way of using CORBA has nothing to do with the concept of distributed objects.

2.8   SOA Terminology

Let's talk a bit about terminology. As usual with evolving concepts, different terms are often used for the same things, and a given term can have different meanings. The Glossary at the end of the book contains definitions of the most important SOA terms. However, I would like to introduce here a few terms you'll see throughout this book. I'll present others later, when we get into the details.

To begin, we'll need terms for the roles systems have when they communicate via services. The terms I use in this book are "provider" and "consumer":

- A *provider* is a system that implements a service (a business functionality) so that other systems can call it.

- A *consumer* is a system that calls a service (uses a provided service).

Requestor is often used as another word for consumer (especially in the Web Services world). This is a more technical term based on the fact that a service consumer sends a request to the provider to call a service (although this is not always the case, as you'll see in Chapter 10). I will use "consumer" throughout this book.

You might also hear and use the usual terms for roles in distributed systems, *client* and *server*. Indeed, a provider is the server of services, while the consumer is the client using them. However, the terms "client" and "server" are used in so many different contexts that I prefer to and recommend that you use "provider" and "consumer" instead.

If you want to use a generic term for both the provider and the consumer, you can use the term *participant*. A service participant is a system that is a service provider or a service consumer (or both). Again, there are alternatives in common usage. For example, in the Java™ world, the term *service agent* has evolved.

2.9 Summary

- Here is my summarizing definition of SOA:

    SOA is an architectural paradigm for dealing with business processes distributed over a large landscape of existing and new heterogeneous systems that are under the control of different owners.

- The key technical concepts of SOA are services, interoperability, and loose coupling.

- The key ingredients of SOA are infrastructure, architecture, and processes (including the metaprocess of establishing SOA, governance).

- The key success factors for SOA are understanding, governance, management support, and homework.

- SOA is neither a specific technology nor a silver bullet. There are places where SOA is appropriate and places where it is not.

- Web Services are *one* possible way of realizing the *infrastructure* aspects of SOA. Using Web Services is often recommended because it seems to be becoming established as the standard technology.

CHAPTER THREE

Services

IN THIS CHAPTER, WE'LL EXPLORE THE MEANING OF THE TERM "SERVICE" AND ITS ASSOCIATED concepts (such as interfaces and contracts).

As for SOA, there are multiple definitions of the term "service." For this reason, I will again quote definitions from various existing sources, such as the OASIS SOA Reference Model, Wikipedia.org, and some books. I will then present my personal definition of the term.

To get a complete picture of what services are, you'll have to read further in this book. The goal of this chapter is to provide a general definition that will serve as a base for later discussions in this book.

3.1 Services

The OASIS SOA Reference Model [OasisSoaRM06] states:

> The noun "service" is defined in dictionaries as "The performance of work (a function) by one for another."

This can mean everything or nothing. As with the term SOA, it is hard to find an exact, useful definition of the term "service" because so many definitions exist. Again, I have collected some of these definitions and put extracts of them in sidebars throughout the chapter. You'll find some common phrases and attributes as you read them, but you will also find a lot of differences in the context, level of abstraction, and wording. As in the previous chapter, I'll begin by presenting my understanding of services.

WIKIPEDIA DEFINITION OF SERVICE (FEBRUARY 19, 2006)

A "Service" is (ideally) a self-contained, stateless business function that accepts one or more requests and returns one or more responses through a well-defined, standard interface. Services can also perform discrete units of work such as editing and processing a transaction. Services should not depend on the state of other functions or processes. The technology used to provide the service, such as a programming language, does not form part of this definition.

3.1.1   Services Represent Business Functionality

SOA is focused on business processes. These processes are performed in different steps (also called *activities* or *tasks*) on different systems. The primary goal of a service is to represent a "natural" step of business functionality. That is, according to the domain for which it's provided, a service should represent a self-contained functionality that corresponds to a real-world business activity. In other words, business people should be able to understand what a service does (see the "Business-Driven Versus Technically Driven Business Interfaces" sidebar).

Of course, when you design a system, the question of how to find and/or design services arises. And, as always in IT, there is no easy answer to this question. This is really a matter of business process management (BPM), discussed in Chapter 7.

3.2 Interfaces and Contracts

Technically, a service is an interface for (multiple) messages that return information and/ or change the state of an associated entity (backend). Or, as Yefim V. Natis, a Gartner analyst who co-coined the term SOA, wrote in [Gartner03]:

> Essentially, SOA is a software architecture that starts with an interface definition and builds the entire application topology as a topology of interfaces, interface implementations and interface calls. SOA would be better-named "interface-oriented architecture."

According to this, it is difficult to make the definition of "service" more concrete. Everything that can be used as an interface, and represents a self-contained business functionality can be a service.

BUSINESS-DRIVEN VERSUS TECHNICALLY DRIVEN BUSINESS INTERFACES

Note that a business-driven interface is different from a technically driven business interface. For example, a technically driven business interface might be designed as follows:

```
customerOP(action, // "create", "read", "change", "delete"
           id,      // customer id or null
           name,    // new customer name or null
           address, // new customer address or null
           account) // new customer bank account or null
```

It is a business interface because it allows you to create a new customer, read or modify his/her data, or delete that data. However, this interface is technically driven, probably by a direct mapping to a corresponding database interface.

In contrast, a business-driven interface might look like this:

```
createCustomer(name,    // new customer name
               address, // customer address
               account) // customer bank account

readCustomer(id)        // customer id

changeCustomerAccount(id,     // customer id
                      account) // new customer bank account

changeCustomerAddress(id,     // customer id
                      address, // new customer address
                      check,   // true: verify address
                      modify)  // true: fix address if possible

deleteCustomer(id)      // customer id
```

Note the following differences:

- Instead of having one signature, you have five. Each operation's name describes the basic functionality from a business point of view. In addition, there are no parameters that do not make sense for each particular functionality (for example, for the deletion of a customer, you only need the customer ID).

- Operations for reading and writing have different levels of granularity. In this case, you have the ability to change a customer's address or bank account independently, but when you read customer data, you get both. Such differences are typical for business processes.

- Specific operations might have additional parameters. In this case, the operation for changing an address has additional attributes that specify whether an address check should be performed and whether the address might even be modified according to the address check (e.g., replacing "NewYork" with "New York").

—continued—

In fact, if you let business people design interfaces on a case-by-case basis, they'll look different from interfaces driven, for example, by the underlying database design. Service orientation clearly prefers business-driven over technically driven interfaces, although this does not mean that you should not think about possible synergy effects. Start the design based on the requirements, not based on the implementation.

However, technically and semantically, there are different kinds of interfaces. One type of interface is a *signature*, which describes the input parameters, output parameters, and possible exceptions.

Simply knowing the signature is not enough to use a service, though. As a consumer of a service, you want to—indeed, must—know the complete behavior and semantics of the service. In other words, the interface should be *well defined*.

The behavior of a well-defined interface should be unambiguous, but in practice, this goal is often hard to reach. In addition, some aspects of a service might be consumer-specific. This especially applies to nonfunctional aspects, such as attributes related to Quality of Service (QoS) and service-level agreements (SLAs).* For this reason, you might lay out the relevant information in *contracts*. A contract is the complete specification of a service between a specific provider and a specific consumer. From a consumer's point of view, it defines "everything you have to know when using this service," so that (ideally) no doubts remain.

In practice, you usually start to describe a service with a well-defined interface. Then, when a specific consumer wants to use the service, you define a specific contract based on the well-defined interface. The individual contracts will reflect the necessary resources you need to provide the service according to the specific nonfunctional commitments. For instance, while all consumers use (or can use) the same formal interface to call a service, consumers may make different numbers of calls at different times.

As an example, a call center frontend might call a service 100,000 times per day, with the peak hours being between 8 a.m. and 6 p.m. On the other hand, a consumer running batch requests during the night might have to make up to 50,000 calls between midnight and 2 a.m. It is the task of the service provider to provide enough resources to satisfy all of the SLAs. Service infrastructures might also provide the ability to priorize different service

---

* The word "service" in "service-level agreement" means something different from the word "service" introduced here as a SOA concept. SLA refers to the service level of an agreement, not a level agreement for a service. In other words, when we talk about SLAs for services, we're talking about agreements about the service levels of those services.

calls, so that some consumers get better response times than others. In that case, different response times might also become part of the individual contracts.

What it means technically to exchange "messages" is a different question. In principle, different so-called "message exchange patterns" are possible. For example, a service might be provided as a synchronous call, where the consumer blocks and waits for a response, or it might involve a notification that is sent to subscribing consumers to inform them about a change in state (which might or might not be called an "event"). In the latter case, no response is expected. See Chapter 10 for details on message exchange patterns.

3.3 Additional Service Attributes

If you go through all the service definitions in this chapter (and other definitions outside this book), you will find references to a lot of additional attributes that services "may," "must," or "should" have. However, there is no common understanding about whether these additional attributes are really required for services. Here are some typical questions to which different people will give different answers:

- Do services have to be stateless?
- Do they have to be implemented as Web Services?
- Should they be coarse-grained and/or composable?

Care must be taken here. My definition of a service is that it should be an IT representation of a business functionality defined by a (well-defined) interface. Services should also typically be self-contained. Some other attributes usually apply, but I don't believe that any of these other attributes are fundamentally required.

In practice, things differ. In your concrete SOA, you may require some—but not all—of the additional service attributes discussed here, and you may find that some kinds of services have attributes that others do not. For this reason, we usually classify different kinds of services according to their attributes (see Chapter 6 for details).

The details of the possible attributes services can have can be pretty complicated. The various attributes will be discussed throughout this book, according to the general topics of the chapters. However, to provide an initial overview, I'll introduce them here. Where appropriate, I will refer you to other places in the book where you can find further details.

3.3.1 Self-Contained

All definitions of SOA agree that it is a design goal that services be self-contained (independent, autonomous, autarkic). However, some dependencies always exist. For example, services may share at least some fundamental data types (such as string). Be careful with more complicated fundamental data types, though. The goal is to minimize dependencies so that a SOA is appropriate for distributed systems with different owners. See Chapter 4 for details.

3.3.2   Coarse-Grained

Services are abstractions that hide implementation details from the consumers. But you pay a price for this abstraction: slower running times. For example, switching from remote stored procedures to service calls might slow down data access by a factor of between 5 and 10 (see Section 13.2). For this reason, it is usually better to have one service call transfer all the necessary data between a provider and its consumer(s) instead of having multiple service calls processing the same amount of data.

In addition, coarse granularity helps to separate the internal data structure of a service provider from its external interface. Having a service for each access to a service attribute (i.e., a service for each setter and getter) would result in distributed objects (see Section 2.7), which increases the dependencies between distributed systems.

Some definitions recommend that services should always be coarse-grained, but this recommendation has problems. One problem is how to tell when granularity is "coarse." For this reason, the OASIS SOA Reference Model (see [OasisSoaRM06]) says:

THE OASIS SOA REFERENCE MODEL'S DEFINITION OF SERVICE

See [OasisSoaRM06]

The noun "service" is defined in dictionaries as "The performance of work (a function) by one for another." However, service, as the term is generally understood, also combines the following related ideas:

- The capability to perform work for another

- The specification of the work offered for another

- The offer to perform work for another

These concepts emphasize a distinction between a capability and the ability to bring that capability to bear. While both needs and capabilities exist independently of SOA, in SOA, services are the mechanism by which needs and capabilities are brought together.

…

The consequence of invoking a service is a realization of one or more real world effects. These effects may include:

1. information returned in response to a request for that information,
2. a change to the shared state of defined entities, or
3. some combination of (1) and (2).

In most discussions of SOA, the terms "loose coupling" and "coarse-grained" are commonly applied as SOA concepts, but these terms have intentionally not been used in the current discussion because they are subjective trade-offs and without useful metrics. In terms of needs and capabilities, granularity and coarseness are usually relative to detail for the level of the problem being addressed, e.g., one that is more strategic vs. one down to the algorithm level, and defining the optimum level is not amenable to counting the number of interfaces or the number or types of information exchanges connected to an interface.

Another problem with the recommendation of coarse granularity has to do with performance considerations. Processing a lot of data takes time, and if a consumer doesn't need this data, that time is wasted. See Section 13.3 for details.

3.3.3 Visible/Discoverable

To call a service, you have to know that the service exists. Often there is a public place where you can search for a service, and/or that describes all the details of a service. However, services can also be discovered by word of mouth. See Chapter 17 for more on this topic.

3.3.4   Stateless

Sometimes, services are defined as being (ideally) stateless. Statelessness is one of the most confusing aspects of services, because some state is always involved. The questions are where and for how long the state exists, and whether it is a technical or business state. This issue is discussed in Section 15.1.

3.3.5   Idempotent

If you call a service that modifies something, and you get no confirming response, you have a problem. Did the modification happen, and you just didn't get the result, or did the service call get lost before the modification occurred? If you're in doubt, and you can resend the service call without getting into trouble, your service is *idempotent*. That is, idempotency is the ability to redo an operation if you are not sure whether it was completed. This makes life a lot easier, so having idempotent services is always a goal (if the price isn't too high). Still, there are cases where this goal difficult to achieve. See Sections 10.4 and 15.2 for details.

3.3.6   Reusable

Avoiding redundancy is a general goal of software development. That is, ideally each functionality should be implemented only once. One common business case for SOA is that it leads to better reusability because all systems that need a certain functionality just call the same service. This is possible, but it has its limitations. One limitation has to do with performance (Chapter 13 gives several examples of performance/reusability tradeoffs that should be considered). As a result, reusability may be a goal, but not a rule.

3.3.7   Composable

Services can use/call other services. That is, broader kinds of business functionality can be broken into smaller steps, which are themselves services. This is why a SOA will often contain a category of "composed services" (see Section 6.3 for details). From a business point of view, the issue of composing services and decomposing business processes leads to business process modeling, which is discussed in Chapter 7.

3.3.8   Technical

Sometimes, SOA definitions also allow so-called "technical services" that don't necessarily represent self-contained business functionalities. For example, if you have a SOA infrastructure for business services, you can use this infrastructure to exchange technical data. In this case, you might argue that you have technical services, or that you used the SOA infrastructure in itself, knowing that business services belong to another level of abstraction. Do whatever is appropriate, but keep in mind that it is the goal of SOA to concentrate on business functionality. See Section 6.6 for details.

3.3.9 QoS- and SLA-Capable

As stated earlier, a service contract should include everything a caller should know to call the service. For this reason, sooner or later you will start to specify nonfunctional attributes, including QoS and SLA attributes having to do with runtime performance, reliability, and so on. However, at the beginning, SOA will work even if services don't have these attributes. (Believe me, your consumers will tell you if your service is not fast or reliable enough!)

3.3.10 Pre- and Post-Conditions

According to the idea of "Design by Contract" (invented by Bertrand Meyer), pre- and post-conditions help specify the semantic behavior of services. The pre-conditions define the specific obligations a service consumer has to meet when calling the service ("state the constraints"). The post-conditions guarantee the specific properties of the system and/or output when the service runs successfully ("state the benefits"). See [DesignByContract] for details.

3.3.11 Vendor-Diverse

SOA is a concept for large distributed systems, and these systems are usually very heterogeneous (see Section 2.2.3). Thus, being able to use different platforms and different products for implementing services is a usual requirement. However, this is more a property of SOA than an attribute of services.

3.3.12 Interoperable

High interoperability is a core requirement of SOA. In the sense that services can be called from any other systems, they are inherently interoperable. But again, this is more a property of SOA than an attribute of services.

ERIC NEWCOMER AND GREG LOMOW'S DEFINITION OF SERVICE IN "UNDERSTANDING SOA WITH WEB SERVICES"

See [NewcomerLomow05] p. 58

From a business perspective, services are IT assets that correspond to real-world business activities or recognizable business functions and that can be accessed according to the service policies that have been established for the services.

...

From a technical perspective, services are coarse-grained, reusable IT assets that have well-defined interfaces (a.k.a. service contracts) that clearly separate the services' externally accessible interface from the services' technical implementation.

3.3.13 Implemented As Web Services

As discussed in the previous chapter, many definitions of SOA claim that it should be implemented with Web Services. I will discuss whether this recommendation makes sense in Chapter 16. For now, I'll just reiterate that Web Services is not the same as SOA. Web Services might be an (obvious) way to implement SOA, but SOA as a concept is not tied to any specific technology.

3.4 Summary

- Here is my summarizing definition of "service" in the context of SOA:

  A service is the IT realization of some self-contained business functionality.

- By focusing on the business aspects, a service hides technical details and allows business people to deal with it.

- Technically, a service is an interface for (multiple) messages that are exchanged between provider(s) and consumer(s).

- The complete description of a service from a consumer's point of view (signature and semantics) is called a "well-defined interface" or "contract." A contract is agreed individually between a certain provider, and a certain consumer, and usually includes nonfunctional aspects such as SLAs.

- There are several attributes that services may (or, according to some definitions, must) have. According to my understanding, they are situation-dependent; services will almost always have different attributes, and should be classified according to those attributes.

CHAPTER FOUR

Loose Coupling

SOA APPLIES TO LARGE DISTRIBUTED SYSTEMS. SCALABILITY AND FAULT TOLERANCE ARE KEY TO THE maintainability of such systems. Another important goal is to minimize the impact of modifications and failures on the system landscape as a whole. Thus, loose coupling is a key concept of SOA.

This chapter will discuss the motivations for this concept (for large distributed systems), exploring variations of loose coupling from the technical and organizational points of view. This topic will demonstrate that SOA is a paradigm that leads to special priorities when designing large systems. However, again, there is no rule prescribing which kind or level of loose coupling you should employ. This decision must be made based on your specific circumstances.

4.1 The Need for Fault Tolerance

We live in crazy times. The market rules, which means you won't usually have enough time to create well-elaborated, robust system designs. If you're not fast enough, flexible enough, and cheap enough, you'll soon find yourself out of the market. Thus, you need fast, flexible, and cheap solutions.

Fast and cheap solutions, however, can't be well designed and robust. Consequently, you will have to deal with errors and problems. The important point here is fault tolerance. The most important thing is that your systems run. According to [ITSecCity02], a flight-booking system failure may cost $100,000 an hour, a credit card system breakdown may cost $300,000 an hour, and a stock-trading malfunction may cost $8 million an hour. As these figures show, fault tolerance is key for large distributed systems. When problems occur, it is important to minimize their effects and consequences.

4.2 Forms of Loose Coupling

Loose coupling is the concept typically employed to deal with the requirements of scalability, flexibility, and fault tolerance. The aim of loose coupling is to minimize dependencies. When there are fewer dependencies, modifications to or faults in one system will have fewer consequences on other systems.

Loose coupling is a principle; it is neither a tool, nor a checklist. When you design your SOA, it is up to you to define which kinds and amount of loose coupling you introduce. However, there are some typical topics you might want to consider when you think about loose coupling in your system. Table 4-1 lists them (this list is an extension of a list published in [KrafzigBankeSlama04], p. 47).

TABLE 4-1. Possible forms of loose coupling in SOA

	Tight coupling	Loose coupling
Physical connections	Point-to-point	Via mediator
Communication style	Synchronous	Asynchronous
Data model	Common complex types	Simple common types only
Type system	Strong	Weak
Interaction pattern	Navigate through complex object trees	Data-centric, self-contained message
Control of process logic	Central control	Distributed control
Binding	Statically	Dynamically
Platform	Strong platform dependencies	Platform independent
Transactionality	2PC (two-phase commit)	Compensation
Deployment	Simultaneous	At different times
Versioning	Explicit upgrades	Implicit upgrades

This table is far from being complete, but it's pretty typical for large distributed systems. Note again that this is not a checklist. There is no SOA certification saying you conform when all or at least 50 percent of the forms of loose coupling are in use. However, it would be very strange if none of these forms of loose coupling were used in your SOA. If this were possible, your system would appear not to have the common requirements of large distributed systems with different owners. That's OK, but you shouldn't call your solution SOA. (Well, it may help you get money and resources for it, but beware of false impressions.)

If there is such a fine list of aspects of loose coupling, and minimizing dependencies is good, you might be wondering why you don't simply use all these forms of loose coupling in each SOA. The answer is that there is a price to pay for loose coupling, in that it makes systems more complex. That means more development, and/or maintenance effort.

To explore how the forms of loose coupling listed in Table 4-1 can help and the costs they can incur, let's examine some more closely. Most of these topics will be discussed in more detail later in the book, so I've included references to future chapters where appropriate.

4.2.1   Asynchronous Communication

Probably the most well-known example of loose coupling is asynchronous communication (see Figure 4-1). Asynchronous communication usually means that the sender of a message and its receiver are not synchronized. Think of it like sending an email. After you send a message, you can continue your work while waiting for an answer. The recipient might not be available (online) when you send the message. When she comes online, the message gets delivered, and she can process it and send a response if necessary (again, with no requirement that you be available/online when she sends it).

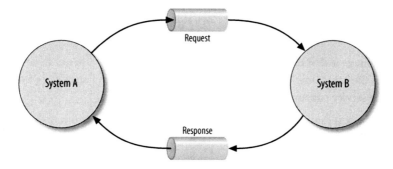

FIGURE 4-1. Decoupling by asynchronous communication

One problem with asynchronous communication occurs when the sender needs a reply. With asynchronous communication, you don't get replies to your messages immediately. Because you don't know when (or whether) a reply will arrive, you continue your work and start to perform different tasks. Then, when the response arrives, you have to deal with it in an appropriate way. This means that you have to associate the answer with the original request (e.g., by processing something like a "correlation ID"). In addition, you have to process the reply, which usually requires knowledge of some of the initial state and context when the request was sent. Both correlating the response to the request, and transferring the state from the request to the response, require some effort.

> **NOTE**
> See Chapter 10 for a discussion of different message exchange patterns (MEPs) and Section 15.3.3 for details about correlation IDs.

The situation gets worse when you send a lot of asynchronous messages. The order in which you receive responses might be different from the order in which you sent the messages, and some of the awaited responses might not arrive (or arrive in time). Programming, testing, and debugging all the possible eventualities can be very complicated and time consuming.

For this reason, one of my customers who has hundreds of services in production has the policy of avoiding asynchronicity whenever a request needs a reply. Having found that debugging race conditions (situations caused by different unexpected response times) was a nightmare, and knowing that maintainability was key in large distributed systems, the customer decided to minimize the risk of getting into these situations. This decision involved a tradeoff because performance was not as good as it might have been with more asynchronous communication.

As this discussion demonstrates, there are two sides to introducing asynchronous communication in SOA (or distributed systems in general):

- The advantage is that the systems exchanging service messages do not have to be online at the same time. In addition, if a reply is required, long answering times don't block the service consumer.

- The drawback is that the logic of the service consumer gets (much) more complicated.

Note that when discussing asynchronicity, people do not always mean the same thing. For example, asynchronous communication from a consumer's point of view might mean that the consumer doesn't block to wait for an answer, while from an infrastructure's (ESB's) point of view, it might mean that a message queue is used to decouple the consumer and provider. Often, both concepts apply in practice, but this is not always the case.

4.2.2   Heterogeneous Data Types

Now, let's discuss my favorite example of loose coupling: the harmonization of data types over distributed systems. This topic always leads to much discussion, and understanding it is key to understanding large systems.

There is no doubt that life is a lot easier if data types are shared across all systems. For this reason, harmonizing data types is a "natural" approach. In fact, when object-orientation became mainstream, having a common *business object model* (BOM) became a general goal. But, it turned out that this approach was a recipe for disaster for large systems.

"WHAT A SHAME THAT WE CAN'T HARMONIZE ANYMORE"

A while ago, I gave a talk about SOA that included my usual claim that you have to accept that you can't harmonize data types on large systems. A senior systems architect came to me during the coffee break and said, "Isn't it sad how bad things have become in our industry when we even can't harmonize data types anymore? In the past we were able to analyze and design our systems." It sounded like a criticism of the younger generations of software developers, who are able to do only one thing: copy and paste.

My answer was as follows: "You might be right. In our crazy times, we simply do not have enough time for careful and long analysis and design. The marketing guys rule the world, and if we don't deliver in time, we are out of the market (even if we have better quality). But be careful, and don't underestimate the level of complexity we have reached now by connecting systems. Remember, there is no central control any longer, and if there were it wouldn't work. If we had harmonized an address type before we shipped the Internet protocols, the Internet would never have become reality. Large-scale systems need the minimal consensus you can provide to be successful. Note that you still can harmonize data types when things run."

The first reason for the disaster was an organizational one: it was simply not possible to come to an agreement for harmonized types. The views and interests of the different systems were too varied. Because large distributed systems typically have different owners, it was tough to reach agreements. Either you didn't fulfill all interests, or your model became far too complicated, or it simply was never finished. This is a perfect example of "analysis paralysis": if you try to achieve perfection when analyzing all requirements, you'll never finish the job.

You might claim that the solution is to introduce a central role (a systems architect or a "model master") that resolves all open questions, so that one common BOM with harmonized data types becomes a reality. But then, you'll run into another fundamental problem: different systems enhance differently. Say you create a harmonized data type for customers. Later, a billing system might need two new customer attributes to deal with different tax rates, while a CRM system might introduce new forms of electronic addresses, and an offering system might need attributes to deal with privacy protection. If a customer data type is shared among all your systems (including systems not interested in any of these extensions), all the systems will have to be updated accordingly to reflect each change, and the customer data type will become more and more complicated.

Sooner or later, the price of harmonization becomes too high. Keeping all the systems in sync is simply too expensive in terms of time and money. And even if you manage to succeed, your next company merger will introduce heterogeneity again!

Common BOMs do not scale because they lead to a coupling of systems that is too tight. As a consequence, you have to accept the fact that data types on large distributed systems will not be harmonized. In decoupled large systems, data types differ (see Figure 4-2).

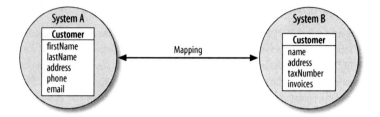

FIGURE 4-2. *Decoupling by using different data types*

Again, there is a price to pay for this decision: if data types are not harmonized, you need *data type mappings* (which include technical and semantic aspects). Although mapping adds complexity, it is a good sign in large systems because it demonstrates that components are decoupled.

The usual approach is that a service provider defines the data types used by the services it provides (which might be ruled by some general conventions and constraints). The service consumers have to accept these types. Note that a service consumer should avoid using the provider's data types in its own source code. Instead, a consumer should have a thin *mapping layer* to map the provider's data types to its own data types. See Section 12.3.1 for a detailed explanation of why this is important.

Again, there are two sides to introducing this form of loose coupling in SOA (or distributed systems in general). Having no common business data model has pros and cons:

- The advantage is that systems can modify their data types without directly affecting other systems (modified service interfaces affect only corresponding consumers).

- The drawback is that you have to map data types from one system to another.

Note that you will need some fundamental data types to be shared between all applications. But to promote loose coupling, fundamental data types harmonized for all services should usually be very basic. The most complicated common data type I've seen a phone company introduce in a SOA landscape was a data type for a phone number (a structure/record of country code, area code, and local number). The trial to harmonize a common type for addresses (customer addresses, invoice addresses, etc.) failed. One reason was an inability to agree on how to deal with titles of nobility. Another reason was that different systems and tools had different constraints on how to process and print addresses on letters and parcels.

NOTE

If you are surprised about this low level of harmonization, think about what it means to modify a basic type and roll out the modifications across all systems at the same time (see Section 18.4.9 for details). In practice, fundamental service data types must be stable.

Does this mean that you can't have harmonized address data types in a SOA? Not necessarily. If you are able to harmonize, do it. Harmonization helps. However, don't fall into the trap of *requiring* that data types be harmonized. This approach doesn't scale.

If you can't harmonize an address type, does this mean that all consumers have to deal with the differences between multiple address types? No. The usual approach in SOA is to introduce a composed service that allows you to query and modify addresses (composed services are discussed in Chapter 6). This service then deals with differences between the backend systems by mapping the data appropriately.

Note that with this approach, there's still no need to have one common view to addresses. If you get new requirements, you can simply introduce a second address service mapping the additional attributes to the different backends. Existing consumers that don't share the additional requirements will not be affected.

4.2.3 Mediators

A third form of loose coupling has to do with how a service call performed by a consumer finds the provider that has to process this request. With a "point-to-point" approach, the sender sends the request to one specific physical system using its physical address. This is like sending a letter to a specific postal address, such as 42 Broadway in New York, NY.

This is a tightly coupled approach. What happens if the receiver moves houses? What happens if the receiver is out of order, or is getting flooded with too many messages? Mechanisms for failover and load balancing are required. That is, you need some kind of intermediary to switch between different physical receivers.

In principle, there are two kinds of mediators:

- The first type tells you the correct endpoint for your service call *before* you send it. That is, you still have point-to-point connections, but with the help of these mediators, you send your service calls to different addresses. Such a mediator is often called a *broker* or *name server*. You ask for a service using a symbolic name, and the broker or name server tells you which physical system to send your request to. This form of mediation requires some additional intelligence at the consumer site.

- The second type chooses the right endpoint for a request *after* the consumer sends it. In this case, the consumer sends the request to a symbolic name, and the infrastructure (network, middleware, ESB) routes the call to the appropriate system according to intelligent routing rules.

In practice, very different flavors of both forms of mediation occur. For example, there are service buses that send messages using a broadcasting approach, so that the sender sends a request to a logical receiver, and any of the different providers providing the requested service can process the call. On the other hand, Web Services are technically point-to-point connections, where you typically use a broker to find the physical endpoint of a request, and/or you insert some so-called interceptors that route your request at runtime to an available provider.

Chapter 5 will discuss details of how to deal with mediation in an ESB.

4.2.4   Weak Type Checking

Another good example of the complexity of loose coupling has to do with the question of whether and when to check types. Most of us have probably learned that the earlier errors are detected, the better. For this reason, programming languages with type checking seem to be better than those without (because they detect possible errors at compile time rather than runtime).

However, as systems grow, things change. The problem is that type checking takes time and requires information. In order for the SOA infrastructure (ESB) to check types, it needs to have some information about those types. If, for example, types are described using XML, the ESB will need the corresponding XML schema file(s). As a consequence, any modifications of the interface will not only affect both the provider and the consumer(s), but also the ESB. This means that mechanisms and processes will be required to synchronize updates with the ESB. And if the ESB uses adapters for each provider and consumer, you might have to organize the deployment of these updates to all adapters. This is possible, but it leads to tighter dependencies than a policy where interface modifications affect only providers and consumers. For this reason, it might be a good idea to make the ESB generic. In general, interface changes should only affect those who use the interface as a contract, not those who transfer the corresponding data. If the Internet had had to validate the correctness of interfaces, it would never have been able to scale.

Now, you might come to the conclusion that you should always prefer generic interfaces to strict type checking in large systems. The extreme approach would be to introduce just one generic service for each system, so that the service interfaces never change: all you change are implementations against the interface. Note, however, that at some stage, your system will have to process data, and whether you can rely on that data being to some extent syntactically correct will affect your code. So, in places where business data gets processed, strong type checking helps. The only question is how stable the data is.

Say, for example, that your services exchange some string attributes. If the attributes are pretty stable, a typed service API that specifies each attribute explicitly is recommended. When a new attribute comes into play, you can introduce a new (version of the) service with the additional attribute. On the other hand, if the attributes change frequently, a key/value list might make sense. The right decision to make here depends on so many factors that a general rule is not useful. For these kinds of scenarios, you have to find the right amount of coupling as the system evolves. Note, however, that explicit modeling of attributes makes it easier to write code that processes the data (for example, you can easily map data in different formats when composing services in so-called orchestration engines). On the other hand, having no generic approach would be a very bad mistake when binary compatibility is a must. For example, a technical header provided for all service messages should always have some ability to be extended over the years without breaking binary compatibility (see Section 15.4).

4.2.5   Binding

Binding (the task of correlating symbols of different modules or translation units) allows a form of loose coupling that is similar to weak type checking. Again, you have to decide between early binding, which allows verification at compile or start time, and late binding, which happens at runtime.

4.2.6   Platform Dependencies

In Table 4-1, there are two forms of coupling that deal with the question of whether or not certain platform constraints apply. Making a decision about the general one, platform dependencies, is easy. Of course, you have more freedom of choice if platform-independent solutions are preferred over strong platform dependencies. The second form is discussed next.

4.2.7   Interaction Patterns

A special form of platform dependencies has to do with which interaction patterns are used in service signatures (i.e., which programming paradigms are provided to design service interfaces). Which are the fundamental data types, and how can you combine them? A wide range of questions must be considered:

- Are only strings supported, or can other fundamental data types (integers, floats, Booleans, date/time types, etc.) be used?
- Are enumerations (limited sets of named integer values) supported?
- Can you constrain possible values (e.g., define certain string formats)?
- Can you build higher types (structures, records)?
- Can you build sequence types (arrays, lists)?
- Can you design relations between types (inheritance, extensions, polymorphism)?

The more complicated the programming constructs are, the more abstractly you can program. However, you will also have more problems mapping data to platforms that have no native support for a particular construct.

Based on my own experience (and that of others), I recommend that you have a basic set of fundamental types that you can compose to other types (structures, records) and sequences (arrays). Be careful with enumerations (an anachronism from the time when each byte did count—use strings instead), inheritance, and polymorphism (even when XML supports it).

In general, be conservative with types, because once you have to support some language construct, you can't stop doing so, even if the effort it requires (including the ability to log and debug) is very high. For more on data types, see Section 15.5.

4.2.8 Compensation

Compensation is an interesting form of loose coupling. It has to do with the question of transaction safety. If you have to update two different backends to be consistent, how can you avoid problems that occur when only one update is successful, resulting in an inconsistency? The usual approach to solving this problem is to create a common transaction context using a technique such as *two-phase commit* (2PC). With this approach, you first perform all the modifications on both backends, except for the final "switch to the updated data"; then, if no system signals a problem, the final commit performs the update on both systems.

2PC is one of the most overhyped attributes of middleware. Whenever there is an evaluation of middleware, the question of whether 2PC is supported arises. However, in practice, 2PC is rarely used in large systems because all the backends have to support it, it requires some programming effort, and it binds resources. The main problem is that all systems have to be online, and have to provide resources until the modifications are complete on the last system. Especially when there is concurrent data access, this can lead to delays and deadlocks.

A more loosely coupled way to ensure overall consistency is *compensation*. In this approach, you modify the first backend, and then modify the second backend; if only one modification is successful, you then "compensate" for the problem appropriately. For example, you might revert the successful modification to restore the consistent situation that existed before the modifications began, or send a problem report to an error desktop where somebody can look into the details and deal with it manually.

The advantage of compensation is that system updates don't have to be performed synchronously (some backends might even be offline while they are being updated). The drawback is that you have to explicitly provide and call services that revert previous services or programs for manual error handling.

BPEL, the process execution language of Web Services, directly supports compensation (see Section 7.4.2).

4.2.9   Control of Process Logic

Process-control decisions can also lead to different forms of coupling. Having one central component controlling the whole process logic creates a bottleneck because each involved system must connect with it. Failure of such a central component will stop the whole process.

On the other hand, if you have decentralized or distributed control (where each component does its job and knows which component will continue after) you avoid bottlenecks, and if some systems fail, others can still continue to work. See Section 7.6 for details.

4.2.10   Deployment

Whether you require that system updates be deployed simultaneously, or at different times, is related to coupling. Of course, systems are bound more tightly to each other if it is required that they update synchronously. The more loosely coupled approach of updating at different times, however, leads to a very important drawback: the need for migration, which leads to versioning (see Chapter 12).

4.2.11   Versioning

Your versioning policy also has something to do with tight or loose coupling. If a system provides certain data types that are used by a consumer, you'll have problems when the provider adds new attributes. If the provider introduces a new type version, the consumer will have to upgrade explicitly to this new type; otherwise, the provider will have to support both types. If, on the other hand, the provider just adds the attribute to the existing type, this might cause binary compatibility issues, and require the consumer to recompile its code or use another library.

With a more loosely coupled form of data type versioning, the consumer won't have to do anything as long as the modifications are backward compatible.

However, as discussed in Section 12.3, achieving loose coupling here can be very complicated. Again, it's up to you to decide on your policy by discussing the pros and cons.

4.3   Dealing with Loose Coupling

The forms of loose coupling discussed in this chapter are only some (more or less typical) examples. Again, note that there are no hard and fast rules: you will have to decide on the appropriate amount of loose coupling for your specific context and architecture.

I have seen very different decisions made with regard to different types of coupling. As I mentioned earlier, the policy of one of my customers was to avoid asynchronous communication whenever possible, based on the experience that it led to race conditions at runtime that were very hard, or even impossible, to reproduce in a development environment, and therefore almost impossible to fix. Another customer in the same domain had a policy that synchronous calls were allowed only for reading service calls because the performance was not good enough for writing service calls.

Note that you might also have to decide about combinations of forms of loose coupling. For example, one important decision you'll have to make is whether an ESB should be separated from a backend via a protocol, or via an API (see Section 5.3.3). Separating via an API usually means that the ESB provides libraries each backend or backend adapter has to use. So, deployment and binding become issues. On the other hand, using a common API, you can hide some aspects of synchronous or asynchronous communications inside the ESB.

You might ask which forms of loose coupling are typical. To my best knowledge, there is no answer. All I can say is that the larger systems are, the more loosely they should be coupled.

4.4 Summary

- Loose coupling is a fundamental concept of SOA (and large distributed systems in general) aimed at reducing dependencies between different systems.

- There are different forms of loose coupling, and you will have to find the mixture of tight and loose coupling that's appropriate for your specific context and project.

- Any form of loose coupling has drawbacks. For this reason, loose coupling should never be an end in itself.

- The need to map data is usually a *good* property of large systems.

The Enterprise Service Bus

PART OF **SOA** IS THE INFRASTRUCTURE THAT ALLOWS YOU TO USE SERVICES IN A PRODUCTIVE SYSTEM landscape. This is usually called the *enterprise service bus* (ESB).* As you'll see in this chapter, there are different opinions about the exact role and responsibilities of an ESB. Part of the reason for the different understandings of ESBs is that there are very different technical approaches to realizing an ESB. This chapter will also explore the consequences of some of these approaches.

5.1 ESB Responsibilities

To run SOA in practice, you need a way of calling services. This infrastructure is the technical backbone of the SOA landscape (sometimes also called the "backplane").

It is the responsibility of the ESB to enable consumers to call the services providers supply. This sounds simpler than it is. Depending on the technical and organizational approaches

---

* As is often the case, there are many meanings for this acronym. I guess it's just a coincidence that ESB also stands for Empire State Building, or *Star Wars Episode V: The Empire Strikes Back.*

taken to implementing the ESB, this responsibility may involve (but is not limited to) the following tasks:

- Providing connectivity

- Data transformation

- (Intelligent) routing

- Dealing with security

- Dealing with reliability

- Service management

- Monitoring and logging

These tasks may need to be carried out for different hardware and software platforms, and even for different middleware and protocols.

The ESB's main role is to provide interoperability. Because it integrates different platforms and programming languages, a fundamental part of this role is data transformation. As [Chappell04] states:

> Data transformation is inherently part of the bus in an ESB deployment. Transformation services that are specialized for the needs of individual applications plugged into the bus can be located anywhere and accessible from anywhere on the bus. Because the data transformation is such an integral part of the ESB itself, an ESB can be thought of as solving the *impedance mismatch* between applications.

This alone can be tough, especially when performance issues come into play (see Chapter 13). The usual approach is to introduce a specific format to which all the individual platforms and APIs map. For Web Services, this format is usually SOAP (see Section 16.2.3).

Another fundamental ESB task is routing. There must be some way of sending a service call from a consumer to a provider, and then sending an answer back from the provider to the consumer (other message exchange patterns exist, as you'll see in Chapter 10, but this is what is technically necessary). Depending on the technology used, and the level of intelligence provided, this task may be trivial, or may require very complicated processing (see Section 5.4.2 for details).

The other responsibilities of an ESB (which I will discuss in Section 5.4) are usually extensions of the core task of providing interoperability. Whether the mechanisms to deal with these tasks are integral or even inherent parts of an ESB, or simply add-ons is a moot point. The important issue is that you know which parts of your system are responsible for which tasks, and which teams are responsible for providing and maintaining them.

For example, one might argue that it is the task of an ESB to provide the technical ability to deal with business processes, and thus, that a business process engine protocol such as BPEL (see Section 7.4.2) must be part of the ESB. On the other hand, one might argue that BPEL is just one specific platform that helps provide composed services, and therefore should not be part of the ESB. There's no doubt that it is a good idea to harmonize the way you compose services that are able to run in process engines. But whether you consider this harmonization as being part of the ESB design, or of a general architecture that uses the ESB, is first and foremost an organizational question. (That's not to say it is not an important question—I have seen many SOA problems that were caused by unclear responsibilities.)

5.2 Heterogeneous ESBs

Note that there is no requirement that the ESB be homogeneous. Although it might be better to have only one technology for running services, this is rarely the case. SOA, by its very nature, accepts heterogeneity. That includes heterogeneity in middleware and protocols. Even with a standard such as Web Services, multiple instantiations of it will differ. And sooner or later, a new standard or new version of the standard that makes things better and easier will be introduced. As soon as you start to use the new standard (alongside the old technology), your ESB will become heterogeneous.

In my experience, in practice, ESBs of significant size are heterogeneous. As an example, consider Figure 5-1, which shows the situation one of my customers was in during 2006.

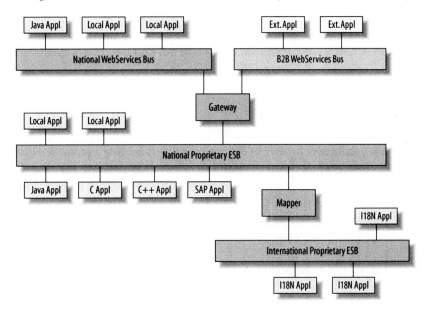

FIGURE 5-1. Example of a heterogeneous ESB

Their first ESB used the technology of a proprietary EAI vendor (the ESB was originally considered to be an EAI bus). When they merged with another company in a different country, however, it turned out that using the same proprietary middleware technology didn't guarantee interoperability. They had to implement a mapper between the two different proprietary ESBs. As the SOA grew, and Web Services became more and more of a de facto standard, it also became necessary to support this protocol, so they realized a gateway technically mapping the original proprietary bus to a Web Services bus. (In fact, for security reasons, the gateway maps to two different Web Services buses, one for internal use and one for B2B communication.) Note that the Web Services gateway over time mapped to different versions of Web Services. Currently, three different versions are supported (using different SOAP protocols). However, the mapping to external service providers always requires some custom coding to deal with all the different abilities of Web Services that must be mapped to the internal proprietary format.

Interestingly, at the same time, the company was working on a second generation of a company-wide ESB based solely on a new generation of Web Services technology. This at first meant that in practice, the ESB landscape was even more heterogeneous because all these ESB approaches were in use.

Note that conceptually, the ESB depicted in Figure 5-1 is *one* ESB. Using this ESB, every system can connect to every other system throughout the landscape. It's just a technical detail that some participants deal with different protocols than others.

Ideally, changing the technology of the ESB should have no impact on providers and consumers. They should be able to use the same API, and only the mapping should change. That is, from the providers' and consumers' points of view, the service API should be transparent. However, this usually requires that the ESB's responsibilities include the service APIs for any specific platforms. If an ESB requires only a specific protocol, consumers and providers have to deal with modifications of this protocol. This is discussed in the next section.

5.3 ESB Differences

Technically and conceptually, ESBs can differ widely. On one hand, your solution might not involve any specific tool or piece of software at all. Just defining a protocol might be enough (in this case, the ESB would delegate a lot of tasks to the providers and consumers). On the other hand, an ESB might consist of several tools and programs that run centrally, and/or decentrally and are used by service designers, implementers, and operators. In this section, I'll provide an overview of the different approaches to help you understand the consequences of specific ESB designs.

5.3.1 Point-to-Point Connections Versus Mediation

One aspect where ESB technologies differ is in the amount of coupling they provide for the physical connections. Does the consumer have to know the exact address ("endpoint") of the service provider, or does the ESB provide some mechanism that brings consumer requests to the correct providers?

If the consumer has to know the endpoint, it sends each request to a specific receiver. Such a connection is called a *point-to-point* connection (see Figure 5-2). The problem with this type of connection is that the call fails if the physical receiver is not available.

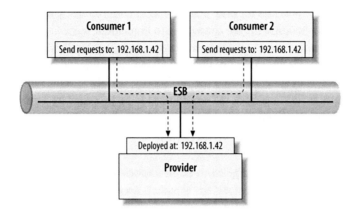

FIGURE 5-2. An ESB providing point-to-point connections

If the consumer does not have to know the endpoint of the provider, it instead identifies the provided service by a tag or symbolic that the ESB interprets to find an appropriate provider (see Figure 5-3). The tag usually contains the service name, and might contain some additional attributes that influence the routing. For example, the ESB might process a priority or have different policies for different consumers. In this case, the ESB plays the role of a mediator or broker, which leads to a loosely coupled infrastructure (see Section 4.2.3).

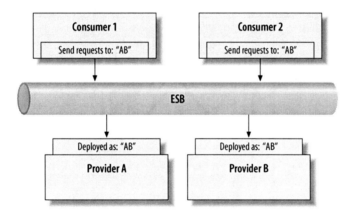

FIGURE 5-3. An ESB mediating connections

The advantage of the indirect approach is that the ESB is able to deal with dynamic modifications of the SOA landscape. Multiple systems can provide a given service, which allows for load balancing and failover (if one system fails, requests can be sent to the remaining provider systems).

To configure the indirect approach, the ESB might process deployment information at startup time (using a configuration file), or at runtime (letting each provider register itself when it is available).

If an ESB technology provides for only point-to-point connections, you can still realize loose coupling. One option is for the consumers to implement some kind of indirection by asking a broker or name server where to send requests before actually sending them. Note, however, that this approach usually only allows consumers to retrieve endpoints to send requests to at start time, or when the first service call of a specific type is made. To process endpoints at runtime, each call would need to be preceded by a call to a broker, which would cause significant overhead and introduce a bottleneck.

5.3.2   Interceptors

The other way an ESB based on a point-to-point protocol can support indirect service calls is by providing so-called "interceptors" or "proxies." An easy approach is to replace the physical endpoint that provides a service with a piece of hardware or software that serves as a load balancer. The consumers still use an official endpoint, which delegates the real task: when messages arrive, the load balancer sends them to the different physical service providers that it knows about (see Figure 5-4).

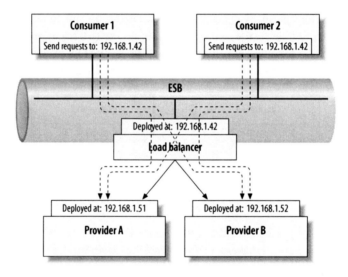

FIGURE 5-4. An ESB with a load balancer for provided services

A more complicated ESB approach provides an interceptor or proxy for each provider and for each consumer. In this case, the consumer will communicate in a "point-to-point" fashion only with its specific interceptor. The interceptor will route each call to the appropriate provider, using its specific interceptor (see Figure 5-5).

In this scenario, the magic of intelligent routing and other ESB services is completely encapsulated from the outside world by interceptors. In fact, internally, a totally different protocol can be used (see Figure 16-4 in Chapter 16 for an example).

Note that the Web Services protocol is an inherently point-to-point protocol. Just exchanging services between two systems requires no tools or programs, but you have to

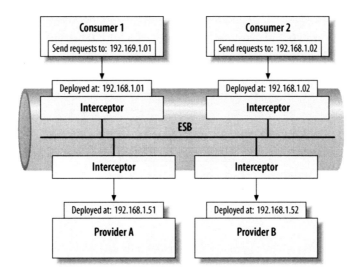

FIGURE 5-5. An ESB using interceptors

know and specify the endpoint of a service call in your consuming process. However, as [PulierTaylor06] points out:

> Web service standards contain no provisions for load balancing and failover. If left alone, a failed or overloaded web service has no way of routing SOAP requests to alternative web sites.

Still, load balancing and failover are core requirements for large distributed systems. For this reason, sooner or later each ESB based on Web Services will incorporate interceptors (see Section 16.3.2 for an example of the details). These interceptors might also help to deal with other aspects of an ESB, such as security and monitoring (discussed in Section 5.4).

5.3.3 Protocol-Driven Versus API-Driven ESB

Conceptually, two different approaches are possible regarding where the responsibility of an ESB begins from the providers' and consumers' points of view. With the *protocol-driven* approach, the ESB defines a protocol, and the providers and consumers send and receive messages according to this protocol (see Figure 5-6). Web Services, which require a SOAP protocol, might be an example for this approach.

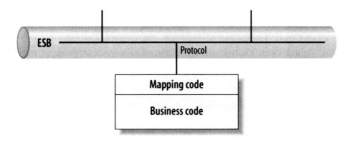

FIGURE 5-6. Connecting to a protocol-driven ESB

With the *API-driven* approach, the ESB defines platform-specific APIs (such as Java inter-faces), and the providers and consumers use these APIs for service implementations and service calls (see Figure 5-7).

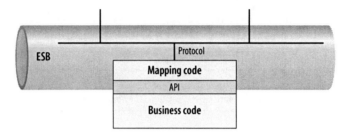

FIGURE 5-7. *Connecting to an API-driven ESB*

The difference between these approaches has major a impact on development processes.

When the ESB defines only a protocol, the details of how consuming and providing pro-cesses are developed are completely outside the scope of the ESB (and its associated team). The infrastructure team does not have to provide tools and/or libraries for mapping the APIs for service calls and service implementations to the required protocol. Instead, each partici-pant (provider and consumer) can choose which tools to use to enable them to send service calls, and provide service implementations that fulfill the requirements of the ESB protocol. If a new platform comes into play, it is the task of the providers and consumers that use this platform to provide adapters to the ESB protocol. The team responsible for the ESB is not involved (except in helping to identify any problems caused by the new adapters).

When the ESB is responsible for the APIs, the problem of mapping service calls and service implementations to well-formed messages that participants can send over the ESB is the task of the team providing the ESB. Providers and consumers can concentrate on the busi-ness functionality. If new platforms get integrated, it is the responsibility of the ESB to provide solutions for corresponding APIs (i.e., to provide code generators and libraries). However, libraries and code generators provided by the central infrastructure team become an important part of the development and deployment processes of each provider and consumer.

The principal tradeoff here has to do with how independent the infrastructure team and development teams for the providers and consumers are. The protocol-driven approach gives providers and consumers more responsibility. Their whole development process is technically independent from the infrastructure, provided it fulfills all the requirements of the ESB protocol. This decouples the infrastructure from system development, but it raises the risk of problems in system development because many individual ways of mapping an internal API to a protocol can arise. In principle, each development team has to solve the same problems, and if the protocol changes, it is up to each provider and consumer to update its individual mapping.

Usually, the protocol-driven approach leads to a third layer of the model of distributed communications (see Figure 5-8). At the bottom of the model, there is a pretty stable protocol, at the top, there is an API for calling and implementing services, and in the middle, there is a layer responsible for mapping the API to the protocol. This middle layer can be provided by platform-specific teams, company-specific teams, third-party vendors, and so on.

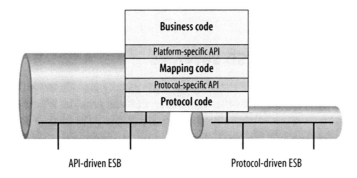

FIGURE 5-8. Layers from business to protocol code

You can find the same layers in the Internet. The transport layer contains the stable protocol HTTP(S). To send data over this protocol, different vendors provide consuming clients (browsers), or implementation tools (web site engines or platform-specific libraries), which provide the mappings to platform-specific interfaces such as Java, HTML, and so on.

In SOA, a protocol-driven ESB leads to a situation where each consumer and provider maps the protocol specified by the ESB to a platform-specific business interface. For example, some code is required to transfer a Java interface to a Web Services protocol. The questions are which tools are used to generate this code, and who is responsible for its generation and maintenance. Often, it's up to the providers and consumers, but a recommended or certified standard tool (provided by the infrastructure team or a third-party team) might be used to generate this code.

In contrast, an API-driven ESB provides APIs for the business teams, making protocol details transparent to providers and consumers. As a consequence, the providers and consumers need (generated) libraries, and a process is required to distribute them.

When the protocol-driven approach is used, problems can occur when a protocol gets modified, or if it does not ensure interoperability. If the protocol changes, each provider and consumer has to modify its mapping (generator) accordingly. This can become expensive. And, if the protocol is not good enough to guarantee interoperability, you might end up having to maintain and verify each individual connection between a provider and a consumer (bringing back a problem that the ESB should have solved). Note that Web Services, which are inherently protocol-driven, currently have the problem of a lack of interoperability (see Section 16.3.1 for details).

There is no doubt that protocols will change over time. For this reason, sooner or later all companies using Web Services consider adopting a mapping layer, which is part of the ESB (but I have also seen different teams being responsible for the ESB and a common mapping layer). Having a central team for providing solutions to map between the business APIs, and the protocol APIs, also solves the problem that code generators for protocol mappings usually lead to very different APIs, which means that you can't easily switch to different service code generators (see Chapter 18).

5.4 Value-Added ESB Services

As mentioned at the beginning of this chapter, ESBs usually provide more than just connectivity. Let's briefly explore the other services an ESB can provide. Where it's relevant, I will refer you to later sections where these topics are discussed in further detail.

5.4.1 Data Mapping

As introduced in Section 4.2.2, loose coupling usually leads to a situation where only a few fundamental and stable data types are defined as a common data model. For all other kinds of information, providers define their own data types. In addition, Section 12.3.1 will demonstrate that versioning of data types can even lead to a situation where services supplied by the same provider use different data types for the same data. As a consequence, a consumer should have a thin mapping layer to map the provider's data types to its own data types.

Of course, an ESB can deal with the need for data mapping and data transformation. As discussed earlier, it depends on how you define the responsibilities of the ESB. The layer that maps between the protocol-specific and platform-specific APIs might also be able to map data types. Alternatively, the ESB might be able to define proxies that map data types inside the protocol. Of course, both approaches require some way to specify the mapping.

These days, some vendors try to solve this problem by introducing a common object model inside the ESB, which of course disables the effect of loose coupling. Be very careful when a vendor attempts to sell you *master data management* (MDM) as a central part of your SOA. It might be appropriate, but it also might be the opposite of what you need.

5.4.2 Intelligent Routing

In this chapter, we have discussed some aspects of routing messages, especially dealing with technical aspects, such as load balancing and failover. However, from a business point of view, you might also need different ways of routing messages. For example, messages might be assigned different priorities, or you might even deal with messages differently according to their contents. The latter is known as *content-based routing* (CBR).

For example, you might see that a postal address inside a message uses an old form of zip code (e.g., five rather than nine digits for a U.S. address, or four rather than five digits for a German address). A message containing a zip code in the older format could be routed to a special provider that transfers it into the new format.

Of course, this way of dealing with message contents requires that the ESB have some semantic understanding of at least some parts of the services. In other words, it is not just the provider and consumer that depend on the exact interface of a service. Be very careful with this approach. In principle, you can add some common properties that an ESB might process, but to be able to scale, they should be part of a message header (see Section 15.4 for more on this).

5.4.3 Dealing with Security

In most SOA landscapes, sooner or later security becomes an issue because some restrictions regarding consumers' ability to call services and see the results apply. For this reason, an ESB might provide some way to deal with the different aspects of security. This topic is discussed in Chapter 14.

5.4.4 Dealing with Reliability

Different protocols offer different forms of reliability. It is not necessarily the case that a protocol ensures that a message is delivered "once and only once." In fact, the Web Services protocol HTTP does not inherently guarantee delivery. Some other protocols might, for example, guarantee that a message will be delivered "at least once."

For this reason, an ESB should define how it will deal with reliability issues. How faults and technical errors are handled may be influenced by the protocol used by the ESB, but the ESB itself can add some mechanisms to change this behavior. Chapter 10 will discuss this in detail.

5.4.5 Service Management

As your SOA landscape grows, sooner or later you will run into the problem of managing all your services. This might be a business topic, if analysts and designers are looking for a way to find existing services and reuse them in new business processes, or there might be a technical requirement to be able to deploy and run a service infrastructure. Chapter 17 will discuss this topic.

5.4.6 Monitoring and Logging

You can't put enough effort into developing your ESB's ability to support logging and monitoring. Remember that the ESB becomes the technical heart of your running business processes, and the way you implement, debug, and maintain local processes is now distributed over multiple systems. That means, in fact, that your ESB becomes your debugger for distributed processes. For this reason, you should establish concepts such as correlation IDs and tools that support monitoring and debugging over distributed systems. See Section 15.3 for more details on this topic.

Note that monitoring and logging should include which consumer is calling a service, and how long a specific service call takes. This is important to withdraw a service (see Section 11.2.2) and monitoring SLAs.

5.4.7 Business Activity Monitoring (BAM)

One argument in favor of an ESB, which is often even used as a possible business case for SOA, is the idea that the ESB will enable *business activity monitoring* (BAM). The idea is that the ESB allows you to monitor messages in such a way that you can learn about the state of your business on the fly, and react very quickly.

For example, you might monitor the times at which certain services are called, which might help you to optimize the way the marketing department places advertisements. As another example, with BAM, if something unusual happens (e.g., certain services are called more or less often than usual), you might immediately be able to spot some business opportunities, and be able to react before your competitors. It's a bit like data warehouse processing, except that you're monitoring and processing behavior instead of the data generated by this behavior.

Of course, I can't say whether this concept will sound reasonable to you, or suit your circumstances. Technically, it should be no problem to detect "unusual" behavior by monitoring service calls. The (technical and organizational) question is how to map this information into useful business input. Establishing a process where unusual service call behavior leads to a bell ringing in a corresponding business department might be enough.

In any case, BAM requires that the ESB be able to monitor service calls on the right abstraction layer. That is, you need to be able to monitor on the messages layer, and process the collected data centrally. You also need some way to process and correlate all the messages for logging and debugging reasons, as just described, so usually, this isn't really a new requirement.

5.4.8 Service Implementation Support

Sometimes, the question of how an ESB can support the implementation of services arises. Regarding the composition (orchestration) of services, people often recommend including a process or workflow engine such as BPEL for Web Services as part of the ESB. Providing both together does create some synergy effects. For example, your ESB monitoring can include a graphical representation of the running processes. Or, as [Chappell04] states:

> The process flow capabilities of the ESB make it possible to define business processes that are local to an individual department or business unit, and that can also coexist within a larger integration network. This is something a hub-and-spoke integration broker or a BPM tool can't do very well on its own.

However, be careful here. Starting with SOA, you might easily be able to specify a common process engine to use. But just as it's difficult to provide a common implementation platform for databases or other systems, you might have problems keeping implementation platforms for (process) services homogeneous. See Sections 7.4.4 and 9.1 for more about this topic.

5.5 Summary

- An enterprise service bus (ESB) is the infrastructure of SOA.

- Its purpose is to provide interoperability (connectivity, data transformation, and routing) combined with some additional services such as security, monitoring, and so on.

- An ESB can be heterogeneous (and often is).

- Whether the ESB is protocol-driven or API-driven is a fundamental decision.

- A protocol-driven ESB defines a protocol that providers and consumers have to match, but it is up to the providers and consumers how to match that protocol. The ESB and connected systems are decoupled in such a way that they do not share any code, so the ESB does not have to deploy libraries for the systems. The drawback is that any protocol changes force the providers and consumers to make corresponding updates.

- An API-driven ESB provides an API for providers and consumers to use to implement and/or call services. This allows protocol details to be transparent, but requires some way for the ESB to deploy generated code, and/or libraries to the providers and consumers.

- There are different value-added services that an ESB might provide. The most important is the ability for distributed debugging.

- Business activity monitoring (BAM) allows you to monitor the ESB, so you can learn about your business in real time and react accordingly. This might create some business opportunities and market advantages.

CHAPTER SIX

Service Classification

AS DISCUSSED IN **CHAPTER 3,** THERE ARE DIFFERENT WAYS TO DEFINE SERVICES, AND SERVICES CAN have different attributes. Even within the same context or landscape, services can differ. For this reason, it's impossible to formulate one common, concrete definition of the term. The variety of business functionality is enormous, and services serve very different purposes and play very different roles. Some services read data; others write it. Some services have simple, fast effects; others perform complicated workflows. Services might have access to no, one, or multiple backends. As with objects in object-oriented programming, there is an enormous variety among services. Thus, it makes no sense to try to deal with all of them in the same way. Correspondingly, it makes sense to categorize services when common differences among their properties become clear.

In this chapter, I will discuss some different categorization approaches. As usual, I won't prescribe general rules, but rather will try to provide a good starting point from which you can make decisions for your concrete SOA.

Of course, there are multiple ways to classify services. I'll begin with a technically driven approach that is pretty common in the community (although different terminology is sometimes used). I start with this approach because, in my opinion, it is the best way to categorize services in such a way that it is easy to introduce different SOA layers and stages of expansion. I will then discuss some other methods of categorizing services that I've encountered in books and project experiences.

6.1 A Fundamental Service Classification

My favorite starting point for service classification introduces the following three categories:

- Basic services
- Composed services
- Process services

This is a categorization you can find in many publications, although the exact terminology differs slightly. For example, [KrafzigBankeSlama04] refers to "basic" services, "intermediate" (composed) services, and "process-centric" (process) services. (In addition, they introduce a fourth fundamental category called "public-enterprise" services; see Section 6.5.1.) In [Erl05]'s categorization, "business services" match most closely with what I term basic services, and the term "process services" covers what I term both composed and process services (see the later section "Categorization according to Erl"). [BloombergSchmelzer06] uses the term "atomic services" instead of basic services.

Based on these three service categories, you can define three different service layers and stages of expansion (see Figure 6-1):

- The first stage of expansion is a so-called *fundamental* SOA, which has only a service layer of basic services.
- The second stage of expansion is a so-called *federated* SOA, which in addition to the basic services has a layer of composed services (this layer might be called an orchestration or composition layer).
- The third stage of expansion is a so-called *process-enabled* SOA, which has a third layer for process services.

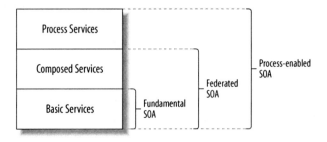

FIGURE 6-1. Fundamental service layers and stages of SOA expansion

Let's go through the different categories, layers, and stages of expansion step-by-step.

6.2 Basic Services

The first stage of expansion provides only basic services, which are services that each provide a basic business functionality and that it does not make sense to split into multiple services. Usually, these services provide the first fundamental business layer for one specific backend or problem domain. Typically, these services are short-term running and conceptually stateless (see Section 15.1.1). Thus, synchronous calls may be useful.

The role of these services is to wrap a backend or problem domain so that consumers (and higher-level services) can access the backend by using the common SOA infrastructure.

There are two types of basic services:

- Basic data services
- Basic logic services

6.2.1   Basic Data Services

Basic data services read or write data from or to one backend system. These services typically each represent a fundamental business operation of the backend.

Basic services encapsulate platform-specific aspects and implementation details from the outside world, so that the consumer can request a service without knowing how it is implemented.

These services should provide some minimal business functionality. That is, there should be no technical interface, as in a service that returns a database table (see the "Business-Driven Versus Technically Driven Business Interfaces" sidebar in Section 3.1). Instead, basic data services typically either read and return or write chunks of data that usually belong together, according to the business needs. That is, business guys should be able to understand what these services do.

[Allen06] defines the following "guidelines for achieving an optimum level of granularity for a lowest level service":

- It should be possible to describe the service in terms of function, information, goals, and rules, but *not* in terms of groups of other services.
- The function set of a service should operate as a family unit that offers business capability.
- A single role should take responsibility for the service.
- The service should be as self-contained as possible. Ideally, it should be autonomous.

Typical examples (in this case, for customer services) are services that:

- Create a new customer.
- Change the address of a customer.
- Return the address of a customer.
- Create a new contract/portfolio/account.

- Return a list of customers according to some search criteria.

- Return a customer's balance.

- Send an ordered item to a customer.

- Return the number of customers.

- Return details on a customer's payment practices.

It is important that these services encapsulate or abstract in such a way that some problems are solved. In this case, the services should encapsulate technical details and alleviate the danger of inconsistencies on the backend. Thus, it is an important goal that these services not be able to create inconsistencies on the backends on which they operate. In fact, basic services should have the so-called ACID properties, which means that they should be:

Atomic
> This means that the call of the service either succeeds or has no effect. Ensuring this property is the task of the backend that provides a service.

Consistent
> This means that after the service call, the backend is left in a legal, consistent state. Thus, no service call should be able to bring a backend into an inconsistent state.

Isolated
> This means that a service being processed by a backend is not influenced by other service calls running on the same backend at the same time. That is, a read service should return data that is consistent in itself.

Durable
> This means that after a service call succeeds, it is guaranteed that the effect is persistent. That is, no system failure is able to undo the result of the service call by accident.

6.2.2   Basic Logic Services

Basic logic services represent fundamental business rules. These services usually process some input data and return corresponding results.

Compared with basic data services, basic logic services are a minority. Typical examples of basic logic services might be services that:

- Define product catalogs and price lists.

- Define rules for changing customer contracts.

- Return whether a year is a leap year.

- Define allowed dates, which might be constraints or extensions of real dates (for example, there exist banking dates such as June 31, to simplify some processings).

However, often these services are also wrappers of the backend systems that provide this functionality (for historical reasons). Thus, the border between basic logic services and basic data services is not always clear. This is not a problem, because in a SOA all basic services, whether they are data or logic services, are usually treated in a similar way. If there is a significant difference in basic services, it is usually between reading and writing services (see Section 6.5.2).

6.2.3 Fundamental SOA

By introducing basic services you get the first stage of expansion of SOA, called *fundamental SOA* (this term is taken from [KrafzigBankeSlama04]).

With basic services introduced, service consumers can use an ESB to process the business functionality that one backend is responsible for (see Figure 6-2).

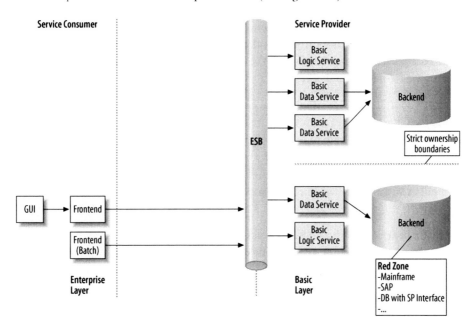

FIGURE 6-2. Fundamental SOA

What is meant by "backend" is open. A backend may be anything that is responsible for a specific group of data and functionality. The important point here is that this backend plays a clear and more or less unique role.

Technically, a backend can be a database, a host, a mainframe, an SAP system, a rules engine, a group of J2EE servers, a remote connection to another company, and so on. It might consist of one or multiple systems. It is the task of the basic service adapters to hide the technical details and provide a common service API so that the backend can be accessed through the ESB.

Organizationally, a backend is usually something you can identify in your organizational structures. It is a system (or a group of systems) that from a business point of view plays a specific role and is maintained by a specific group of people. It provides a certain general functionality, such as booking, customer management, order management, and so on.

What this means in practice can differ widely, due to historical (and hysterical) reasons. Usually, the question of system and backend boundaries is a general question of the overall domain model of a company, which is supported by organizational structures.

When drawing an overall picture of a large system, I often describe these backends as being the "red zone." This is an American football* term referring to the last 20 yards of a football pitch. When the ball reaches this area, the situation becomes critical because play is more condensed (with only 20 yards of room for moves) and dangerous (in that you're close to the point where games are won and lost). Both conditions are also true for backends of IT systems: they contain and manage core business data and functionality in a very condensed form (without added features such as ergonomic user interfaces and so on), and because this data represents the essence of the company, mistakes and misuse can have important consequences. In one banking project I heard the term "juristic data" used for the data processed here, because all the data that might be juristically relevant for the company was stored in the backend.

The most important consideration for backends is that they must not become inconsistent or corrupted. Basic services must therefore ensure that external systems can access these backends without being able to corrupt them. That is, they should hide the technical details. In addition, due to the philosophy of services, a basic service should represent a self-contained business functionality. This functionality should be atomic, in the sense that it either succeeds or has no effect. In either case, the backend remains consistent in itself.

Note that a basic service should never access more than one backend. It should wrap this single backend (which might internally be composed of multiple systems) in such a way that external systems can do something useful with the data on the backend. Typical examples of such services include services that create a customer, update a customer's address, query an address, search for a customer, and so on.

Note that in large systems, there are always multiple backends with redundant data. For example, you might have a CRM system and a billing system that both hold certain items of customer data (ID, address, and so on). In this case, you would have different basic services for each backend that allow modification of this data. For example, both the CRM system and the billing system would provide a basic service that allows a customer's address to be changed. It is not the task of basic services to ensure consistency across backends. That is the responsibility of higher services or (if these don't exist yet) the frontends calling the basic services.

The advantage of this approach is that it is clear which team is responsible for basic services (the team also responsible for the backend), and that team can concentrate on

---

* American readers might wonder why I add "American" to "football." You might argue that this is a tautology because the other football is called "soccer." However, in other parts of the world "football" is usually the term used for soccer, so this clarification helps people from other countries to understand which sport I mean here.

fulfilling the need to provide external access to their backend without the danger of it becoming corrupted.

The systems that consume basic services can be very different. They can be simple clients or batch programs, or multilayered clients. From their point of view, the basic services they call store and retrieve data or provide basic data transformations. That is, the basic services are at their bottom layer. On top, there might be additional layers for additional business processing and presentation. These layers might even be physically separated, as, for example, in portal software where a server provides contents for an Internet browser.

If these clients are allowed to perform tasks such as changing a customer's address, it is their responsibility to ensure consistency across all backends by calling the appropriate basic services for the different backends.

Note that SOA does not require that these basic service interfaces be harmonized. Although that would be nice, it is typically not the case. (This aspect of loose coupling is discussed in Section 4.2.2.) Names and attributes of similar basic services provided by different backends might differ, and it is the task of the consumer of the basic services to deal with these differences.

However, it doesn't make sense for each frontend to have to constantly deal with the fact that there are multiple backends that deal with customer data. Clearly, it would be preferable for a frontend to be able to make changes globally across backends. This is where composed services come into play.

Note, however, that in a large system it is not always easy to maintain consistency by giving this responsibility to higher layers that have to ensure that multiple calls to multiple backends are consistent. To facilitate matters, it should be clear which system is the master and which systems have derived data, and corresponding synchronizations should apply. Note that these synchronizations are usually outside the scope of SOA. Synchronizing backends is not part of a distributed business process. Therefore, you usually won't use services to synchronize data (although technically you might use the service infrastructure to perform this task).

6.3 Composed Services

The second stage of expansion adds composed services. These represent the first category of services that are composed of other services (basic and/or other composed services).

In SOA terminology, composing new services out of existing services is called *orchestration*. Like in an orchestra, you combine different "instruments" to perform tasks that are more complex than those possible with a single instrument. These services might therefore also be called *orchestrated services*.

These services operate at a higher level than basic services, but they are still short-term running and conceptually stateless. To use a workflow term, a composed service represents a *micro flow*, which is a short-running flow of activities (services, in this case) inside one business process.

6.3.1 Composed Services for Multiple Backends

Composed services are typically services that access multiple backends and therefore are composed of multiple basic services. A typical example is a service that updates redundant data on multiple backends. For example, large systems may contain the same customer data in different backends (in a system local to one company redundant customer data might be found in the CRM and billing systems, while in a system spanning multiple companies the same customer data might be found in each company's CRM system). By providing a service that changes a customer's address on all the backends, you can ensure consistency across the backends (unlike with basic services, which are responsible for consistency on only one backend).

A more complicated example would be a service that changes a phone contract. Unlike a simple change of address on different backends, in a case such as this different backends might need different updates. The update of the customer data is different from the updates inside the billing system and the core network dealing with the real phone calls.

A third example of a composed service would be a service that transfers money from one backend to another backend. In this case, the composed service would call one basic service that withdraws money from one backend and another basic service that pays the money into another backend.

The latter two examples immediately raise the issue of transaction safety. What happens if the first service call succeeds but the second fails? Again, from the consumer's point of view, such services should have the ACID properties (discussed earlier in Section 6.2.1). Thus, they should either succeed or have no effect. This means that if only one of the two basic service calls fails, you must undo the successful service call and return a failure.

6.3.2 Composed Services for One Backend

Composed services may also map or adapt existing services in some way. Such services might also be referred to as "adapter services."

These services might be useful to provide a different interface for a service that, for example, has a different name, more or fewer attributes, and so on. Typical applications would be to provide backward compatibility or to map services to a required interface.

6.3.3   Federated SOA

Having both basic and composed services leads to the expansion stage I call *federated SOA* ([KrafzigBankeSlama04] calls it *networked SOA*). This stage introduces an additional layer for composed services (see Figure 6-3).

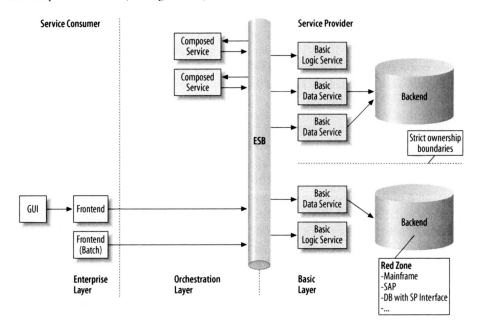

FIGURE 6-3. Federated SOA

As discussed earlier, a typical example of a composed service might be a service that makes a global modification of a customer's address by calling the appropriate basic services of all backends where the address is kept (see Section 15.1.1 for a possible implementation). This service would have to:

- Know which backends must be informed to update the address.
- Map the attributes of the new address to the specific attributes provided by the individual basic services of the different backends.
- Deal with error handling (i.e., react appropriately if one or more address updates fail).

The last aspect is the important part to ensure consistency across all backends. While in this scenario it might be fine not to have all backend updates occur at the same time, for other business processes, overall consistency is crucial. For example, in the case of transferring money from one backend to another, both the basic service responsible for withdrawing the money on one backend and the basic service responsible for depositing the money on the other backend have to be successful, or the transfer as a whole should fail. A composed service for such a task should be programmed such that at the end of the service call, either both basic services have succeeded or both have failed.

Note that the often-taught approach for handling such a requirement—introducing transaction safety by performing a two-phase commit (2PC) using a common transaction context for both basic service calls—is usually not appropriate, because it is either not possible or too expensive. You might be surprised how seldom 2PC is really used in large systems. Instead, a more loosely coupled approach called *compensation* (see Section 4.2.8) is typically used.

Compensation in this scenario means that you call both services independently from one another, and if only one basic service succeeds while the other fails, you "compensate" by doing something appropriate. What the appropriate reaction is depends on the circumstances. For example, you might call a third service to roll back the effects of the successful service call (i.e., the first backend might provide an additional service that is able to undo the money withdrawal, which the composed service can call if the service call on the second backend fails). Another reaction would be to put this case on an error desktop where the inconsistency can be resolved manually (this approach might also be used in the event that the rollback fails).

Although compensation makes the business process more complicated, it has several benefits:

- The backends do not need to provide technical support for a common transaction context (note that the backends might even be plain files).

- Implementing basic services becomes easier.

- Maintaining transaction safety over long-running business processes is almost impossible, or at least very resource-intensive. For example, say your service creates a new customer on multiple backends so it can process an order for that customer. Performing the whole process in one transaction context would require that all systems involved share a common transaction context.

Note that when compensation is applied, backends might have to log that a part of a business process was reversed. Suppose that to place an order for a new customer, you first create the customer in your backend systems. If the order fails for some reason, the backend systems may need to preserve the information that a new customer was created and then immediately withdrawn.

6.3.4 Security

The introduction of composed services raises another issue: security. Conceptually, the ESB provides interoperability. So, even when a composed service is provided to allow a task such as updating a customer's address consistently across all backends, consumers still have the ability to call the low-level basic services that allow individual changes on each backend. This reintroduces the danger of inconsistencies appearing across backends. So, we need some mechanisms that help to guarantee that those basic services are called only by higher services. Implementing such restrictions is discussed in Chapter 14.

Note that in general it is still useful for consumers to be able to call basic services. For example, a consumer might call a basic service to retrieve a customer's current address. The layer of composed services does not completely hide the layer of basic services. That is, from a business point of view, it doesn't matter whether a service is a basic or a composed service. The only important point is whether it fulfills the necessary business functionality. What type of service it is is just an implementation detail.

6.4 Process Services

The third stage of expansion adds process services, which represent long-term workflows or business processes. From a business point of view, a process service represents a *macro flow*, which is a long-running flow of activities (services) that is interruptible (by human intervention).

Unlike basic and composed services, a process service usually has a *state* that remains stable over multiple calls. (See Section 15.1.2 for a discussion what it means to be stateful.)

A typical example of a process service is a shopping-cart service. Its state would contain the contents of the shopping cart, perhaps combined with some customer data so that the customer's order could be maintained and manipulated over multiple sessions. Depending on the design, the process may end with the customer's final order being placed, or even with the delivery of all ordered items.

Because process services are typically stateful, you have to provide certain features in your SOA to maintain that state over multiple sessions (see Section 15.1.2) and still provide linear scalability so multiple service calls can be dealt with (see Section 15.1.3). Thus, you might provide the ability to change clients and frontend channels during the process.

A typical example would be a service that allows a customer to order a new insurance policy. The customer might begin the process online, through a company's web portal. During the process, other frontends (such as a back office or call-center client) might request data from the actual process and update it. The process would then end with the policy either being implemented for the customer or canceled for whatever reason.

Another aspect to consider with process services is failover—that is, whether and how to keep the process state when one system with the current state fails. These extra requirements are the main reason for having a separate category for these kinds of services. The other reason is that from a business point of view, long-running process services usually have different qualities from short-running composed services.

While [KrafzigBankeSlama04] claims that it is fine not to distinguish between composed and process services, [Erl05] uses the term "process services" for both service types. Again, it's up to you to categorize appropriately.

6.4.1 Process-Enabled SOA

Introducing process services leads to the stage of expansion called *process-enabled SOA* (again, this term is taken from [KrafzigBankeSlama04]). As stated earlier, the additional layer for process services enables you to manage processes that might be started and controlled by different frontends and be interrupted by human intervention (see Figure 6-4).

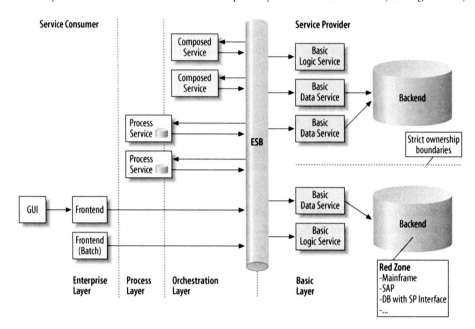

FIGURE 6-4. *Process-enabled SOA*

Note, however, that BPEL as a Web Service standard does not provide any ability for the running process service to trigger human interaction, which has important consequences for the general design of systems (especially frontends). See Chapter 9 for details.

6.4.2 Service State Versus Backend State

When dealing with process services, you have to make an important design decision. Should the process state be maintained in a backend, or in the service itself? The question has to do with how relevant the state of the process is for your business:

- If the process data becomes "juristic data," it is probably more appropriate to manage the state in an ordinary backend.

- If the process data is just some persistent data that has no essential relevance for your business, stateful services are fine.

A typical sign of data having juristic relevance is that the customer/caller gets a unique ID (order number, booking number, etc.) for the process that she can refer to days, weeks, or even years later. In other words, if you have to be able to say something about the state of a process later, the process data should be persisted in a backend.

For example, if you have a business process for a customer creating a bank account, the related data will clearly be juristic. Even before the process is completed (say, because you're waiting for passport identification or a credit rating), you have to manage that customer's data in your backend system(s).

On the other hand, if you have a shopping-cart service that allows a user to keep track of items she may want to order, the related data doesn't become juristic data until the customer elects to place the order and pay for the items in the shopping cart. So, it's not a big deal if the customer has to open a new shopping cart if she ends the session and then decides to continue later. For convenience, however, you might offer to persist the shopping cart's state over multiple sessions. Then, of course, you'll need some functionality that enables clients to find the running processes later. If convenience is your big business advantage or you want to persist all the items customers have ever selected (with or without buying them), such a shopping cart can become part of a backend system providing multiple basic services for shopping-cart access.

Again, this is a design issue (influenced by business requirements). The important thing is to understand the difference between maintaining state in a service and in a backend. Misunderstanding this can easily lead to a situation where stateful process services silently become backends, with the interesting consequence that these backends are wrapped by process services instead of basic services. This doesn't help to make your system landscape more maintainable. This is an important issue that you should always consider when introducing business process and workflow systems.

6.5 Other Service Classifications

As stated earlier, the categorization approach I just presented is only one possibility. In addition to the categories and layers introduced in the previous section, several other categories and layers might exist. For example, you might introduce special layers to separate external services from internal services. You might also divide a process layer into different sublayers, according to certain technical and/or business rules. Or, according to your domain model, you might have some composed services that deal only with your domain, while others deal with multiple domains.

Also bear in mind that fundamental SOA, federated SOA, and process-enabled SOA are not the only possible stages of expansion when establishing SOA. For example, one important stage of expansion is when service management (with service repositories) comes into play (which is somewhat independent from the stages). See Chapter 19 for a more detailed discussion of establishing and implementing SOA.

I have observed and read about several other service categorizations that you might find helpful. I'll present some of them here.

6.5.1   Dealing with Different Types of Consumers

One way to categorize services is to differentiate them according to their target audience. That is, some services may be internal, while others are for the public; likewise, some services might be for a particular department, while others are for the whole company.

The reason for these distinctions is that these services usually have different requirements in terms of security and stability (in the sense that the interface remains unmodified). While "local" services might not need any special security procedures, services for the public usually should run with special security settings (see Chapter 14). Conversely, while publicly available services for anonymous crowds of users usually have very high requirements regarding stability and robustness, "internal" services can more easily be modified. In addition, service-level agreements (SLAs) might differ. For example, external service consumers might need 24/7 availability, while internal users require availability only during business hours (or vice versa).

Other differences may also exist between internal and publicly available services. For example, they might use different interface technologies. While internally there might be good reasons to use proprietary solutions, the goal for public services is typically to provide a very common interface (such as Web Services).

In any case, having different kinds of consumers might lead to different tools, processes, and service lifecycles. It's a good idea to deal with these differences by using different service categories for them.

[KrafzigBankeSlama04], for example, introduced a service category called "public-enterprise services." Services in this category require special security mechanisms, because of the lack of control over the service consumers.

Another distinction that I have seen is between national services and international services. The company in question has offices in different countries, which use different infrastructures and have partially different processes. International services are those that need support within all infrastructures and/or cover business processes that are common across countries.

In cases such as this, there might be a special requirement for the same service to behave differently in different contexts (perhaps because of political, cultural, or historical factors in the different countries). There are different options for dealing with this situation. One option is to design different services for each country (e.g., rating_de( ), rating_us( ), etc.). In this case, the service consumer needs a way to get routed to the right service. This could be handled by the routing capabilities of the ESB, via configuration management, or by providing different calling implementations. Another option is to give all of those services the same name and provide some kind of polymorphism. That is, when the caller calls the rating( ) service, some tricky settings should choose the right implementation. This could be done by deploying different service implementations in different locations or via configuration management or routing features of the infrastructure (ESB).

In any case, if you have such a requirement, it is probably a good idea to introduce a special service category for these kinds of services, because special processes and tools must be provided for them.

6.5.2 Reading Versus Writing Services

Another obvious distinction that can be made is the distinction between reading services (services that do not modify the state of a corresponding backend) and writing services (services that do).

By definition, reading services have special attributes and usually introduce fewer problems: they are inherently idempotent (see Sections 3.3.5 and 15.2) and usually do not require transaction contexts for different backends or rollbacks in the event that they only partially succeed. Writing services, on the other hand, often require an additional amount of security so that modifications can be traced. For this reason, all writing services might need additional technical data that identifies the caller (which might even lead to them becoming stateful—see Section 14.3.4).

Note, however, that some systems also require logging and traceability for each read access. Services that don't manipulate data from a business point of view technically might still have a lot of commonalities with writing services because they write log or history entries.

Reading services are often less stable than writing services. The reason is that extensions to reading services ("Oh by the way, could we also get the following attribute and display it in our frontend?") do not affect complicated business processes, while modifying attributes for writing services might have impacts in a lot of places. For the same reason, writing services are more often used in composed or orchestrated services. Reading services are primarily used by frontends to display data (see Section 9.2 for details).

One of my customers has another reason for separating reading and writing services. When they update their systems to a new release, the systems are down for several hours. Most of their services are reading services, however, which means they can mirror the data during the updates and continue to provide those services. Only writing services must be turned off. The deployment rules for reading services are therefore different from those for writing services, so categorizing the services along those lines makes sense.

6.5.3 Business Categorizations

The motivations for the categorization approaches introduced so far were mainly technical (i.e., driven by the fact that the different types of services are treated differently by processes and tools). In other words, these categorizations lead to differences in your infrastructure (including the corresponding processes).

Of course, services also differ from a business point of view, in terms of their roles and responsibilities. Several publications introduce service categories according to this point of view. I'll present a few approaches here.

Categorization according to Erl

In [Erl05], Thomas Erl introduces a categorization of services whose terms are similar to a possible classification of class categories in object-oriented modeling. As a foundation for the definition of different SOA layers, he introduces the following service categories:

- *Application services* are services that "contain logic derived from a solution or technology platform."

- *Business services* are services that "contain business logic." Similar to the basic services introduced earlier, they might be further divided into:

  — Task-centric business services

  — Entity-centric business services

- *Process services* are services that "represent a business process as implemented by an orchestration platform and described by a process definition."

While you might argue that this categorization isn't very different from the one I introduced earlier (business services correspond to basic services and process services include composed services), the "application services" category introduces some uncertainty. First, this seems to be a category of services that do not provide business functionality, which is in a sense a violation of the term's definition: a service should always represent some business functionality (actually, it's relatively common to have at least some services that deviate from this rule; see Section 6.6 for more information). Second, this classification introduces the possibility of services that both contain logic from a solution/technology platform and provide business logic. [Erl05] introduces a new term for them: *hybrid services*.

[Erl05] also introduces some additional service categories:

Integration services
> These are application services that "act as an endpoint to a solution environment for cross-application integration purposes."

Wrapper and proxy services
> These are integration services that "encapsulate and expose" or mirror "logic residing within a legacy system."

Utility services
> These are application or business services that "offer reusable logic."

Controller services
> These are services that act "as the parent service to service composition members"; in other words, they coordinate other services to "contribute to the execution of an overall business task."

Other service-type terms used include *activation services, coordinator services, registration services,* and so on.

All of these terms have to do with a certain role, property, or ability of the services. However, the different categories do not lead to differences in the infrastructure. Therefore, in my opinion, these terms are usually more important from a business modeling rather than an architectural point of view (which does not mean that they are *not* important).

It's up to you to find the most helpful way to categorize your services. Even inside the same project or systems, different categorizations might be useful. It's important to research your system's details and consider the alternatives.

Categorization according to Allen

In [Allen06], Paul Allen also specifies three key types of (business) services. However, here business-case aspects such as risk and market differentiation matter (see Figure 6-5).

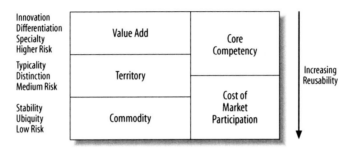

FIGURE 6-5. Characteristics of service types according to [Allen06]

The three key types are as follows:

- *Commodity services* are general services that each participant of the business market has to have. They are universal, stable services, sufficiently established to be used at low risk and with maximum reuse in mind. These services are candidates for outsourced functionality or standard products.

- *Territory services* represent functionality that is essential and central to a specific business. They are common but volatile. Examples include services that provide business rules.

- *Value-added services* are services that reflect the special value an organization brings to the market. They differentiate a company from competitors and usually are highly innovative.

Categorizing services in this way gives you some idea about the stability of a service, the importance it has for the company, and possible risks involved in introducing and maintaining it.

6.6 Technical and Infrastructure Services

I have proposed as a defining characteristic of services that they represent some business functionality, but in fact, in most SOA landscapes there are some common services that are not provided to represent business functionality. These are often called *technical* or *infrastructure services*.

Such services typically use the service infrastructure to provide some "additional" functionality. That is, if you know how to call a business service, you can use the same interface to do something useful but not necessarily business-specific. Typical examples are services that provide technical or infrastructural support. These services might:

- Query deployment information

- Monitor runtime statistics

- Print, log, or trace

- Enable or disable components and systems

- Verify interfaces

From a pure SOA point of view, these are not services, because services should always represent some kind of business functionality. On the other hand, if you have a service infrastructure, why not use this infrastructure for other purposes when it helps?

In essence, this is a question of terminology. While you may call these kinds of services "services," you should always mark them as something special. It should be clear that they serve a particular purpose, so that business teams do not get the impression that services do not necessarily have to represent business functionality. If possible, it may be best to avoid explicitly calling them services.

The application services category introduced by [Erl05] (see "Categorization according to Erl" earlier in this chapter) raises similar issues. A typical example might be a service interface for legacy systems (i.e., services that map existing database procedures, 3270 terminal escape sequences, or SAP BAPIs). Historically these might not represent self-contained business functionalities, but technically you might take them as starting point for your service landscape. Again, be careful about introducing the impression that services do not have to represent self-contained business functionalities, because it's important to maintain a clear abstraction layer that hides technical details.

6.7 Beyond Services

Are services all there is to a distributed system landscape?

No, definitely not. Recall that SOA is a concept for business processes distributed over multiple backend systems with different owners. In your company, several other processes will exist. For example, if the CRM backend has a specific client that maintains the backend or deals only with the data of this backend, it is usually not appropriate to let this client communicate with the backend only via services. The price, in terms of both complexity and performance, is usually too high. What the right technology to implement such a client is is another question. Of course, you might benefit from conceptual abstractions SOA introduces, but don't let services become your "golden hammer" and start treating every problem like a nail.

Also bear in mind that tasks such as synchronizing redundant data over multiple backends are not distributed business processes. Again, you might use the service infrastructure to perform these tasks, but don't come to the conclusion that they are service-oriented.

6.8 Summary

- Services typically fall into different categories. It is up to you to find the appropriate categories to deal with the differences services in your context.

- Based on how you categorize your services, you can define corresponding service layers and stages of SOA expansion.

- The fundamental service classification specifies basic, composed, and process service categories. The corresponding stages of expansion are fundamental SOA, federated SOA, and process-enabled SOA.

- Basic services should always belong to only one backend system and are responsible only for consistency inside this backend.

- Composed and process services are responsible for consistency over multiple backends.

- The usual approach to force consistency across multiple backends is compensation, not transaction safety or two-phase commit (2PC).

- When designing long-running processes, think carefully about whether to implement them as stateful process services or to keep the state in a backend, providing basic services to perform state transformations.

- Other categorizations might be possible and useful. They don't necessarily have to lead to clear, distinct service types.

- Your SOA landscape may include technical or infrastructure services. Strictly speaking, they don't fulfill the major service requirement of providing self-contained business functionalities. Consider carefully how to name and deal with these services.

- Services are not a silver bullet for any type of communication between distributed systems. Their primary purpose is to allow distributed business processes. Synchronizations between redundant master and slave data, decoupling frontends, and so on are different tasks.

CHAPTER SEVEN

Business Process Management

I N SOA, SERVICES ARE TYPICALLY PARTS OF ONE OR MORE DISTRIBUTED BUSINESS PROCESSES. THUS, the main motivations for services come from business processes. And, of course, the question of how to identify services arises. This leads to the terms of business process management (BPM).

This chapter discusses BPM from a SOA perspective, including the topics of business process modeling and orchestration. I will introduce some BPM tools and standards (such as BPEL), and I'll present possible processes for identifying new services according to new business requirements.

Note that entire books and web sites have been devoted to the subject of BPM. This chapter is only an overview, with a focus on developing services in a SOA context (spiced with my experience). The following two chapters will discuss organizational and technical consequences of what is discussed here.

7.1 BPM Terminology

Let's begin with some terminology. There is a bit of confusion about the management and modeling of business processes, so first I'll try to clarify things a bit.

The confusion starts with the acronym BPM itself, which can stand for two different things. Usually, it stands for *business process management*, which is a general term that refers to all activities related to managing and improving business processes. As [BloombergSchmelzer06] states:

> Business process management usually refers to a technology-enabled means for companies to gain visibility and control over long-lived, multistep processes that span a wide range of systems and people in one or more organizations.

Alternatively, BPM may stand for *business process modeling*, which is the modeling of business processes or parts thereof. According to [BloombergSchmelzer06]:

> Business process modeling is a set of practices or tasks that companies can perform to visually depict or describe all the aspects of a business process, including its flow, control and decision points, triggers and conditions for activity execution, the context in which an activity runs, and associated resources.

According to these definitions, business process modeling usually is a part of business process management. Thus, I've chosen to call this chapter Business Process Management and include some sections about business process modeling. When I use the abbreviation BPM, I usually mean business process management.

Another source of confusion can be the difference between business process management and workflow management. Both foster a mainly process-oriented perspective on systems and organizations, and the terms are often used interchangeably. If you want to differentiate between the two, you can think of a business process as being more general:

- A business process describes *what* has to be done (including input and output). It might include manual activities and might use any kinds of resources.

- A workflow describes *how* a certain result can be reached. It looks further into the details of all the steps or activities.

Thus, you might say that you can break down a business process into smaller and more concrete steps, and that at some level of abstraction those activities or process steps are part of a *workflow layer*. Figure 7-1 gives one possible representation of this concept, but note that the exact number of layers and terminology may differ. For example, sub-subprocesses might be named *tasks*, and some might consider tasks to be part of a workflow layer.

SOA standards are also affected by this terminology confusion. For example, according to this distinction, the Business Process Execution Language (BPEL), discussed later in this

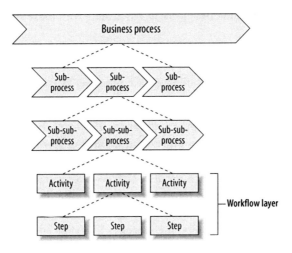

FIGURE 7-1. Example of a business process hierarchy with a workflow layer

chapter, would be part of a workflow layer. However, because BPEL uses the general terminology of business processing, I will use the term *business process* throughout this book even when (according to some) strictly speaking a workflow is meant.

7.2 BPM and SOA

Services are parts of business processes. For this reason, you have to think about business processes to bring services into play.

Business process management, however, is a huge topic. It deals with aspects such as analyzing the business (including needs and opportunities), implementing and integrating business strategies, monitoring and optimizing business processes, establishing corresponding tools and culture, and aligning business with IT.

Talking about BPM in relation to SOA, it is clear that the lowest-level activities of a decomposed process are services. From a business point of view, it doesn't matter whether these services are basic or composed services. What counts is that the services perform necessary business functions. Process services, however, are something different, because they serve to represent complete business processes (or parts thereof).

Now, the question is, how do you identify the services that represent or become parts of your business processes? Here, we are talking about the general fundamental topic of system design. How do you break a system or functionality into smaller parts (called services) so that you can implement it? And how can these services be designed in a more general way so that you can reuse them in different scenarios?

In general, there are two different approaches to dealing with these kinds of problems:

- In the *top-down* approach, you decompose a problem, system, or process into smaller chunks until you reach the level of (basic) services.

- In the *bottom-up* approach, you build business processes by composing services into more general chunks.

All experts agree that in practice, a pure application of either of these approaches does not work. Of course, you can design your processes from the top down, which will help you to understand what is needed and what might be a "natural" separation of activities. However, ignoring existing realities might result in high costs compared with an approach that also takes the existing bottom layer into account. On the other hand, designing business processes from the bottom up introduces the danger of proposing technical details and constraints to very high levels, making the processes inflexible and unintuitive.

[BloombergSchmelzer06] puts it as follows:

> Your approach to SOA should be both top-down (through process decomposition) and bottom-up (exposing existing functionality as Services and composing them into processes). If you take only a top-down approach, you're likely to recommend building Services that are technically difficult or complex to implement. Taking solely a bottom-up approach can yield Services you don't need or, even worse, Services that don't fulfill the requirements of the business.

So, in practice, a mixture of both approaches is appropriate. (There are many different names for such a mixed approach, such as "middle-out," "middle-ground," "meet in the middle," or just "agile.")

Usually, your aim should be to fulfill a real business need. That is, a new or modified business process or a new functionality should come into play. However, you should also respect what you already have (adapting IT reality).

7.3 Example for BPM with Services

Let's take a look at what implementing a new business process with SOA might look like.

Say you want to realize a new business process. You have the new business process on top and the existing backends, which might provide some basic business functionalities represented as services, on the bottom (see Figure 7-2).

Typically, you'll begin with a top-down decomposition to:

- Decide which process steps are manual and which ones are IT-supported.

- Separate the whole process into smaller chunks according to *when* they are performed and *which systems* are responsible for them.

- Break down complex aspects into more manageable steps.

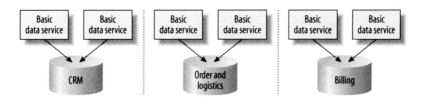

FIGURE 7-2. Starting point for a new business process

The result of this task (which might be called *high-level design* or *solution design*) is a rough idea of how the process should be performed in practice (see Figure 7-3). One important reason for this design process is to determine which IT systems are responsible for which parts of the process. Remember that we're talking about distributed processes. To go into further detail, you first need to identify the systems involved, so you know which people to discuss the details with.

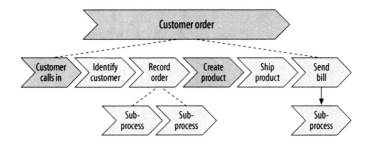

FIGURE 7-3. High-level or solution design

An interesting question arises when services come into play: at which level of abstraction do you design subprocesses and/or activities as services? There is no general answer for this question. You might argue that any IT-supported activity should be a service, or you might disagree with that statement. For example, business rules might be extracted and modeled in special rule engines, and you might or might not consider rules to be services. You'll have to develop your own procedure for designing processes and identifying services (see Figure 7-4).

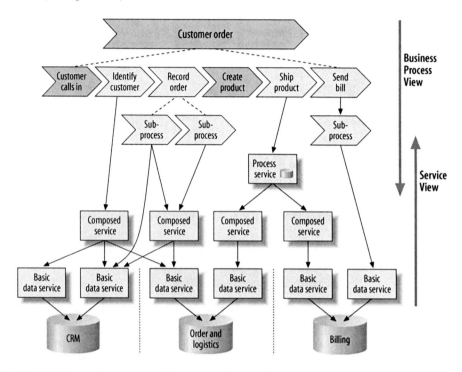

FIGURE 7-4. At some stage, processes, subprocesses, and activities become services

Tooling has a big impact. When you start to use a tool to design and execute services as parts of processes, you are definitely on the level of services. But whether a specific process or subprocess is just drawn by hand, modeled graphically (but in a form that cannot be executed) by a business-process-modeling tool, or modeled by an IDE as a process service that can be executed by a process engine will depend on your specific situation. The only hint I can give is that the "right" way to break down functionality into chunks of appropriate abstraction is something that evolves. Start small and grow.

In any case, the more you decompose a process, the more you should take existing services into account. That is, if you need customer data, you might look for existing services that fulfill your needs instead of focusing on specifying a new service that provides all the necessary data. However, be aware that the existing services might fulfill their tasks slightly differently than you expect, which can have an impact on your process design. For example, you might need a certain attribute relatively late in the process, but if a service you called early in the process has already returned this attribute, you won't need to call another service for it later. With this in mind, you'll have to design your process in such a way that you can keep the value of this attribute from the service call where it's returned to the moment when you really need it.

As another example, writing services might require certain data you originally planned to create or request later in the process. In this case, you might modify the process to suit the existing services, or you might add a service that is able to perform the functionality without this data and then provide another service to set the data later, as planned.

How do you know you're doing it right? There is an important answer to this question: through learning and experience (which might be written down as design principles, patterns, and policies).

Generally speaking, starting with anything that works and seems to be appropriate is probably fine. This is usually a better approach than starting a huge research project to find out the best way to design your first service. Remember that perfectionism is typically too expensive. If problems with the design arise later, you can fix them. Your whole business requires flexibility to improve, and flexibility also enables to you learn from experience. Note, however, that you have to take the time to review and understand what went wrong and what worked well.

What we're really talking about here is *iterative development*. In my opinion, iterative development is the only way you can realize complex systems in reasonable amounts of time. With this approach, you start with a small extract of the whole system and realize an appropriate solution. Then you grow, adding new functionality, redesigning existing solutions, and refactoring existing behavior. As a result, your system becomes better and better, fulfilling more and more requirements in appropriate ways. However, you must accept that you will never achieve perfection, and your task will never be done (unless your system and your business die). See Chapter 19 for more details on establishing SOA.

7.4 Business Process Modeling

In the previous section, I used a graphical notation to draw the different layers and relationships of a business process. This is one example of a business process model. [BloombergSchmelzer06] provides the following general definition of a (business) model:

> A model is in fact just a representation of the process that allows companies to document, simulate, share, implement, evaluate, and continually improve their operations.

With SOA, these models play an important role because standards evolve to enable process modeling in different tools. Some tools even allow you to execute modeled processes with process engines.

7.4.1 Using Business Process Modeling Tools

Figure 7-5 shows the general role a business process modeling tool or engine can play. Such a tool can be used to compose ("orchestrate") new composed or process services out of existing services. In addition, you might have the ability to execute and monitor the resulting composed or process services in a business process engine, ideally using the abstraction layer of the model.

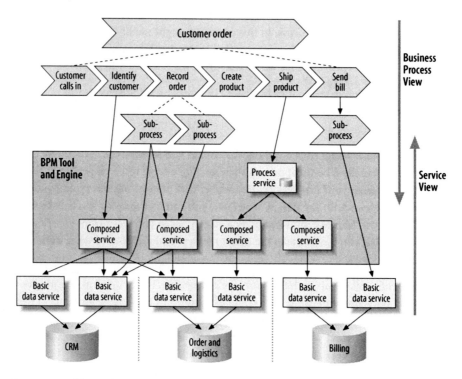

FIGURE 7-5. Modeling and executing composed and process services with BPM tools and engines

Figure 7-6 shows an example of such a BPM tool (ActiveBPEL, an open source business process engine; see [ActiveBPEL]). The major work area shows the current business process (service) under development. Around it there are areas for the lists of existing services and process elements to create the process from. You can also debug and monitor processes running in the engine.

The vision is to enable users to "Plug and Play" business processes by dragging and dropping activities and control structures onto a graphical model. This approach will allow business experts (as opposed to IT experts) to design, modify, monitor, and debug business processes or parts thereof (a pretty old vision promised by tool vendors to bridge the business/IT gap).

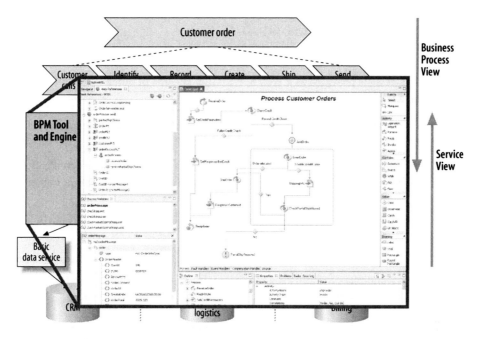

FIGURE 7-6. Modeling with a tool such as ActiveBPEL

7.4.2 BPEL

The Business Process Execution Language plays a fundamental role in modeling and running business processes in tools and engines. BPEL has such momentum in the SOA movement that it is rapidly becoming the standard for designing and running business processes.

Conceptually, BPEL is an XML language for describing business flows and sequences, which in themselves are services. Language elements provide the ability to call services, process responses, and deal with process variables, control structures (including timers), and errors (including compensation).

BPEL was initially designed by IBM, Microsoft, and BEA as a combination of IBM's Web Services Flow Language (WSFL, see [WSFL]) and XLANG, a notation for the automation of business processes based on Web Services. Nowadays, OASIS is specifying the standard (see [WS-BPEL] for details).

A simple BPEL file might look as follows:

```
<?xml version="1.0"?>
<process name="changeAddress" ...>
  <variables>
    <variable messageType="..." name="...">
  </variables>
  <flow>
    <receive .../>    <!-- for this request (operation and input) -->
    <invoke .../>     <!-- call other service -->
```

```
      <assign .../>     <!-- map data -->
      <reply .../>      <!-- return data -->
    </flow>
  </process>
```

The whole ‹process› is provided as a Web Service that consists of different operations. Roughly, the XML file is organized as follows:

- The ‹variables› section allows you to define process variables. Similarly, you can define error handlers and links to other services.

- Next, you define a top-level activity, which usually is a ‹sequence› (an ordered collection of subactivities to be performed sequentially) or a ‹flow› (which defines one or more subactivities to be performed concurrently).

- A ‹receive› activity is usually the beginning of an operation. It defines the operation name and input data.

- Various activities then define the process. These activities include calling other services with ‹invoke› and mapping and assigning data with ‹assign›.

- Finally, a ‹reply› activity allows you to end the process and return output data.

Although in principle BPEL is human-readable, reading and writing BPEL files manually is tedious and error-prone. Usually, you should use a BPEL tool to design and execute a process.

Note that BPEL does not standardize the notation, so BPEL processes might look very different in different tools and engines. However, the behavior of a BPEL process should be standardized in such a way that it doesn't matter which tool it gets edited in or which engine executes it.

The full name of BPEL was initially BPEL4WS, before it was renamed WS-BPEL (following the usual Web Services naming conventions). It follows Web Services conventions because the "processes" (which can just be composed services) it is used to create are provided as Web Services. So, to call these processes or services, which might themselves be called by other processes or services, you have to be able to call Web Services (which are technically provided inside BPEL engines).

This raises the question of whether this business process modeling standard is usable only for Web Services technologies. The answer is no. There are two parts to the processes and services composed as BPEL XML files: one describes the structure of the business process, and the other defines a binding of this structure to concrete technical operations that are invoked or used. A standard binding to Web Services is provided, but you can use other bindings. This means that, in practice, you can compose processes and services that use different middleware and even native technologies such as J2EE calls (it's no surprise that the Oracle BPEL tool provides direct support for using database queries as basic services). Of course, you'll have to find out how portable these bindings are when switching to another BPEL engine.

7.4.3 Other Business Process Modeling Standards

BPEL is not the only business process modeling standard available. Figure 7-7 provides an overview.*

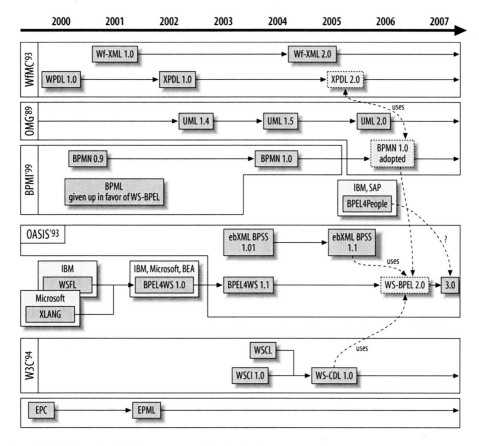

FIGURE 7-7. Overview of business process modeling standards

You can distinguish between the following main branches of the BPM standards evolution:

- The most famous branch is currently BPEL, discussed in the preceding section.

- Another major branch started with the Workflow Management Coalition (WfMC), which was founded in 1993 to specify a standard for workflow management systems. The first standard was Workflow Process Definition Language (WPDL), but the current process-definition standard came under the influence of XML and is called XML Process Definition Language (XPDL). See [WfMC] for details.

---

* Thanks to Dr. Martin Bartonitz, who drew the initial diagram as part of a German article discussing the evolution of BPM standards (see [Bartonitz05] and [Bartonitz06]) and generously gave permission to use it.

- The third important standard is the Business Process Modeling Notation (BPMN), which was initially defined by the Business Process Management Initiation but is now maintained by the Object Management Group (OMG). See [BPMN] for details.

Other standards involved include:

- Wf-XML, a standard provided by the WfMC to define how to install a process definition (defined with BPEL or XPDL) into a process engine.

- UML (Unified Modeling Language), which provides some graphical notations (especially activity diagrams) that can be used for process flows.

- WS-CDL (Choreography Definition Language), a standard to specify business processes via choreography (see Section 7.6).

- BPSS (Business Process Specification Schema), which is part of the ebXML standards (XML specifications for electronic business; see [ebXML] for details).

- EPC (Event-driven Process Chain), which is now supported by an EPC Markup Language (EPML) interchange format. This format is (maybe more in Europe) used with SAP/R3 and ARIS.

Only BPEL and XPDL are provided for engines, and BPEL currently has no notation support (hence it is sometimes called the "business process assembler"). For this reason, companies work hard to be able to transfer other modeling languages and notations into BPEL and XPDL. However, this is harder than it sounds. While it may not be too complicated with simple scenarios, transferring more complicated scenarios from one model to another can be very difficult. Note that recently the OMG has started working on a standard to transfer business process models. This standard is called the Business Process Definition Metamodel (BPDM; see [BPDM] for details).

The most important notations are BPMN (see Figure 7-8), UML, and EPC. Unlike BPEL, which is a pure XML format to specify business processes, these graphical notations are what guarantee that business process diagrams look the same.

So, which standard should you use? Again, there is no firm answer. BPEL has the most momentum in the SOA community, and especially in the more technical Web Services world. For business people, however, BPMN and EPC seem to be more intuitive, and fully supporting BPMN is an advantage of XPDL. The race is still open, and at this point I have no idea which standard will ultimately be adopted.

7.4.4   Business Process Modeling with BPEL in Practice

As stated previously, BPEL currently seems to have the market momentum. However, that doesn't mean that the concept of Plug and Play business processes works as naïve assumptions might suggest. In practice, the following aspects may hinder the realization of that vision:

- To compose and/or orchestrate services, you need services. That means the whole vision of Plug and Play business processes requires a stage of SOA expansion where you

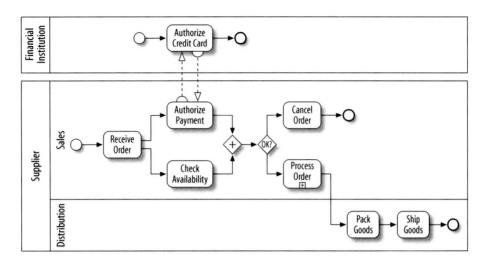

FIGURE 7-8. Example of a BPMN diagram

have enough existing services available to compose new ones. If you don't have the right services, you will have to implement new basic services to realize a solution.

- BPEL can be considered a business process assembler. Engines can execute BPEL by processing the elements of this modeling language. However, as stated earlier, this level of abstraction might not be appropriate for business people. Furthermore, there is not yet a standard notation for BPEL. Business people seem to find specific business process notations such as BPMN and EPC a lot more intuitive and useful. Possible solutions might be for business and IT people to design and maintain BPEL diagrams together, or for modeling transformations from BPMN/EPC to BPEL to be used.

- The whole concept of composition and orchestration works only from a functional point of view. Nonfunctional aspects such as security, SLAs, and so on are not covered. What does it mean for security aspects and SLAs when different services with different service contracts are composed? As far as I know, there is no support for this aspect of composition yet.

- Designing and implementing business processes might be done at different layers of abstraction. For example, due to performance reasons, one logical service call might turn out to need to be implemented as two different service calls (see Section 13.3.2 for an example). The question is how to deal with these different kinds of abstractions when you have one tool for both design and implementation.

- Although BPEL has error-handling support—for example, it provides the ability to define compensation handlers (see Sections 4.2.8 and 6.3 for some discussions about compensation)—attempting to model complex business processes including error-handling results in huge diagrams. Additional features might prove necessary and be introduced in the future.

- Finally, modeling languages have their limits. They are provided for typical scenarios of business logic, using common control structures and data mappings. When processes contain complex business logic, BPEL is probably not appropriate. Note, however, that this might also be a sign of bad design; it may be preferable to refactor out complex business logic as an auxiliary service.

The newness of BPEL is also a source of problems, as there are still some functionality and portability issues in the tools and engine. This situation will probably improve over the years, but it is currently a factor you may need to take into account.

In my experience, using BPEL to design and maintain common business processes can be appropriate. This is best done by business and IT experts sitting together. The higher abstraction definitely helps, but has its limits. Again, start small and evolve.

7.5 Other Approaches to Identifying Services

The example we just looked at for defining business processes and services was driven by concrete requirements: the need for new business functionality leads to one or more new or modified business processes, which require the use of new, existing, or modified services. This is a highly iterative and incremental approach. However, it is not the only possible approach.

In a private conversation, Torsten Winterberg presented four different ways to discover services:

Process decomposition
By breaking down a process into smaller chunks (steps, activities), you identify the individual services required.

Domain decomposition
By analyzing the domain, you end up with useful services to provide.

Business event tracing
By analyzing and monitoring what triggers business functionality, you define appropriate services.

Bottom-up
By examining what you have (existing backend interfaces or "natural" technical interfaces), you identify appropriate wrapping services to introduce.

Domain decomposition leads to an approach that is often called "portfolio management," which I'd like to discuss further.

7.5.1 Portfolio Management

One more general service design approach is to try to find out how services should be designed to fit different requirements. Instead of implementing one version for the first consumer and then :modifying or supplementing it with other versions for additional consumers, with this approach you try to analyze all the requirements so that you can design services in such a way that they are useful for several consumers. As a result, you can reuse these services from the beginnings of their lifecycles.

Indirectly, Grady Booch (father of UML and IBM fellow) recommends this approach in [Dreyfus06]:

> A better pattern for identifying good services involves defining crisp abstractions. Throw some essential usage scenarios against your system. Focus on the points of intersection where the success of multiple scenarios all depend on a narrow set of software. Within striking distance of those intersects, you will find the place to dig for services, at the granularity suggested by the nature of those scenarios.

The problem here is, again, to find the right depth of analysis. Large distributed systems are too big to realistically be able to analyze all the requirements and find a perfect design. It's easy to fall into the trap of "analysis paralysis": if you try to achieve perfection (making all the right decisions and creating the right solutions), your task will never get done.

So, you might take Grady Booch's advice into account, in the sense that looking at different usage scenarios might help you to find the right design and granularity for your services. But beware that an approach that starts to perform a complete system analysis for a large distributed project usually is a recipe for disaster.

Portfolio management has a major risk, which is that you will design and realize certain elements based on assumptions that turn out to be wrong. The You Ain't Gonna Need It (YAGNI) principle refers to the risk that your predictions of what will be needed in the future won't necessarily be accurate.

However, there might be very good reasons to realize solutions based on assumptions. Sometimes you don't have a choice, because you're designing something new for the market that might or might not turn out to be useful. If it is useful, it might bring you a big market advantage. Nevertheless, you should know the risk.

7.5.2 Don't Switch Off Your Brain

Saying that you should be careful about attempting service design based on profound analysis or, even worse, just on some assumptions does not mean that you should blindly ignore everything you know when you design and realize your services. I didn't say that you should turn off your brain.

Taking many elements into account is something that separates the best designers and implementers from the worst.

The YAGNI principle warns against investing *significant* effort based on assumptions. Too often these assumptions turn out to be wrong, and you usually pay for your mistakes throughout the whole lifetime of your software because the system gets increasingly complex. However, making some assumptions can be useful. As an example, say you need a service that returns the address of a customer, but your consumer only needs the town and street. In this case, it's pretty obvious that the service should also return the zip code if it's available in the backend system. This will not require much additional effort but may prove very useful in the future if a different consumer turns out to need that information as well.

If you can design a service such that it will support multiple scenarios without expending a disproportionate amount of effort, you should do so. The point here is not to fall into the trap of trying to achieve perfection.

7.6 Orchestration Versus Choreography

We have already explored the idea of designing higher services and processes by composing them out of existing services. This approach is called *orchestration*. Here are its characteristics:

- There is one central controller that coordinates all the activities of the process.
- You can apply the composite pattern, which means that the whole composition itself can be used as a service.

However, this is not the only way to design or execute processes. Another common approach involves collaboration between different parties, which are each responsible for one or more steps. In this scenario nobody controls the process as a whole, and it might even be the case that nobody knows about or understands the process as a whole. This approach is called *choreography*.

When you analyze processes in practice, you usually end up in a process based on choreography. Each person, department, or company involved can tell you what they do: "If I get the document I do the following…and then I pass it to XYZ." Their control and knowledge ends as soon as they give up control to the person, department, or company responsible for performing the next step.

Of course, you can also design processes in this way. In fact, because this kind of process design avoids centralized control, it might scale better. The drawback is that finding out the state of the process or the reason for misbehavior can become a nightmare (as anybody knows who's dealt with such processes in large companies or agencies).

Here are some analogies to illustrate the difference between orchestration and choreography:

- First, the names themselves lead to the analogy of an orchestra controlled by a conductor versus a performed, choreographed dance where the participants react to external influences such as music and the behavior/movements of their peers.
- A second analogy is the model of control for the flow of traffic at an intersection. In this case, orchestration would involve a traffic light (controlling when each vehicle gets to cross), while choreography would compare to a roundabout, where there is no central

control; there are only some general rules specifying that vehicles approaching the intersection have to wait until there is room to enter the circle, turn right (or left in the UK), and then take the appropriate exit.

Both analogies demonstrate that choreography depends highly on two things: collaboration and the specification of some general rules so that the collaboration doesn't lead to chaos.

7.6.1 Choreography and SOA

Usually, SOA is more or less understood as an architectural concept where business processes are designed using orchestration. In fact, BPEL is a pure orchestration language, and composability is often considered to be a fundamental attribute of services (see Section 3.3.7).

Nevertheless, choreography is an issue. For example, there are Web Services standards dealing with choreography, and of course the approach of having one process service controlling a whole business process has its limits. Orchestration usually leads to a limited scope of one controlling system. Choreography leads to a more global view of the system, accepting that control can be distributed among the different parties.

One typical approach, which has the character of choreography, is to implement (business) process chains (see Figure 7-9). The business starts by calling one service that performs some task, which then triggers another service to perform another task, which in turn triggers yet another service to perform a third task, and so on. Each service performs some task or activity and triggers one or more consecutive services that perform further tasks or activities. These services would typically be categorized as basic or composed services, but not as process services. Also, because the services give up control, they usually trigger consecutive services without waiting for responses. This leads to the concept of services called by one-way messages or events, which in turn leads to the concept of event-driven architecture (EDA).

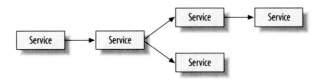

F I G U R E 7 - 9 . A business process chain realized as services

One-way messages, events, and EDA will be discussed in Chapter 10. To anticipate one of that chapter's topics here, there are different opinions about the relationship between EDA and SOA. Some claim that it is a supplementation of SOA, and others claim that the combination of SOA and EDA results in something new (what they, however, call "SOA 2.0" or "Advanced SOA" then).

All I can say here is that choreography is useful, but time will have to show how to provide special support and tools for it and which terminology should be used.

7.7 A Few More Things to Think About

As I stated at the beginning of this chapter, business process management and business process modeling are complex tasks. This chapter was only able to present general concepts, typical tools, and some practical experiences, which I hope will be helpful.

This topic connects with SOA topics presented in other chapters:

- Chapter 8 will discuss the consequences of BPM and SOA for the structure of companies and organizations.

- Chapter 9 will discuss the consequences of BPM and SOA for the overall system design (including the impact to frontends and backends).

- Chapter 10 will provide some more details about one-way messages and events that lead to event-driven architectures (EDA) and (business) process chains.

- Chapter 11 will discuss the service lifecycle, which starts when services are identified as part of a high-level or solution design.

- Chapter 19 will discuss how to establish SOA, which includes a careful growing of business processes realized with SOA.

I also recommend that you read other books about SOA written from a business point of view (see, for example, [Allen06], [BloombergSchmelzer06], or [Spanyi03]).

However, the best recommendation I can give is to use your experience, and to pay attention to the experiences of those who have been through it already. Your context will always be in some way special, and claims I read like "BPM is top-down while SOA is bottom-up" or "Middle-out is a recommendation for design, which is not the beginning (the beginning is modeling)" only reinforce my feeling that the only "right" approach is the one that works for you and your company.

7.8 Summary

- Business process management (BPM) and business process modeling provide approaches to identify services that are parts of distributed business processes.

- In practice, process design is a combined top-down and bottom-up approach, which involves decomposing processes into smaller chunks (steps and activities, which are represented as services) while taking existing system landscapes and services into account.

- Another typical approach for identifying necessary services is portfolio management. However, with this approach you'll have to deal with the risk of providing services nobody ends up needing.

- There are multiple standards for designing and executing business processes, some of which have standardized notations. These standards allow you to use different tools and engines. The most important notation standards are BPMN, UML, and EPC. The most important business process standards that engines can execute are BPEL and XPDL.

- BPEL seem to have the market momentum for business process execution. It can be considered a business process assembler that enables you to define "processes" that can serve as composed or process services using Web Services technologies. Internally, BPEL processes can use different formats, although a Web Services binding is standardized. The BPEL format itself is tedious and error-prone, so you need to use appropriate tools and/or model transformations.

- Composing new services out of existing services is called "orchestration." Orchestration results in a model where there is one central controller that coordinates all activities of a process.

- Another form of business process design is choreography. Unlike orchestration, this approach is defined by collaboration of different parties, each controlling some steps or activities (services). Examples of this approach include business process chains, where each activity (service) triggers one or more consecutive activities (services). If the trigger is an event, this leads to event-driven architectures.

CHAPTER EIGHT

SOA and the Organization

THIS CHAPTER WILL DISCUSS HOW **SOA'S** DISTRIBUTED PROCESSING AFFECTS THE ORGANIZATION AND structure of companies and enterprises. We'll focus on key success factors of SOA that impact organizations as a whole. As a consequence, you will come to understand why SOA is fundamentally a business strategy rather than an IT strategy.

8.1 Roles and Organizations

Chapter 7 discussed different ways of designing business processes and services. One question not discussed was who (or which role, from an organizational point of view) is responsible for such designs. This leads to the general question of responsibility for distributed processes.

8.1.1 From Monolithic Systems to Distribution

SOA is a concept for distributed systems. But while distributed processes are a reality now, systems and companies are often formally structured in a way that doesn't really support distribution. The dominating structures of companies are departments, which maintain specific systems that have grown over the years. These systems typically started out as projects, but the results of those projects needed to be maintained, so corresponding departments were founded. Now, when these companies need some new functionality, they tend to either give the corresponding task to an existing department, which realizes the new functionality in its monolithic system, or launch a new project, which results in a new department being created. The departments usually have their own client applications, so the average internal or external customer or call center agent has to deal with many different clients (see Figure 8-1).

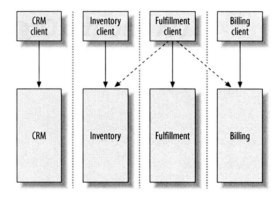

FIGURE 8-1. Departments lead to monolithic systems

Nowadays, integration and distribution are becoming increasingly important. So, although companies still have monolithic department-oriented structures, the departments and systems are starting to work together (with greater or lesser degrees of success and ease).

Sooner or later, you will learn that distributed business processes change this old department-oriented model. Having distributed processes means that you need distributed planning, distributed design, distributed realization, and distributed operation. This does not work with a department-based philosophy creating monolithic systems (sometimes called "fiefdoms" because the chief of the department behaves like the lord of the manor, ruling and controlling everything to his advantage and that of his department).

[Spanyi03] puts it as follows:

> While each functional group often does a great job of managing the work process contained inside its turf, they are less adept in the coordination of work across department boundaries—the essence of overall enterprise performance from the customer's perspective. In other words, "enterprise business processes" are those that touch more than one department, group, or internal fiefdom in the company and largely determine a company's overall effectiveness.

One major consequence of distributed processing is that there is not necessarily one department responsible for the whole process. But if no one department is responsible, who is? Some organizational structures are required to supplement departments:

• For the development of new distributed functionality, you need a *project-oriented* organization structure.

- For the maintenance of cross-department functionality (such as process services), you need some *cross-domain* departments.

Some companies might have such structures already. For example, fulfillment or order management departments might be cross-domain departments. Regarding the project-oriented development of new distributed functionality, however, let's go into some of the details of "solution management."

8.1.2 Solution Management

Developing any new functionality can be a project with an impact on several different departments (or business units, companies, or teams). For this reason, you need to introduce the role of a project manager to manage and accompany the project throughout its lifetime (from the first idea to the deployment of the realization). One company I know of names this role the "solution manager" (see the "Solution Management by Example" sidebar). The following discussion explains how this role is involved in the successful realization of a new functionality.

If there is a need for a new functionality or business process, the project or solution manager begins by creating a high-level design to determine the impact on existing systems. This process identifies which domains (companies, departments, teams, etc.) to get into contact with to discuss the details. Obviously, the departments responsible for specific backends still play a fundamental role. They provide and maintain the core of all business processes, data, and basic business rules. But this role is only one important role for the business (process) as a whole. The project or solution manager has to bring data and capabilities together to serve business needs.

For example, to introduce a bonus system into a company, you might add a new system to manage bonuses, extend existing services to deal with bonuses, and provide new services to pay the bonuses or rank customers for bonuses (see Figure 8-2).*

The high-level or solution design is important to identify which departments (business units, teams, etc.) are responsible for which parts of the effort. Only with their help can you compute the business case. With their estimations, you can sum up all the effort and resources required for the realization of the new functionality and compare it with the (expected) return on investment. Based on this, you can decide whether it makes sense to realize the new functionality.

The task of a solution manager doesn't end with the high-level design, though. The solution manager's support is also needed during the realization of a solution, because in practice things always turn out to be different than expected. Also, the danger with distributed solutions is that any one system can break the whole solution.

* Thanks to Eberhard Wolff for this example.

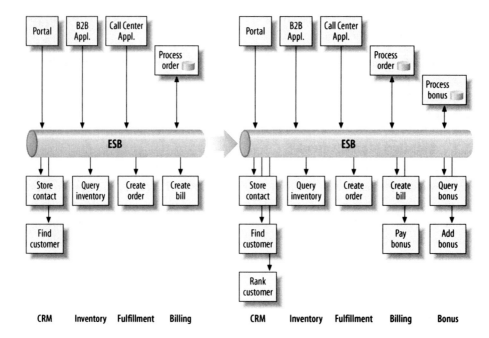

FIGURE 8-2. Projects lead to distributed development

The project is complete when the solution has become part of the existing systems and begins to be maintained just like any other software by existing departments, business units, or operation units. Event then, however, you have to know how to handle errors. As part of your incident management procedure, you need processes to find how and where to fix a problem. If a specification such as a service contract is broken, things might turn out to be easy: just follow the business process from the point where the problem was detected back to the beginning to find out where things went wrong. However, the problem might be conceptual. Then, again, the question is who is in charge of fixing it. For this reason, project or solution managers might even have a role to play when a project is finished (i.e., starting a new project to fix a problem).

8.1.3 Collaboration

All this makes it clear that there is one key requirement for SOA: collaboration. From the formulation of an idea to the maintenance of its realization, distributed systems require collaboration.

Of course, collaboration is difficult in organizations consisting of isolated departments behaving as fiefdoms. In these cases changing the culture of the company will be a key, if difficult, factor in ensuring the success of SOA. When departments are used to being in control, giving up that control to a solution manager and making their own functionality dependent on other departments is a huge move. In addition, because things will not always work smoothly, you might run into the "not invented here" syndrome (where departments and people seek to fulfill specified solutions only, while knowing that things won't work and ignoring signs that announce impending disasters).

SOLUTION MANAGEMENT BY EXAMPLE

One phone company I know of maintains most of its software in such a way that new releases get rolled out three or four times a year. Of course, this software has to match with existing marketing.

The process usually starts with marketing thinking about a new product or raising the need for a process optimization. A solution manager gets the task of making a high-level design and finding out how much the new feature or optimization will cost. Then, before the real development of a new release starts, the solution manager and the affected departments come together to make a release plan. The goal is to maximize the benefits for the company as a whole, at the lowest cost. The departments usually have budgets for each release, and the release plan should ideally use exactly 100 percent of each department's available resources. That is, the goal of the release planning is to give each team tasks that will occupy 100 percent of their development time, and to plan the tasks such that they will create the best possible benefit. Together, these multiple tasks will lead to the realization of complete solutions for the benefit of the company as a whole.

Of course, in practice things are a bit more complicated. For example, developers never have 100 percent of their time free for development (i.e., in agility terms, you need to know the "velocity" of the teams). In addition, you need time to verify that existing functionality is not broken. In fact, only the first half of the allotted development time is typically reserved for the development of new functionality. The second half is for integration and bug fixing. Last but not least, you must be aware that all your planning can become worthless if a competitor suddenly introduces a new feature. You'll have to match this feature as soon as possible, which changes all existing plans.

However, experience shows that having the right project-oriented structure for such a case will help you to react fast. Distributed development also means distributed resources that help to develop solutions. If an organization has the appropriate structure, this can become a big market advantage.

Departments that are organized as profit centers can also be a problem, because profit centers tend to prioritize their own benefit over the general benefit of the system or company. Any cultural model that has the potential to undermine collaboration can jeopardize success.

Because SOA is a strategy that makes the concept of distribution more explicit, you can easily run into trouble if your organizational structure is not prepared for it. For this reason, SOA might serve as a problem detector. SOA will make it clear how well a culture of collaboration has been established.

If collaboration is not established, however, SOA can be blamed for it ("before SOA, everything was better"). In fact, because collaboration is a hard task, some companies might claim that the price of distribution is too high and switch back to department-oriented software development.

8.1.4   Management Support

With all this in mind, it is clear that another key success factor for SOA is management support. SOA is a strategy that has a lot to do with the culture and structure of a company. Collaboration is key, and CEOs as well as CIOs must understand the impact SOA will have on their organizations.

This also means that they must allow enough time for the corresponding processes to be set up, and not expect that all the promised benefits will be realized in a year. SOA is a strategy that must be established over the course of several years.

8.2 Funding Models

There is no doubt that sooner or later you will need funding for your SOA strategy as a whole. Consequently, you will have to define some general aspects (such as the infrastructure, policies, patterns, and so on) and provide general solutions. This is considered to be part of SOA governance, which is discussed in Chapter 19.

One question related to this topic is which model should be used to pay for SOA and new services. The main problem is that the business case of SOA depends on some concepts that will only pay off when they scale. For example, having an integrated, reusable service doesn't pay off for the first communication between a provider and a consumer, but it does when there are multiple providers and consumers. Likewise, loose coupling might not pay off for the first solution, but it does when you have multiple solutions that have to run and scale.

So, who should pay for the implementation of a new service? In principle, there are a lot of possible funding models for services:

- The first consumer of or solution needing a service has to pay for its development.
- All consumers of a new service have to pay for its development.
- Providing a new service is an investment of the provider and there is a pricing model so that each call of a service has an associated cost.
- There is a pool of resources to fund the creation of new services.

In practice, for distributed processes (typically some functionality inside a company or a network of collaborating companies), I have only seen the first and last of these models used. The other options lead to funding and pricing models that are hard to maintain or require unnecessary effort. However, this might change when the culture of SOA is established.

Note that again these models lead to collaboration instead of the idea of profit centers. Of course, you can also introduce and realize distributed processes among profit centers, but then you have to make a judgment about the worth of each solution and service so that the consumers can pay for the effort appropriately.

Of course, collaboration has its limits. Say, for example, that a solution turns out to be inappropriate, but an appropriate solution would require that one department (or business unit or company) be given a lot of additional resources, while another department would save resources. Ideally, for the realization of the solution the resources saved could be transferred to the department where the additional effort is required. However, in practice this almost never works officially, due to organizational and functional constraints (although I have seen it happen in an environment with a pragmatic culture).

Similarly, improvements in processes often require investments of effort now that will pay off later in terms of maintenance. But when it comes to the question of whether to invest for better maintenance or provide new business features based on pure designs, new business features usually win. Otherwise, you might find yourself out of the market (in which case your investments and excellence won't help you). So, finding the right balance—which, by the way, also requires collaboration—is still an issue.

8.3 Summary

- SOA is a strategy that impacts a company or organization as a whole.
- Distributed processing requires collaboration, because you need distributed planning, distributed design, distributed realization, distributed operation, and distributed incident management.
- SOA leads to a combination of department-oriented structures responsible for data and core business rules and project-oriented structures responsible for designing and realizing solutions for business requirements.
- The role of project or solution manager is required to coordinate among departments. This person is responsible for creating a high-level design, providing support during the realization of the solution, and assisting in maintenance efforts.
- There are different funding models possible for realizing new processes and services. Most common are funding pools and models where the first consumer or solution to require the service pays the development costs.
- Collaboration and top management support are key success factors for SOA.

CHAPTER NINE

SOA in Context

SO FAR, WE HAVE EXPLORED THE CONCEPTS OF SERVICE-ORIENTED ARCHITECTURE AND EXAMINED THE organizational consequences of implementing SOA. However, in practice SOA is only *one* aspect of the overall architecture of a system landscape. SOA has to do with how systems communicate to perform distributed processes. Those distributed processes are initiated by frontends or batch processes and store their data in backends, and the way SOA organizes the communication has an impact on both the frontends and the backends.

This chapter will situate SOA in the context of the global picture of SOA-based system landscapes. We'll begin by examining different ways of modeling a SOA-based architecture. Then we'll discuss topics such as work sharing between SOA and frontends, and specific questions regarding connectivity to backends.

9.1 SOA-Based Architecture Models

Diagrams of a SOA-based system landscape may look very different, depending on the illustrator's intentions and point of view. Such illustrations may focus on business, domain, logical, or technical aspects of the landscape.

9.1.1 Logical Architecture Models

An architecture model focusing on the business or logical aspects of a system landscape might look like Figure 9-1.

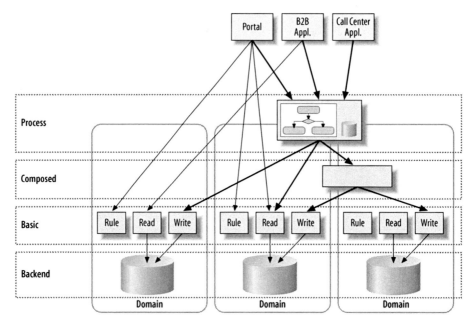

FIGURE 9-1. A logical SOA-based architecture model

Inside your landscape you have different domains, which play specific roles and have specific responsibilities. A domain usually is something you can identify in your organizational structure. For example, it might be a company, a division, a business unit, a department, or a team. The important point is that it should be a "natural" entity with clear responsibilities.

A backend in this model represents the technical system and its associated data and capabilities, for which the domain is responsible. Technically, it can be a single system, a collection of different systems, or even a component of a system shared with other domains.

Ideally, with a perfect domain/IT alignment, system boundaries would match business boundaries. But in practice, for historical (and hysterical) reasons, this is often not the case. In these circumstances, should domains be defined by technical or organizational aspects? I recommend using organizational boundaries, because the purpose of this decision is to define who is responsible for the services associated with a domain.

As written in Chapter 7, basic services are provided by specific domains. Figure 9-1 shows three types of them: reading and writing services, which are basic data services according to the classification of Chapter 6, and rule services, which are basic logic services that provide general business rules. These services wrap the technical details of the backend.

Composed and process services, in contrast, won't necessarily belong to a single "natural" domain, because they often combine business functionality from different domains. So, who is responsible for such services?

As mentioned in Chapter 8, you might have a cross-domain department that handles these issues. For example, the solution managers discussed in that chapter might belong to a "process department" responsible for cross-domain services. This department would, of course, be a domain in itself, although you might not consider it to be a "natural" business domain. In other words, according to your domain model, there might be "cross-department" domains responsible for overall processes. (I have also seen fulfillment and order management departments playing this role.)

If you do *not* have cross-domain departments, you need some way to assign cross-domain services to specific domains, because somebody has to be responsible for such services. In this case, the assignment of a service to a domain should be part of your solution design.

Note that there can also be hierarchies of domains, making the rules governing responsibilities more complicated. For example, you might have subdomains providing basic services and domains providing two categories of composed services: the first category would use services inside the domain, while the second category would also use (basic) services of other domains.

However, be careful about making too many rules. Remember that SOA is a concept that supports heterogeneity, including in organizational structures. A domain (company, department, etc.) that provides five services will probably look different from a domain that provides hundreds of services.

9.1.2   Mixed Architecture Models

What if you want to include some technical details in your diagrams, instead of just focusing on the business or logical aspects of your system architecture? A slightly more technical view of the landscape introduced in the previous section might look like Figure 9-2.

In this figure, you can see both logical and technical aspects of the architecture. It contains the following new aspects:

- All service calls are now shown as being routed through an ESB (which has the consequence that you can't see which composed and process services call which basic services).
- Process services might be implemented (and managed) by a BPM engine or tool.
- All basic logic services providing business rules are implemented in a rules engine.

Although it includes some technical details, this view still demonstrates the overall architecture from a domain-driven point of view. It is important to understand that this second view does not contradict the first one. They are just different views of the same landscape.

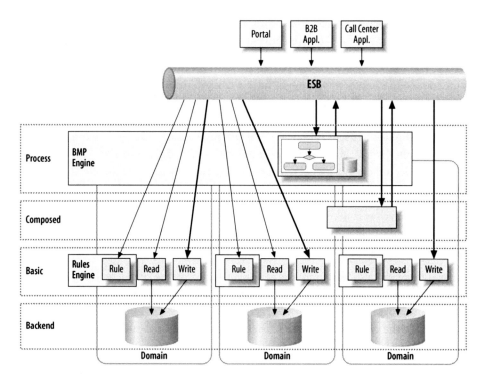

FIGURE 9-2. A SOA-based architecture model covering logical and technical aspects

9.1.3   Technical Architecture Models

An even more technically driven view might look like Figure 9-3.

In this diagram, the technical aspects of the system landscape dominate. The ESB is in the center. Domains provide only basic data services and composed services; basic logic services and process services are separated, because special tools are provided for them.

Looking at this model raises the question of whether and in what sense a domain is responsible for its basic logic services (rule services) and/or process services. We run into a conflict here. While logically a rule service belongs to an ordinary business domain, it might be better to manage all the rules in a common domain associated with a rules engine.

Likewise, defining all the process services in a common central place may be desirable: it allows you to get an overall impression of all your business processes at design time and runtime.

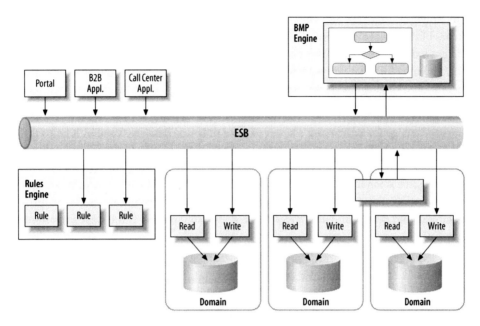

FIGURE 9-3. A technical SOA-based architecture model

9.1.4 Choosing the Right Architecture Model

I've heard a lot of arguments for and against the different models discussed here. How to deal with process and rule services is a central question. There are a few points to consider:

- On the one hand, a domain should be responsible for all its business logic. For this reason, it should control not only basic reading and writing services but also basic logic services, and process services if this makes sense from a business point of view.

- On the other hand, having a common BPM tool and engine and/or a common rules engine managed by one team helps to get synergy effects for tools and allows there to be one common view for all processes and business rules.

Tool vendors tend to prefer the technical model, because it allows them to bundle together things you can buy. The ESB, BPM tools, and rules engines might even be considered to be a common SOA suite (or an "advanced ESB"). Combined with a repository that manages all the services, this approach gives you one homogeneous way to manage your whole business. Only the implementation details of basic services would be outside this central scope. Using good tools, you could easily get an overview of all your services, business rules, and business processes both at design time and at runtime.

Note, however, that SOA and large systems are designed to allow heterogeneity. Just as you are likely to have different platforms and programming languages, you might have different ways to implement processes and rules. For example, because BPEL has limitations, you may find that you have to implement some process services in an ordinary programming language such as Java.

Again, don't misunderstand me. I am not against homogeneity. If you can achieve it and it is appropriate, go for it. Just as it's better to have only one database vendor, it helps to have only one middleware technology for the ESB, only one BPEL engine, and only one rules engine. However, be wary of falling into the trap of requiring homogeneity even when the price is too high (problems may arise when you try to come to a common agreement, lump together different requirements, and so on). The technical aspects are just implementation details, and ultimately the business point of view is the more important of the two.

Also, don't forget that there is a difference between commonality and centralization. If commonality leads to centralization, your system will no longer scale.

9.2 Dealing with Frontends and Backends

Now, let's discuss some special aspects of integrating SOA with frontends and backends.

9.2.1 Roles and Responsibilities

The first important point to understand is where the frontend ends and SOA starts. We'll focus on frontends that are user interfaces.

Services in SOA are interfaces for B2B scenarios. These scenarios are organized in such a way that a system or component communicates from time to time with another system to read or write some data. Between these service calls, the service consumer uses its business logic to perform its task.

This means that a frontend that acts as a service consumer to some extent controls the overall behavior. This is different from a frontend that has almost no business logic and "only" presents data. For such a frontend, the workflow logically is at the server side (although the control flow still might be on the client side).

In SOA, a service *serves* the consumer; it doesn't control it. This even applies to process services. For this reason, process services usually do not allow human interaction. In fact, BPEL is a "batch language" that can define a service composed of other services. The service might be long running, but it can't interact with a user.

This leads to a specific programming model for the frontends. If frontends just *present* backend data, it's easy. They just call basic reading services, according to user input (search data, logical IDs, and so on).

If the end user wants to *modify* backend data, things get more complicated. With a naïve approach, the frontend would collect user input to, for example, conclude a new contract. The data then becomes an order that is processed by a process service.

However, for complex data, only a specific combination of input data is valid. So, this approach might result in many process services encountering errors because of invalid input data. To avoid this, you have to guide the end user by offering only valid options and checking input early. The interesting question is how to ensure that the user doesn't input invalid data so that process services processing this input over various backends don't fail.

According to Figure 9-4, you start collecting user data while using basic services to limit or validate user input. That is, while the user types in what she wants, different basic services are used to read specific user data and general business data. The former would typically be basic reading services, while the latter would be basic logic services (rule services). With both, you might constrain options or validate user input.

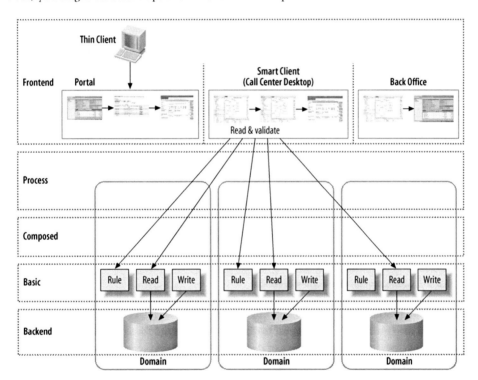

FIGURE 9-4. Frontends read and validate...

Note, however, that you should not validate each input field by calling a service. In practice, it might even be better to have some stable business rules redundantly implemented in the frontend instead of calling a service for each validation (we will further discuss the aspects of redundant validation later).

When the input has been collected, you send the change request to the backend(s) by directly or indirectly calling one or more writing services. Figure 9-5 shows an example of calling a process service that uses composed and basic services to perform a modification on multiple backends.

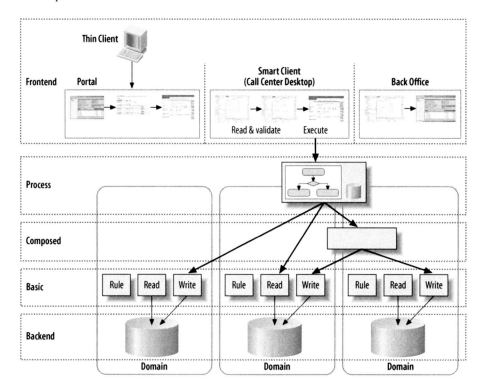

FIGURE 9-5. ...before executing sets of writing services

Note that if a problem occurs you can't interact with the user, because you can't send requests to the frontend. The frontend might even have terminated or ended the session. If you need some interaction all you can do is bring the process into a condition that is regularly checked by some monitors, systems, or users. This might result, for example, in a back office agent intervening to continue a process that has been stopped (see Figure 9-6).

Although this programming model has its limitations, it is not necessarily bad. The roles and responsibilities are clear. For example, in an order management system, the frontends have the task of collecting (and prevalidating) orders. These orders are then executed as process services. While the orders are being processed, frontends can connect to the running processes to get the state, but if a problem occurs all the process can do is enter a state where it blocks until a third party can intervene.

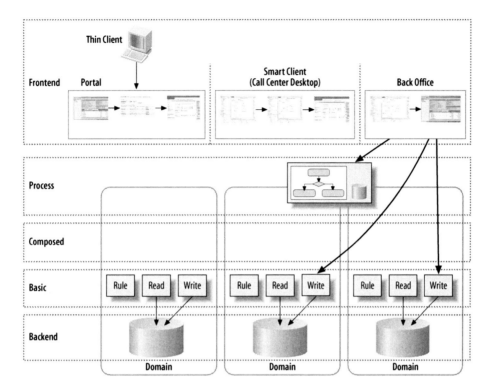

FIGURE 9-6. A back office might continue an interrupted process

There are a few efforts to circumvent the constraint of process services not being able to process user input. One option is the use of *presentation services*, which by some "infrastructure magic" can interact with a user. There is also a white paper called "BPEL4People," by SAP and IBM, which discusses how to support user interaction within the scope of the BPEL standards (see [WS-BPEL4people]).

Be careful about switching to this model, though. It's not necessarily a bad idea, but you should understand how it will influence your whole architecture. Process services will have different semantics, covering more of the workflow concepts of user interfaces and other frontends. In other words, you should make the semantics of process services clear. Are they part of a "backend workflow" running as a kind of batch processing, or are they part of a "frontend workflow" with possible human interaction?

9.2.2 Multilayer Validation

I've mentioned prevalidating input to raise the likelihood that the execution of orders and other business processes will succeed, but this raises the question of *how* you prevalidate user input. In principle, you can use the following basic validation/prevalidation policies:

Validate in the backend

All validation might be done only in the backend(s). In this case, frontends prevalidate nothing. With this approach, if the user fills in a lot of data and the backend rejects it because the problem was caused by the first of several input fields, the end user might become very frustrated. Detecting the problem earlier would have saved a lot of time and effort.

Validate in the frontend

All validation might be done only in the frontend(s). In this case, the backends assume that the service consumers will not send any flawed or inconsistent data. Of course, this is a risky approach, because the frontend(s) might make mistakes or miss certain flaws; this could in turn lead to undefined behavior in the backends, making them inconsistent and/or making them crash.

Redundancy

Both the frontend(s) and the backend(s) might validate independently. The frontend will attempt to catch possible problems upfront, and the backend will ensure that the input it receives is valid. Independent validation might, however, lead to inconsistencies.

Central decision points

Validation might be handled by a common "decision point," which is a service that knows business rules (which apply to specific user data). In this scenario the frontend(s) and backend(s) are the "enforcement points" that enforce the decisions provided by a central service provider, which might technically be a rules engine.* The problem with this approach is that it might lead to a lot of service calls.

In practice, validation usually involves a mixture of these approaches. Backends should always check all input for validity. In general, it is also a good idea to enable frontends to prevalidate the input for services. However, prevalidation can't be perfect; otherwise frontends would implement the whole business logic (including dealing with possible race conditions). In general, you have to deal with the fact that things will go wrong, and provide appropriate processes to deal with this. The aim of prevalidation should be to ensure that process services will "usually" succeed. Be wary of expending a disproportionate amount of effort on prevalidation.

Validating in both the frontends and the backends raises the question of whether to program them independently or use common services (such as rule services). Again, you need a mixture of both. Redundancy is not necessarily a bad thing in itself, and trying to eliminate it may require more effort than it's worth. However, you have to define services for each kind of check you perform, and there's a performance penalty for calling these services repeatedly at runtime. In practice, there should be a central place for business rules that change frequently. For example, such rules might apply to pricing models, product portfolios, contract types, and so on. But having a central service to check whether a date or a salutation is valid and calling it for each input is probably not appropriate.

---

* The concept of distinguishing between a *policy decision point* (PDP) and a *policy enforcement point* (PEP) is a general concept for dealing with consistent common behavior. See Section 14.3.3 for another example.

Note that the business rules are often some kind of master data, and if you provide services for them there is still a question of whether the system should check each input against them, or download the rules, say, once a day and perform the checks locally. You'll have to determine the right validation policies and the right amount of validation for your concrete SOA and SOA-based solution.

9.2.3 Multifrontendchannel Scenarios

It's common for distributed systems to require support for a multichannel approach. A customer might start a business process (such as an order) using an online portal, for example, and continue it via a call center. Likewise, processes started by a call center application might be processed by the back office and monitored by the customer using a portal.

To support this, instead of managing each channel's processes independently, you must be able to switch between different frontend channels. This keeps the processes consistent.

In practice, this means that the process engines must provide abilities to find and identify running processes. Ideally, the identifier is a business ID such as a work request number, but of course people don't always have such IDs at hand (especially if they don't know them yet).

An interesting aspect of this problem emerged when one of my customers realized this scenario. It turned out that different frontend channels used different search criteria, just as they used different views to manage the data. For example, one frontend might start a process for a customer identified by a contract number, while another channel used the customer number. A third channel might use the address of the customer to find the running process.

The question was, how could all the useful search criteria be assigned to a running process? Should each frontend be responsible for assigning all the search criteria for the other frontends? Probably not, because this would take time, and each frontend would have to be modified each time a new frontend needed an additional search criterion. A better solution would probably be for the process engine to get the task not only of processing services but also of making them searchable by enriching them with all the useful search criteria.

9.2.4 Multiapplication Frontends

Another common scenario is that different frontends running on the same system or desktop need the same data provided by a service.

Consider a desktop where you have multiple clients with graphical user interfaces dealing with the same customer. For historical reasons, one frontend provides different business processes from the other frontend(s). Say you start with one frontend, which loads the customer data by calling an appropriate service provided by the CRM department. Now say you need the same customer data in another frontend.

Conceptually, the second frontend would need to call the same service to retrieve the customer data. However, because the data is already on the desktop, this would be a waste of resources. The alternative is to enable direct or indirect local communication between the two frontends:

- Direct data exchange would mean that both frontends establish and manage a communication layer to exchange the data. This, of course, would raise the coupling between the clients, which might or might not be appropriate.

- Indirect data exchange would mean that there is some "magic" that knows that the customer data was loaded by one frontend and can be used by the other frontend. Here, we're talking about something like a local cache for service calls on the consumer side. This might even be part of your ESB (e.g., using local interceptors; see Section 5.3.2). Again, this might or might not be appropriate.

The different solutions affect different areas of programming: while the first approach has nothing to do with SOA (it's a special communication between two frontends or clients), the second approach does and might be supported by your infrastructure (ESB).

Note that both scenarios usually require some kind of local communication, because there has to be some way to exchange information indicating that one frontend is processing the same data as the other frontend. The first frontend, which initially loaded the customer data, will have to at least send the customer number to the second frontend, which performs some further processing with the customer (unless the transfer of the customer ID has to be done manually by the end user).

Because this can be considered an optimization, you should usually start with both frontends calling the same service to load the customer data and see whether this approach causes any problems.

9.2.5   Future Management

Finally, let's discuss another interesting aspect of business processes dealing with multiple backends, which I call "future management." If a customer calls in to change a contract or change an address, this change won't necessarily become valid immediately. That is, customers and business processes as a whole might define modifications that should happen later, at a certain point in time.

So, how do you deal with future modifications? In principle, you have the following options:

- Arrange future management in such a way that the backends can deal with tasks that have to be processed in the future.

- Make future management part of your process management.

With the first approach, you need services that allow modifications of backend states and that take specific dates as parameters. In addition, the backends have to be able to manage tasks for the future. This is a requirement that is often hard to satisfy. In addition to canceling future tasks, the management of conflicting future tasks can become very complicated. For this reason, it is usually better to make future management part of your process management.

If future management is part of your process management, you might or might not choose to make it a responsibility of the usual process engine: either the engine may allow you to delay tasks and provide ways to deal with future tasks, or you may delegate the responsibility of managing future tasks to a special system. In the latter case, your process engine will still be responsible for:

- Running processes directly
- Putting processes for later processing into the system managing future tasks
- Processing those tasks when the system managing future tasks indicates that they should be run

Such a separation between one tool or system running the actual tasks and another tool managing future tasks might help to separate concerns. But, of course, managing actual and future tasks together might also be possible and have some advantages.

9.3 Summary

- There are different models for structuring descriptions of SOA-based system landscapes. While some prefer the logical view, others focus more on technical aspects.

- For the successful management of SOA landscapes, a logical or domain-driven general view considering the technical aspects as "implementation details" provides better scalability and is better able to deal with heterogeneity.

- Process services are backend processes, which usually provide no means of direct communication with the end user. For this reason, frontends dealing with use cases that lead to backend modifications have to use the pattern of collecting the data for the changes interactively while performing the changes without interaction.

- To minimize the danger of process services running into failures, frontends can prevalidate user input according to the actual situation and business rules.

- There are different ways to validate business rules and input data for business functionality. Usually, the backend should validate everything, and the frontend should try to ensure that the common scenarios run smoothly. Validating in both the frontend and the backend can be implemented redundantly or via common services.

- For multifrontend-channel scenarios, you have to deal with the fact that processes initiated by one channel must be researchable by other channels.

- When dealing with multiple clients on the same desktop, you might want to avoid each client calling the same services. You might do this using local communication and/or local caches.

- You have to think about how to deal with future tasks. You may choose to give backends specific abilities to deal with future tasks, or designate a special place where future tasks are managed.

CHAPTER TEN

Message Exchange Patterns

SO FAR, WE HAVE CONSIDERED A SERVICE AS AN **IT** REPRESENTATION OF SOME BUSINESS FUNCTIONALITY THAT technically works by messages being sent between a service provider and a service consumer. The typical scenario we looked at was that of a consumer performing a service call and getting a response. Now it's time to go into the details of the different ways of exchanging messages between providers and consumers. As you will see, there are multiple message exchange patterns (MEPs), which exist on different communication layers. One pattern leads to events and event-driven architectures.

10.1   Introduction to MEPs

There are different ways to exchange data between distributed systems. One fundamental approach to dealing with these differences is to categorize the way chunks of data are exchanged. These chunks of data are called *messages*. Thus, by categorizing different ways of exchanging messages, we get the so-called *message exchange patterns*. MEPs define the sequence of messages in a service call or service operation, specifying the order, direction, and cardinality of those messages.

Note that MEPs are general concepts to describe communications between different systems (or nodes). Discussing all the aspects of messaging and message styles could easily fill a book (see, e.g., [HohpeWoolf04]). Because of space constraints, I will concentrate here on MEPs in the context of SOA. When useful, I will use SOA terms such as "provider" and "consumer" instead of general message terms such as "sender" and "receiver."

10.2 Basic MEPs

There are different approaches to categorizing MEPs. I'll start with two basic patterns and then explain some others based on these patterns.

10.2.1 Request/Response

Probably the most important pattern for SOA is request/response (sometimes also called request/reply). In this pattern, the consumer sends a request message to the service provider and waits for the provider to send a response message (see Figure 10-1). The response message might contain requested data and/or a confirmation of successful processing of the request.

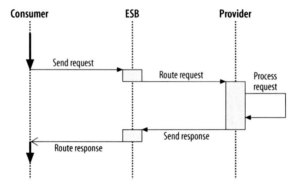

FIGURE 10-1. Request/response message exchange pattern

From a consumer's point of view, such a service call is like a remote procedure call (RPC). That is, the consumer is blocked until the response arrives. You can think of this like a telephone conversation, where you ask a question and wait for the answer before continuing.

Exchanging messages according to this pattern has a big advantage: it makes code pretty simple. A service call is handled like any other function or procedure call. When you need some information or need something to be done, you make your request, wait for the answer or confirmation, and then continue with your work, knowing that the problem has been solved.

The drawback of this pattern is that you cannot do anything else while you are waiting for the response. This typically means either that you need a fast response or that running time doesn't matter. In practice, a provider processing such a request should usually be available and able to send a response in a reasonable amount of time.

If the provider is not available or something goes wrong, the consumer might never get the response and end up waiting forever in a blocked state. Of course, you can introduce timers to start some exception handling if a response does not arrive in a given amount of time, but conceptually you can consider this to be an extended and more complicated MEP based on the fundamental request/response pattern. (For more on this issue, see Section 10.5 later in this chapter.)

Note that you might also arrange to do something else while waiting for the response. For this reason, sometimes people differentiate between blocking and nonblocking request/response patterns (sometimes also called *synchronous* and *asynchronous* request/response patterns). Again, you can consider the latter to be another, slightly more complicated MEP, which is typically called the request/callback pattern (see Section 10.3.1 later in this chapter).

10.2.2 One-Way

If you don't need a response, there is an alternative that's even simpler from a consumer's point of view: send a message, and you're done. This one-way pattern is often also called "fire and forget" (see Figure 10-2).

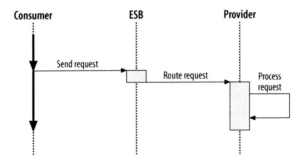

FIGURE 10-2. One-way message exchange pattern

You might wonder why I didn't introduce this pattern first, because it looks like the simplest and most fundamental one. In addition, you might argue that the request/response pattern is just a composition of two one-way messages. However, this is not necessarily the case, for two reasons:

- From a consumer's point of view, a combination of two one-way messages would lead to an *asynchronous* or *nonblocking* request/response (or request/callback) pattern, because the client is not blocked between the time when it sends the initial request and the time when the response arrives (see Section 10.3.1).

- From an infrastructure's (ESB's) point of view, sending two one-way messages would require the sender of the first request (i.e., the service consumer) to be able to receive the second one-way request (which logically is the service provider's response). That means the consumer has to be able to be a provider (i.e., it must be addressable and able to process incoming messages).

The next section explains this in more detail.

10.2.3 Request/Response Versus Two One-Way Messages

Say you've designed a business process in which system A sends a request to system B that necessitates a response from system B to system A. This response might or might not be required to be sent to the process/thread of the original consumer.

If the consumer process (which might be a frontend, a batch application, or a service itself) needs the response for its further processing, it is important that the response is delivered to the specific process instance that performed the initial request (see Figure 10-3).

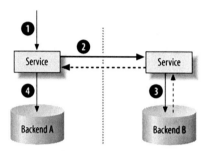

FIGURE 10-3. Two systems connected with a request/response pattern

For example, a CRM service might need to know about a customer's actual payment behavior to determine whether to allow a certain contract option. For this, it calls a service of the billing system. But it needs the response in order to continue to perform the initial service, so it is important that the response is routed to the original CRM service instance. In this case, the consumer must block and wait for the reply.

If, on the other hand, system A needs the response to the request but the specific initial consumer can continue to do its work without getting the response, it is not important that the response be delivered to the process instance that performed the initial request. Instead, you can consider the response message to be another service request back to the system that initiated the first request (see Figure 10-4). In other words, you can use two one-way messages.

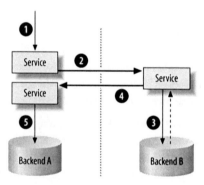

FIGURE 10-4. Two systems connected with two one-way patterns

For example, a CRM service might enable an invoice outside the usual payment intervals. This service might send a corresponding request to the billing system. As soon as the billing system has processed the request, it might call another service in the CRM system to store the new invoice number and date there. (Of course, it must also include the customer ID so that the "response request" corresponds to the right customer.)

Figure 10-5 shows the corresponding sequence diagram for this scenario.

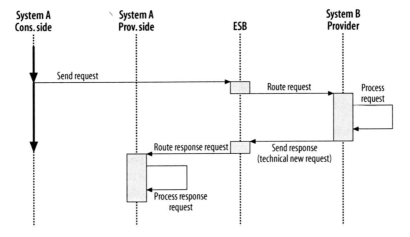

FIGURE 10-5. Two one-way message exchange patterns

As the last example demonstrates, the big advantage of one-way messages is that no process is blocked. That is, the consumer and the provider don't have to be available at the same time. In fact, you can insert message queues in your infrastructure (ESB), so that once a message is sent it is persisted and can't get lost. This is the core of *message-oriented middleware* (MOM) such as MQ and JMS.

> **NOTE**
> Sequences of one-way messages led to the concept of (business) process
> chains, discussed in Section 10.6.

The advantage of the request/response message pattern is that the response is delivered to the same process instance that triggered the initial request.

If you have no support for the request/response pattern in your infrastructure, you'll have to program in the ability for the providing side of the requesting system to find the right instance to deliver the response to. In this case the consumer usually sends an internal "return address" to the provider, which the provider sends back with the response message. The consumer process/thread that processes the incoming response message can then use this information to internally route this response to the right process instance (i.e., the one that initially sent the request).

10.3   More Complicated MEPs

There are many possible extensions to and variations of these two fundamental MEPs. Let's discuss some of the most typical ones.

10.3.1   Request/Callback

Often a process/thread needs some data or confirmation, but doesn't need to be blocked until it arrives. This pattern may be called nonblocking request/response, asynchronous request/response, or just request/callback (I prefer the latter term).

Conceptually, a consumer's API for such a scenario works such that the consumer initiates a request and specifies what to do when the answer arrives. Technically, the consumer might (for example) define a so-called "callback function," which is a function/procedure that is called when the response arrives.

Dealing with asynchronous responses usually leads to more complicated code. For example:

- If you send more than one request/callback message, you have to deal with the fact that the responses may return in a different order from the order in which you sent the requests. That is, you have to correlate the answers to the initial requests. This is usually done by introducing correlation IDs that are passed with the requests and delivered with the corresponding replies.

- You have to make sure that the context for each response is still valid and contains all the information required to process the response.

- In addition, you might have to deal with the fact that no responses arrive for some requests. If the response isn't just providing some additional "nice-to-have" information, you have to be able to verify that no response arrived (for example, by processing some maximum response period) and react appropriately.

The big advantage of this kind of message exchange is that it introduces a form of loose coupling: service providers do not have to be available when requests are sent, and consumers can continue to work while awaiting responses.

Each approach has its pros and cons, so it can be difficult to decide whether to use synchronous or asynchronous request/response scenarios. The right choice depends on factors such as running time, availability of resources, reliability, and maintainability. There is no doubt that asynchronous communications are harder to maintain. But blocking while waiting for responses that (might) take a long time can be a waste of time. As usual, introducing loose coupling removes dependencies but raises complexity (see Section 4.2.1).

Note again that (as discussed earlier) if the response does not necessarily have to get delivered to the same process/thread that sent the request, two one-way messages might be an attractive alternative.

10.3.2 Publish/Subscribe

Sometimes one-way messages may be sent that do not require responses. The reason for sending such messages is usually to inform another system that something has happened or changed. These kinds of messages are often called *notifications* (or *events*, discussed in Section 10.6).

Why might you need to send notifications? Following the usual business process modeling, there might be a general design that defines that a system must notify a specific other system when certain conditions arise. For example, when a billing system has sent a new bill to a customer, a message may be sent to the CRM system to inform the CRM system about the new invoice number.

However, there is another famous pattern that enables a system to register or subscribe for certain notifications or events. This pattern is usually called the *observer* or *publish/subscribe* pattern, and it is one of the fundamental design patterns (see [GoF95]). In general, this pattern allows multiple "observers" to "subscribe" with a system so that it will notify them when a specific situation occurs.

As I've just hinted, in SOA infrastructures you often only see the second part of this pattern: the notification. The subscription might be part of the business process modeling that leads to service designs. That is, at design time a service contract might define that the CRM system gets an event from the billing system each time a customer gets a new bill. Other service contracts (for example, to an online portal) might define that other systems get the same event. As a result, when a customer gets a new bill the service provider "billing system" will automatically send a notification to all the consumers with that clause in their service contracts.

Note that at runtime, a one-way message is sent from the provider to each consumer. This is an exception to the usual request/response scenarios, where the operation starts with the consumer sending a message to the provider.

10.4 Dealing with Reliability and Errors

So far, I haven't said anything about what happens if something goes wrong. Here are some problems you might encounter:

- The service provider detects an error and sends back a fault message instead of a typical response message.

- The service provider is unavailable and therefore cannot receive the message.

- The transport layer for the messages might not be reliable. That is, messages might get lost over the network.

Dealing with these situations can make message exchange patterns a lot more complicated.

10.4.1 Fault Messages

If the service provider (or any other process receiving messages and sending responses) detects an error, instead of sending back the usual response message, it will send back a fault message (see Figure 10-6). Usually, you can define special attributes for these fault messages.

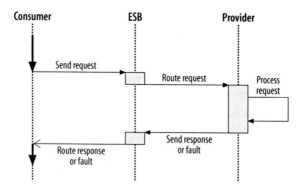

FIGURE 10-6. Request/response with optional fault

Whether and how faults are handled in special cases has to do with the protocol you use. For example, Web Services allow you to specify and deal with special fault messages that are returned by providers in the event that (expected and modeled) errors occur.

10.4.2 Technical Errors

If there is a technical problem that prevents a message from being delivered, the sender must be notified. However, this is more complicated than it sounds. Consider a simple one-way message. If the sender sends a message without expecting any confirmation, at the end of the pattern the consumer has no guarantee that the message was delivered. If the receiver sends a confirmation and the consumer gets it, the initial sender knows that the initial message was delivered successfully. However, the initial receiver does not know that the initial sender has this knowledge. Only if the initial sender confirms the initial receiver's confirmation and all messages are delivered will both parties know that the initial message was delivered and that the other knows that it was.

For this reason, a message exchange that is reliable from both points of view must involve a double confirmation (see Figure 10-7).

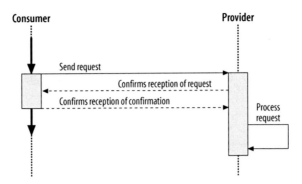

FIGURE 10-7. Robust one-way message exchange

With synchronous communications, these kinds of checks are usually part of the infrastructure. That is, the sender of a (request or response) message should get an appropriate exception if the message could not be delivered successfully (provided that the underlying transport layer doesn't try and/or wait forever).

With asynchronous communication, things can become more complicated. One typical approach is to persistently store all outgoing messages in a message queue, which tries to deliver them at set intervals. In this case, a confirmation may be sent indicating that the messages are reliably on their way. The only question is what happens when a message begins to "molder" in the message queue: you might throw it away, or send an exception to a more general monitoring system. You might expect that in this case the queue also informs the initial consumer, but note that that connection is gone, and in general service consumers are not able to serve as service providers.

Another typical way of dealing with these situations is to retry sending the message until a corresponding response arrives. Note, however, that for this you need idempotent services (see Section 3.3.5). That is, you need to be sure that resending the message will not have unintended consequences. If, for example, you're sending a message that adds a certain amount of money to a bank account, you want to make sure that if the message has to be resent, the effect takes place only once. If you don't get a response to such a message, you won't know whether it was the request or the response that failed. That is, the provider might or might not have processed the service call already.

NOTE

See Section 15.2 for details on how to make services idempotent.

10.5   Dealing with Different MEP Layers

Message exchange patterns always depend on the characteristics of the transport layer or protocol they use. But one layer above or below, things might look totally different. For example, you can provide asynchronous message exchange patterns on synchronous protocols, and vice versa.

To illustrate, let's look again at the example discussed in the previous section about dealing with unreliable protocols. Even if your transport layer is not reliable, you still can provide an API with a reliable interface (see Figure 10-8).

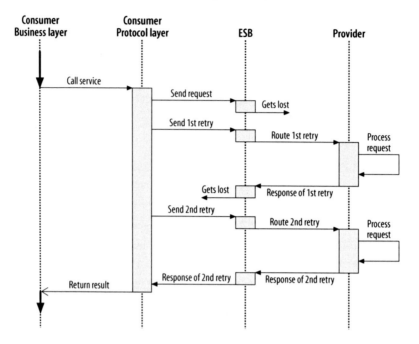

FIGURE 10-8. Reliable service call on top of an unreliable protocol

In this figure, the consumer calls a service. The corresponding API blocks until it receives the response (or an exception). Underneath this API, however, the code is more complicated, because the protocol used is not reliable. In this figure, for example, the first request message sent to the provider gets lost. So, after a timeout, the low-level API of the consumer performs a retry. This message is routed successfully to the service provider. Unfortunately, this time the response gets lost, so the consumer performs another retry. This attempt succeeds, and the requested data is finally returned to the consumer.

In this example, the consumer uses an API for a synchronous request/response MEP, while the low-level protocol is a sequence of request/callback MEPs (the consumer code processes the first successfully delivered response). Note that the protocol itself can also use other MEPs, such as one-way messages, to handle the communication internally.

From a SOA point of view, the interesting issue is which MEPs the protocol supports and which MEPs the APIs support. If the ESB is protocol-driven, the consumers might be responsible for programming aspects such as retries. If the ESB is API-driven, however, the infrastructure team is responsible for providing APIs for different MEPs. In this case, the SOA infrastructure might provide the ability to specify the number of retries and the timeout period between retries. (See Section 5.3.3 for further details on the distinction of protocol-driven versus API-driven ESBs.)

Of course, things can become even more complicated. For example, a retry might be sent because the response took too long to arrive, not because either the request or the response was lost. In this case, the consumer will have to deal with multiple responses.

Figure 10-9 illustrates this scenario. Here, the first request message got lost, so a retry was sent. The retry was successful, but because the result took too long to arrive, a second retry message was sent. This message was processed by another thread of the service provider. As a result, the consumer ended up with two responses (which might not even have arrived in the expected order).

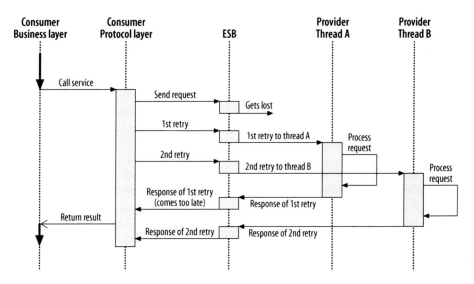

FIGURE 10-9. Dealing with unreliability and late responses

Again, idempotency is a major concern in this scenario. If messages get lost either before or after a service provider has processed them, the consumer, who does not receive the anticipated response, has no way of knowing whether the operation took place. A retry might therefore cause the effect to occur a second time, which can be disastrous if the result is not the same as when processing the request only once. For example, if a request creates something new, that object will be created twice; likewise, if a service call adds $100 to an account, a total of $200 may be added instead. (See Section 15.2 for a discussion of this topic.)

10.6 Event-Driven Architecture

Recently, there has been new hype about an architectural style called *event-driven architecture* (EDA). As its name implies, EDA is a software architecture pattern promoting the production, detection, consumption of, and reaction to events.

To some extent, one-way messages and publish/subscribe messages can be considered to be *events*. These events typically are notifications of significant changes in state that enable those interested in these changes to react accordingly.

For example, an event notifying consumers that a barrier has been placed on a phone company customer might result in all systems that deal with this customer disabling all functionality for the customer.

There is a lot of discussion at the moment about whether EDA is a special form of SOA, an enhancement of SOA, or something different. For example, some analysts and companies have introduced terms such as "Advanced SOA" or "SOA 2.0" to refer to the combination of EDA and SOA (see, e.g., [GartnerEDA06], which strictly speaking compares and combines EDA with "interactive SOA").

In my opinion, the most important distinction has to do with the types of events being sent around. Of course, as with services and objects, you can classify events very differently. One interesting difference has to do with whether the events notify consumers about changes with or without including corresponding data:

- If an event just notifies consumers that customer data has changed and needs to be processed, only a small amount of data will be sent around. Data sent with the event will help consumers decide whether the updates are relevant to them—for example, the new general type of the contract or similar information might be included—but in essence these notifications simply indicate that there are updates that need to be processed.

- If an event includes the data to be processed, it will be more coarse-grained. In this case, the consumer of the event will receive all the information necessary to process this event.

I consider the latter another form of calling a service, with the difference that (after the consumer has subscribed for the event) the provider defines the format and sends it in a one-way fashion. You might view sending notifications around as something different from using services, but you might also consider these processes as special kinds of services that use special message exchange patterns.

Both of the above types of event can be useful in modern distributed systems and business processes. In fact, in almost every SOA landscape I have seen, events have played a significant role. I've often considered this to be just another message exchange pattern of the ESB.

As with SOA, there are different definitions of EDA. Some, for example, do not require the event publishers to know the event consumers. In these scenarios the event consumers subscribe to an intermediary event manager, to which event producers publish the events. This could be handled as part of the ESB.

This decoupling is one reason why EDA is sometimes considered to have a looser coupling than SOA. However, as usual, you pay a price for loose coupling (see Chapter 4). In this case, the provider doesn't know the dependencies. From a resources point of view, this is not a problem because it makes no difference to a provider how many different consumers receive the notifications (unlike with services, where it matters how many different consumers send service requests to the provider). When you want to modify or withdraw events, however, not knowing dependencies might become an issue (unless the provider can get this information from the infrastructure). In fact, not knowing dependencies often results in systems no longer being maintainable.

Interestingly, the resulting process model of an EDA might be different from (or a special case of) the process model of SOA. Instead of composing basic services into composed services or process services, you get something that can be called a "business process chain," or just a "process chain" (see Figure 10-10). Like a supply chain, a business process is organized in such a way that each system plays a certain role and marks the end of its processing as an event so that consecutive processing can follow.

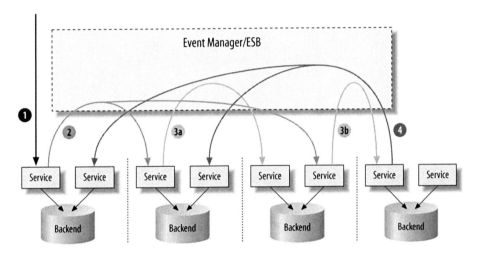

FIGURE 10-10. A process chain

It's like choreography (see Section 7.6): there is no central control. Instead, the process chain is a sequence of (parallel) processings triggered by events. As with choreography, there are advantages and drawbacks. The good thing is that there is no need for a central controlling component, which might turn out to be a bottleneck. The bad thing is that it is more difficult to understand, document, and monitor the whole process or process instances, respectively.

10.7 Summary

- Services use different message exchange patterns (MEPs) that define the order, direction, and cardinality of messages sent around until a specific service operation is done.

- The basic MEPs are request/response and one-way. Also important are the request/callback (asynchronous or nonblocking request/response) and publish/subscribe patterns, and higher patterns dealing with error handling.

- MEPs are layer-specific. For SOA, the MEPs on the protocol and API layers are important.

- Events are a special type of one-way messages. They lead to event-driven architecture (EDA), which can be considered a special case or supplementation of SOA.

- One-way messages and events lead to (business) process chains, which is another way of implementing business processes. Instead of orchestrated services, where there is a central controller for the whole process, you get choreographed services, where each service triggers the next step(s) of the business process.

CHAPTER ELEVEN

Service Lifecycle

SERVICES ARE PIECES OF SOFTWARE, JUST LIKE ANY OTHER SOFTWARE. THUS, THE USUAL LIFECYCLE FOR software development applies. However, there are some differences. Some of them are based on the fact that we talk about both software under development and software under maintenance. In addition, service lifecycles are only parts of more general and distributed development processes. This chapter introduces the service lifecycle and its associated topics.

Note that the service life cycle applies to different artifacts, such as service specifications, service implementations, and test code. For example, Section 16.3.3 discusses the lifecycle for WSDL files (Web Services files specifying services).

11.1   Services Under Development

A service is an IT representation of a business functionality. Thus, services are pieces of software. Although the language and format of this software can differ (for example, depending on the implementation platform and/or the classification of the service), it has the usual lifecycle of any software under development, which at its core consists of phases of design, implementation, integration, and bringing into production (see Figure 11-1).

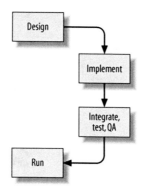

FIGURE 11-1. A typical software lifecycle applies to services

11.1.1 Iterative Service Development

Of course, what we've learned about software development over the past years also applies here: in practice, a waterfall-like approach doesn't work. We make mistakes, we gain experience, and requirements as well as contexts change over time. Therefore, software development usually should be an iterative process, with results from earlier phases adjusted due to experiences encountered at later stages.

However, there is a special aspect of services to consider: a service is part of a more general business process. Thus, any modifications of a service's design or implementation might impact other systems. For this reason, we must think about when it is appropriate to modify a service. We'll begin by looking at the design phase.

The design phase usually produces the specification of the service interface. Ideally this interface includes the semantics and nonfunctional attributes, and it might be part of one or more contracts between the service provider and the (initial) service consumer(s). Therefore, even during the implementation and testing of a service, any changes to its design may impact other systems (as long as the service implementation is not driven by portfolio management, which leads to new services being created before concrete requirements exist; see Section 7.5.1).

Does this mean that you should never modify a service interface (at least, not after it has been published and become part of the interface to another system)? No! This would be a very, very bad move. Don't fall into the old trap of trying to make perfect designs. You will fail. Accept that even the design of a service might change. That is, take into account that interfaces of services under development may need to change, and introduce processes that make modifications during the design of a service possible (if necessary). When a work contract implements the consuming system, this contract should take into account that the service might not yet be solid.

With this in mind, let's modify our initial service lifecycle diagram so it looks like Figure 11-2.

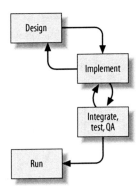

FIGURE 11-2. A software lifecycle with iterations

You might wonder how often it happens that service designs change during their implementation. Of course, the quality of the design has a lot to do with this. The better the design is, the fewer modifications are typically required. Note, however, that market pressure tends to lead to situations where there is no time for solid design. In addition, even the best designers make mistakes, and in large systems people who know "everything" about a topic almost never exist. So, you should expect that modifications of a service design will be common during its implementation. In my experience, less than 50 percent of designed interfaces remain stable during the implementation phase.

As a consequence, in one company I know of, service consumers try to convince service providers to implement their services before the consumers start using those services. Early implementation experiences can help to identify necessary interface modifications. However, this approach means that the service is not integrated with a consumer during the implementation phase. Therefore, some problems are only identified when this phase is over, which can cause other problems.

11.1.2 Service Identification

Usually, a service is not an end in itself. There should be something that leads to its need and design. In fact, as we have seen already, services are parts of a more general business processes. Thus, a typical scenario that leads to a new service being created is the design of a (new) business process, also known as business process modeling (see Chapter 7 for details).

However, this is not the only approach for identifying new services. Another approach is portfolio management, where a department or company introduces new services because they think it make sense to provide these services (usually expecting that they will be used later). Of course, this approach has its risks, which I discuss in Section 7.5.1.

New services may also be introduced to meet new requirements for existing services. If a modification isn't backward compatible, a new service (or a new service version) is necessary. A new service version is typically considered to be, technically, a new service (see Section 11.2.1 and Chapter 12 for details).

So, while there are different reasons for introducing new services, it is common for some sort of procedure to be carried out before the design of a service begins. Usually the phase before design is called "analysis," but this doesn't really fit. I prefer to name the lifecycle step before design "service identification" or "service discovery" (see Figure 11-3), which might be part of a solution design (see Sections 7.3 and 8.1.2).

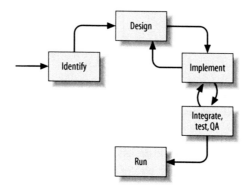

FIGURE 11-3. Starting the lifecycle with service identification

Now, this diagram includes all of the steps taken for a service under development. After identifying that a (new) service is necessary, we design its interface and contract, implement it, and perform the usual tasks to verify its quality (you might call this phase integration, testing, quality assurance, or whatever). Recall that this process is iterative. Tests and integrations might lead to modified implementations, and the design of the service itself may need to be altered.

In rare cases, service development might even lead to experiences that have an impact on service identification. That is, it might turn out that a new service is not useful. However, because this case is relatively rare, I've omitted an arrow leading back to service identification.

11.2 Services in Production

After a service is developed, it is typically used. That is, the software gets deployed into a running system, performing more or less mission-critical business functionality for the company, enterprise, or universe.

There is an important point to understand here. This is the moment at which the software that implements a service transitions from being software under development to software under maintenance. In general, SOA is a concept that combines new software under development with existing software under maintenance. However, for systems under maintenance different rules apply. For example, modifications become much more critical, especially if the systems have different owners. For this reason, we must also look at how to modify and withdraw services in production.

11.2.1 Modifying Services in Production

As soon as a service is in production, it can be used in mission-critical scenarios and business processes. That means whenever you modify such a service (whether its interface or "only" its implementation), you are modifying existing business processes that are in use. And if this results in broken business processes, you're in trouble.

For this reason, we should be careful about drawing an arrow back from the run state of the service lifecycle to previous states. In fact, it is a best practice for services in production to be stable. Whenever you need to modify the behavior of a service in production, you should do this by introducing a new service or a new version of the service, which is independent from the previous version of the service. Also, as discussed in Chapter 12, it is a good approach for the new (version of the) service not to have any impact on existing behavior.

However, there is one common exception to this rule: bug fixes. If you find a bug, you will usually want to fix it in the existing running service, rather than introducing a new version of the service. In other words, the difference between a bug fix and a modification is that you typically want to apply a fix to existing behavior as soon as possible.

With this in mind, we can extend the service lifecycle as shown in Figure 11-4. When services are in a production state (the "run" phase) you can fix bugs, but this should never have an impact on the design. If a bug fix does impact the design, it is actually a modification, which should result in a new service (version) that has its own lifecycle.

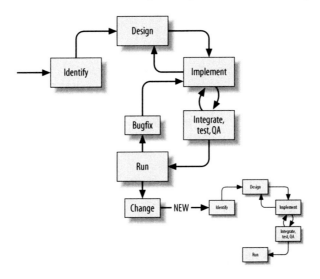

FIGURE 11-4. Service lifecycle with bug fixes and modifications

Of course, in practice there is a gray area between a service under development and in production, as well as between a bug fix and a modification. You might modify a running service without bringing a new service (version) into production, as long as it is in the interest of all consuming systems to perform the modification. And, of course, it can be useful to modify a service that is not yet being used by any consumer. However, you should decide these things based on a general concept so that all service participants are aware of the rules, processes, and lifecycles.

> **NOTE**
>
> Introducing a new service (version) as a modification of an existing service raises the question of how to deal with service versioning. See Chapter 12 for a detailed discussion of this topic.

11.2.2 Withdrawing a Service

One state in the service lifecycle is still missing: dead (i.e., withdrawn from production). This step is shown in Figure 11-5, which illustrates the complete service lifecycle.

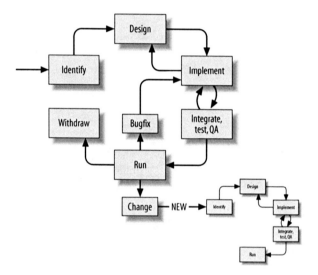

FIGURE 11-5. A complete service lifecycle

Withdrawal is the final step of the service lifecycle. To keep systems maintainable, it is usually important to prevent the number of services and service versions in use from ballooning (especially when versioning policies lead to multiple service versions, as happens when each modification of a service in production leads to a new service; see Chapter 12). This means that obsolete services and service versions should be phased out.

However, in large systems and companies, withdrawing services can be problematic. One issue has to do with resource allocation. Removing existing software is an investment in the maintainability of a system, but because no immediate business advantage may be evident, it often has a very low priority. In fact, system maintenance usually only gains management support when it is nearly too late and the dangers of an unmaintainable system have already begun to become visible.

The fact that distributed systems have different owners further complicates things, because it must be the interest of both the service provider and the service consumer(s) to withdraw a service. It makes no sense to remove a service without collaboration with the consumer(s). If you act unilaterally, the moment you withdraw a service in use one or more consumers will likely call your CEO to complain that a business process is broken and that the only way to restore it is to bring the withdrawn service into production again. Guess what the CEO will decide then?

So, what is the right way to withdraw a service in a distributed system? You should always follow a set procedure, which might be as follows:

1. First, you mark the service as deprecated (with a hint as to which service to use instead).

2. Then you monitor whether (and by which systems) the service is still being used. This, of course, requires some monitoring code, which usually should be part of your enterprise service bus (see Section 5.4.7).

3. If the service continues to be used, you should contact the relevant consumer(s) and discuss a solution. As a result, you should be able to produce a schedule for the final withdrawal of the service.

Because consumers of existing services don't get any direct benefit from service withdrawals, you might have trouble getting their collaboration. Effort is required to switch to a new service (or version); you should recognize this and try to help the consumers understand that they are in fact making an investment in the maintainability of the provider's code. In other words, you should try to create a common understanding of the benefit of an upgrade for the whole system or company.

Of course, an alternative solution is for the provider to provide some concrete incentive for the consumers to switch to the new service/version, so that there is some benefit for all the participants. Sound silly? Well, in practice, this indirectly happens pretty often: "You need a new service? Well, you can get it if you take this opportunity to stop using my deprecated services."

11.3 Summary

- Service implementations are software and have lifecycles just like any other software.
- The lifecycle is usually triggered by some process that identifies the need for a new service (business process modeling with process decomposition, portfolio management, modification of an existing service, etc.).

- Although a service design is usually an interface to another system, you should not fall into the trap of thinking that this interface can't be modified during the development of the service. Be sure that the contracts you define with external providers are specified in such a way that interface updates are possible.

- When a service goes into production, the software switches from being governed by rules for software under development to being governed by rules for software under maintenance. For this reason, generally only bug fixes should be allowed as modifications to existing services. All other changes should result in new service versions.

- Withdrawing a service is an organizational process that requires collaboration.

CHAPTER TWELVE

Versioning

W HEN YOU ESTABLISH **SOA,** YOU CAN'T EXPECT TO BE ABLE TO DO AND ANTICIPATE EVERYTHING AT once. Large distributed systems are never static. Requirements evolve, and new ones appear. Also, as you develop and implement services you constantly learn and improve, and you may want to apply your new knowledge to existing services. Therefore, you need the ability to update and grow.

As discussed in the previous chapter, SOA is a concept that has to deal with existing running solutions and services as well as new requirements that lead to the development of new solutions and services. Therefore, you need a mixture of maintenance and innovation.

This chapter will discuss how to deal with changes to services.

12.1 Versioning Requirements

There are two common reasons why services (and interfaces in general) have to be modified:

- When implementing new business processes you usually become aware of aspects you didn't know about or consider at design time, resulting in services (implementations as well as interfaces) needing to be modified.

- New or modified requirements may necessitate modifications of existing services.

Some people argue that with good design, the first case should not happen. One of my customers even deliberately introduced a process that made it difficult to make modifications once a service interface was specified, in an effort to force stability in the designs.

However, in practice, interfaces are no more stable than any other code. One reason is that people make mistakes (which you should be able to correct when you recognize them). In addition, these days we don't often have enough time for good designs. Finally, reality is always different from what we anticipate.

When you implement business processes, you learn. According to your new insights, you may decide to modify even interfaces. Otherwise, inappropriate or bad designs would remain in your system for years.

Now, given that services change during their development and when they are used in running systems, the question is how to deal with these changes. SOA is a concept for large distributed systems, and you can't require that all systems involved make corresponding modifications at the same time. You need migrations. In addition, you need processes that enable a testing department to test an older revision of a service while a new revision or a bug fix is already under development. You also need to allow service consumers to continue to use an older version of a service even after a new version becomes available.

In principle, there are two different requirements regarding the versioning of services:

- It must be possible to have multiple *versions* of a service running in the same runtime environment. For example, it must be possible for there to exist two versions of a service that returns customer data.

- It must be possible to have multiple *revisions* of a service under development. However, these different revisions don't have to be available in the same runtime environment.

The former is a business-driven requirement, because at runtime you will see that different versions of services are available. I will discuss this first, in Section 12.2. The latter requirement usually leads to the topic of configuration management. I will discuss this later, in Section 12.4.

12.2 Domain-Driven Versioning

Domain-driven versioning enables different versions of the same service to be run at the same time in the same runtime environment. That is, two consumers might call the same service using different interfaces. While one consumer uses a newer version of the service, another consumer might use an older version.

These are plenty of articles about how to deal with this issue, but these articles usually assume additional requirements that have to do with automatic updates of services. However, policies for automatic updates lead to additional complications and requirements.

Instead, I'd like to present a trivial versioning approach that has proven to be appropriate in all projects I have seen so far. Because it keeps things simple, there have to be good reasons not to follow this approach. So, we'll look at this option first, before briefly exploring some alternatives.

12.2.1 Trivial Domain-Driven Versioning

My trivial policy for domain-driven versioning is simply *not* to provide any technical support for versioning. That is, treat every modification of an existing service as (technically) a new service.

If you need to modify a service that returns customer data (say, GetCustomerData( )), you simply introduce a new service that incorporates the modification. Of course, you should make it obvious that this new service is a successor of the other service, which you can easily do by naming the new service accordingly (e.g., GetCustomerData_2( )). To avoid having a special rule for the first version of a service, you might choose to name the first service GetCustomerData_1( ) (see Figure 12-1). With this convention your service names will always have two parts: one that indicates what the service does and one that specifies the version number.

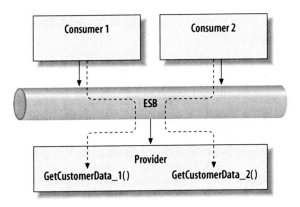

FIGURE 12-1. Two consumers calling two different service versions with trivial versioning

Of course, the costs of bringing a new service into existence are usually higher than those of modifying a service. For this reason, in practice I recommend a slightly relaxed rule for domain-driven versioning: from the moment a service is used in production, any modification that is not simply a bug fix should result in a new service. This rule has two important consequences:

- During development time any desired modifications can be made, and these modifications are not considered to result in new versions. Note, however, that from the moment a service is first used (e.g., in integration tests), the service provider should inform existing service consumers about any modifications and discuss them with the consumers (as should always be the case when a contract changes).

- At runtime, it is possible to fix bugs without creating new versions of the service (which would be more expensive). Of course, this implies that the service interface doesn't change. In practice this might lead to the problem that bug fixes sometimes turn out to be modifications, so that semantically new versions would have been more appropriate. But the price of creating new services for each bug fix is usually higher.

Note that I have not said anything about the question of whether or not the modifications are backward compatible. In fact, this policy applies even for backward-compatible modifications.

Why, you might wonder, shouldn't the provider be able to make changes to existing services without introducing new versions if these changes will not impact the existing consumers? There are two reasons. First, backward-compatible modifications often turn out not to be as "compatible" as expected. A typical example is when an additional attribute leads to longer running times, resulting in the (formal or informal) SLAs of the service being broken (see Section 13.4 for an example). In addition, any modification involves a risk. Introducing a modification as a new service gives you the chance to observe its runtime behavior for only a single consumer; all the other consumers can then switch to the new service when it is clear that everything works fine.

The second reason for not making even backward-compatible changes without introducing new versions is that these changes often result in modified data types. This issue is discussed later, in Section 12.3.

So, to sum it all up, after a service is brought into production, bug fixes are OK, backward-compatible modifications *should* result in new service versions, and incompatible changes *must* result in new versions. Note, however, that there is a gray area: a bug fix might actually be a modification (even a nonbackward-compatible modification). This versioning concept is a policy, not necessarily a law. Its purpose is to give service participants common guidelines so that the normal behavior is clear and intuitive. If in doubt, talk to each other.

The problem with this approach is obvious: there is a danger that you will end up with too many versions. Especially for services that return data (say, customer data), there is a risk that each new consumer will need additional data, so the original service will grow and grow. I've seen this happen. One company I know of that has hundreds of services in production (each version counts) started with the rule of having not more than three versions of the same service in production. In practice, they often wound up having as many as five (and more) versions running simultaneously.

To avoid having too many versions (which hinders code maintenance), you will occasionally need to take services out of production. As discussed in Section 11.2.2, this is usually done in two steps:

1. Declare an old service version as deprecated.

2. Withdraw the deprecated service.

Also bear in mind that in mission-critical systems (which SOA environments typically are), you can remove services only when they are no longer being used. For this reason, you need monitoring for this policy (see Section 5.4.7).

There is always a danger that some consumers will continue to use old, deprecated service versions. Remember that distributed systems have different owners, and that for consumers changing service versions incurs costs but may not result in any direct benefits. However, if old versions are not phased out, the entropy of the system as a whole will get worse and worse. Thus, you might need to escalate things organizationally, or the provider might need to offer consumers some incentive to switch to a new service version.

See Chapter 11 for more details about this topic from a service lifecycle point of view.

12.2.2 Nontrivial Domain-Driven Versioning

We've looked at the trivial versioning policy. What might a nontrivial policy look like?

There are a lot of possible answers to this question. In principle, the options include:

- Provide a mechanism that ensures services are forward compatible. That is, if your infrastructure allows you to provide a hook for future extensions, you can add extensions as needed and mark them as being optional. Existing service consumers will still be able to use the interface as they always have, and new consumers will be able to take advantage of the newer features.

- Introduce techniques that allow you to extend services in such a way that you can specify what should happen with consumers using the older interface. For example, your infrastructure might provide a mechanism to add new attributes, including specifying default values in case these attributes are not present.

- Provide a method of indirection so that different implementations are provided for different consumers. For example, a service broker might be able to determine which version of a service is provided for which consumer.

How these approaches are realized is a different question. As an example, you can use Web Services to deal with using different namespaces for different versions and/or use a UDDI registry (introduced in Chapter 16) as a broker that routes service requests differently. See, for example, [BrownEllis04] for more details about this approach.

12.3 Versioning of Data Types

When different versions of services exist, different versions of data types are also involved (at least, if the services use structured data types). Dealing with this issue can become a lot more difficult than just dealing with different service versions.

Say, for example, that a new attribute for a Post Office box is added to a service that returns data including an address. That is, the existing address type, which has the following attributes:

```
String street
String zipcode
String city
```

gets this new attribute:

```
String postbox
```

Because older versions of the service use the older address type and newer versions of the service use the newer address type, two different address types are in use in the same runtime environment (see Figure 12-2).

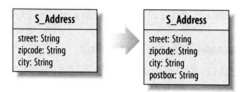

FIGURE 12-2. Two different versions of an address type

The question is how to deal with this fact. In principle, there are three possible options:

- Use different types for typed interfaces.
- Use the same types for typed interfaces.
- Use generic code so that type differences don't matter.

I will discuss these options now in detail.

12.3.1 Using Different Types for Different Versions of a Data Type

When using different types for different versions of a type, you might be tempted to simply apply the same rule I suggested in Section 12.2.1 for naming and distinguishing between the types. However, this situation is more complex, for a few reasons.

The first reason is that modified types lead to other modified types. That is, if a type is used by another type, the other type also changes. For example, if an address type is used by a type for lists of addresses, which is part of a type for customer data, which is used by a type for lists of customer data, a change of the inner address type changes all the other types (see Figure 12-3). As a consequence, you get many types.

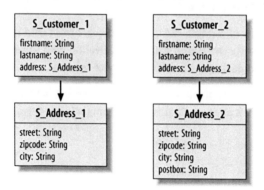

FIGURE 12-3. Modifying a versioned address type that is used by other types

The other reason for the increased complexity is that, in effect, services have different data types for the same kinds of information. In a programming language with type binding, the result of these type differences is that it is not possible to compare, copy, or assign the types as a whole; you have to program utility functions that compare, copy, or assign the different types element by element (ignoring or providing default values for attributes that are not in both versions of the data type). This has consequences for service providers and service consumers:

- As a service provider, you have to use different types for the same kind of information. You might do this by copying and pasting the code that implements the functionality for different types, by implementing functionality for one type and mapping the data to other types, or by using generic code (templates).

- As a service consumer, it might happen that you need a new service that uses the new version of a data type as well as an older service that still uses the old version of the type. Because these types differ, you will have to map data to deal with the same kind of information in both services.

The second point in particular has nasty consequences, because service consumers sooner or later will probably have to deal with different versions of the same type. To help you understand this problem, consider the following example. Say you have two different versions of a service that returns customer data. As discussed earlier, the address types are different: one consumer uses S_Address_1 and the other uses S_Address_2. Now suppose you have another service, called GetInvoiceData_1( ); this service returns invoice data that includes customer data, and it also uses the newer address data type. As a result you get the situation illustrated in Figure 12-4. Note that all these services (including all versions) are used by some consumer(s).

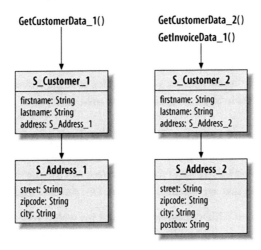

FIGURE 12-4. Different data types for different services

Now say that later an additional requirement is introduced for a consumer that specifies that the service returning invoice data should also return a tax number as part of the customer data. So, you introduce a new service called GetInvoiceData_2() that returns a new data type, S_Customer_3. As a result, you get the situation illustrated in Figure 12-5.

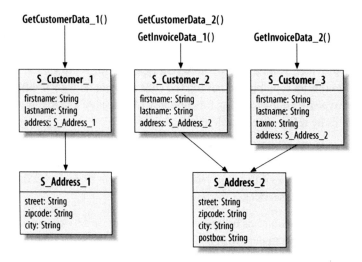

FIGURE 12-5. New attributes result in even more different data types for different services

Now, if a new consumer wants to use both services (GetCustomerData() and GetInvoiceData()), it will find itself in the strange position that two different data types are involved when it uses the latest versions of the two services. Of course, you can avoid this situation by always upgrading all services that use a certain data type when the data type changes for one of the services where it is used, but this leads to a lot of additional service versions.

Note that what is described here is a conceptual problem arising from the fact that you have to support different versions of APIs with structured data types. There are alternatives, some of which will be discussed in the following sections: you might not use structured types, you might not use typed APIs, or you might try to share different versions of a type inside a process. All of these alternatives have their own drawbacks, though.

12.3.2 Using the Same Type for Different Versions of a Data Type

When the same type is used for different versions of a type, this type must contain all the attributes of all the versions of the data type. All services will use the same type, but they will use only those attributes that are specified for them. This policy introduces three problems:

- You have to document which attributes are valid for which service versions. For complex data types or types used in different services, this can become very complicated.

- The data types of older services change over time. This means that these different versions are not binary compatible. As a result, you have to make sure that all libraries of a process are compiled with the same version of a data type. Thus, if a data type changes for a new service and you need this new service, you have to recompile all existing code for all other code that used this data type. If this fails, very nasty runtime misbehavior will occur.

• If you validate input data according to your point of view, you have to make sure that additional attributes do not make your input invalid.

To illustrate, consider again the situation depicted in Figure 12-5. With this approach, the different service versions would all use the same data types, as shown in Figure 12-6.

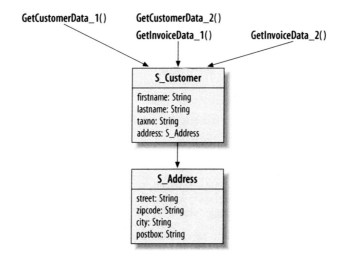

FIGURE 12-6. Different services with different versions sharing the same data types

However, for GetCustomerData_1( ) the taxno and postbox attributes are ignored, and for GetCustomerData_2( ) and GetInvoiceData_1( ), the taxno attribute is ignored. This, at least, must be documented (which is not easy, because when writing the documentation for GetCustomerData_1( ) you don't know about future attributes, and when modifying S_Address, it might not be obvious where it is used).

In addition, if a process uses a library calling GetInvoiceData_1( ) that is compiled for an old version of the data type and later adds a new library calling GetInvoiceData_2( ) that is compiled for the new version of the data type, the problem of binary incompatibility arises. As a result, you might get bugs due to different interpretations of the same memory, which are one of the worst possible kinds of bugs to deal with.

Only if you can ensure that each consumer uses a consistent set of libraries (for example, by providing different library names for each consistent release of all service code) might this policy be appropriate.

12.3.3 Using Generic Data Types

A third option for dealing with different versions of data types is to use only generic code that is able to deal with any data type. In this case, the binary format of the approach with the same types doesn't matter. As a consequence, data types don't matter at compile time; all the processing happens at runtime.

To see the difference, consider what a static API to access the street of the address of a customer returned by GetCustomerData_1( ) might look like:

```
S_Customer_1 custData;
S_Address_1 address;
String street;
input.setCustomerID(id);
custData = serviceAPI.getCustomerData_1(input);
address  = custData.getAddress();
street   = address.getStreet();
```

The same task implemented using a generic API might look as follows:

```
Data custData, address;
String street;
input.setValue("customerID",id);
custData = serviceAPI.getCustomerData_1(input);
address  = custData.getValue("address");
street   = address.getValueAsString("street");
```

Alternatively, the last two lines might be combined into one line:

```
street   = custData.getValueAsString("address.street");
```

This is definitely an option to consider. However, this currently seems to be a very uncommon approach. Especially in the Web Services context, all generators I know of (by default) generate typed APIs, introducing the versioning problems discussed earlier. One reason for this is that without typed APIs you lose the advantage of finding bugs at compile time. Whether or not the path of an attribute is correct is evaluated at runtime. Still, for large systems, this approach might pay off. Maybe it's not so common because typed interfaces seem to be so easy and intuitive (as long as you don't have large applications of the SOA concept). The prototypes probably look fine, and later on it might be too late to change things conceptually.

12.3.4 Summary of Versioning of Data Types

Hopefully, you understand now that versioning of data types is an issue for large distributed systems. I've discussed three options, which all have pros and cons (and, of course, a lot more could be said about all of these options). A fourth option would be to use flat lists of parameters rather than structured data types, but of course this doesn't work when coarse-grained services send around complex data.

As I mentioned previously, the option of using only generic data types is not often used in practice, and it can be hard to provide support for this approach on all platforms of a SOA system. Also, the option of sharing types for different versions is a very dangerous one, because if your process does not ensure that all your libraries are consistent (which is difficult in distributed systems) it can result in very ugly bugs and undefined runtime behavior. In addition, this option reduces your ability to find bugs at compile time. Thus, the first option I presented is the most commonly used. This approach often results in complaints by ordinary programmers about providing such a silly versioning concept, where it is not even possible for providers to have consistent data types. But as we've seen, this is part of the price of distributed systems with different owners: you can't just switch to new services across the board.

As a service consumer, it is a good idea to make your code somehow independent from the versioning of the services called. You should use your own data types, which are mapped to the data types of the services when they are used. For this reason, service consumers usually should have a thin top layer that maps external data types to internal data types (which might or might not be combined with the mapping layer between service APIs and service protocols, as discussed in Section 5.3.3).

However, be careful, and try to keep things simple. You will discuss this approach when you realize that dealing with different versions is an issue. Don't make things too complex by trying to prepare for things that might happen in the future.

12.4   Configuration-Management-Driven Versioning

As introduced at the beginning of this chapter, by "configuration-management-driven versioning" I mean the requirement of having multiple revisions of a service under development in different runtime environments. This requirement leads to the topic of configuration-management tools such as version-control systems.

When you have a set of files and other artifacts that belong together, it must be possible to give them a common label so that you can deal with them as one group. That is, if you model a service, generate interfaces based on the model, implement services against these interfaces, compile libraries out of these implementations, and deploy the resulting libraries, you have to be able to find all the versions of the different artifacts that belong together.

If all the artifacts are files, this is easy. You can use any version control system that is able to label files and support the management of different versions of a file (including showing differences and merging multiple modifications).

If there are artifacts that are not files, you need related mechanisms. For example, if you have a service repository (see Chapter 17) that is implemented in a database, in the repository interface you need support for configuration management or corresponding organizational rules (such as having different repositories for different configurations).

Again, note that it is usually very important at least to be able to show the differences between two versions of an artifact. This might require you to have special tools or scripts (e.g., special database scripts, stored procedures, or Visual Basic scripts for a tool such as Rational Rose).

12.5 Versioning in Practice

It's important to be aware that requirements are likely to change more often than you expect, and also that difficult modifications (particularly those that are not mission-critical) have a tendency to be put off. This means that you may end up with more versions being rolled out more frequently than you expect, and that it may turn out to be harder to than you expect to phase out old versions. Recall the large SOA system I mentioned earlier, which expected to have a maximum of three versions of each service in the same runtime environment. The system had more than 30 service participants and more than 300 services, and there were regularly up to six different versions of individual services in production.

With these difficulties in mind, you should take the following recommendations into account.

12.5.1 Modifications Should Impact Only the Provider and Consumer(s)

Try to make modifying services as easy as possible. In particular, service modifications should impact only the service provider and the service consumer(s)—no one and nothing else. Note that central teams that design the architecture for distributed systems tend to impose more control than is necessary.

For example, your infrastructure might help you by checking service interfaces during the transfer of data. However, this means that each modification must also be deployed to the infrastructure component that does the runtime checking. This leads to more complicated processes and potential bottlenecks.

Thus, inside the SOA infrastructure should be as generic as possible with respect to domain-specific business functionality. Any specific processing that is influenced by different versions of services should affect only the endpoint of the infrastructure (e.g., libraries and proxies for the provider and consumer(s)).

12.5.2 Call Constraints Should be Considered

One of my customers has introduced a concept known as a "call constraint," which is a parameter that each service has that gives the consumer(s) the opportunity to signal a special context that might have an impact on the service implementation. The problem that prompted this innovation was that while services are intended to be (re)used by multiple consumers, in practice the granularity of services often differs because additional attributes can affect running times (see Chapter 13). In addition, it is not always clear at design time which service context will occur in practice, and when such a context might become critical. That is, you don't know ahead of time which attributes it will be critical to return.

The concept of a "call constraints" argument allows you to delay runtime optimizations until the moment when they become necessary. The provider and the consumer agree upon a special flag that the consumer can send inside the "call constraints" argument to indicate that there is a need for special optimizations or a special behavior for that specific consumer. The provider can then implement this special behavior for the consumer without changing the service interface or breaking existing behavior.

This is a useful technique, but you should note some things:

- This is not a general mechanism that consumers can use to specify whether or not the provider should return a certain attribute; it is a formatless flag that both participants must agree upon and that is described in the semantic description (contract) of the service.
- Inside the implementation of a service, you usually have to pass this parameter as part of the "calling context."
- This is a practical approach for the dealing with the fact that when a service enters integration testing or production, some things may become evident that were not clear before. Using this flag can be a lot easier than modifying the service. However, don't do it too often—you might consider these flags as workarounds for future modifications (knowing that nothing remains as stable as a workaround).

For more details about call constraints, see Section 13.3.1.

12.6 Summary

- SOA requires a smooth migration strategy for new service versions.
- The best approach is to treat each modification of a service (in production) technically as a new service.
- If you have typed APIs for services, versioning of service types is also recommended (although there are alternatives).
- To avoid an explosion of versions, you have to introduce processes to deprecate and remove old service versions. This is one reason why it's useful to be able to monitor service calls.
- To become independent from versioning aspects of called services, service consumers usually should have a thin layer that maps external data types into internal data types.
- Service modifications should never affect anyone other than the service provider and consumer(s).
- To be "forward compatible," you might provide an attribute for upcoming call constraints. This enables consumers to signal special needs at runtime, without having to modify service signatures. However, be cautious about making everything generic, because this might introduce a lot of complexity and hidden dependencies.

CHAPTER THIRTEEN

SOA and Performance

IT SYSTEMS HAVE TWO ASPECTS THAT REPEATEDLY BREAK PLANS, CONCEPTS, AND DESIGNS: PERFORMANCE and security. In this chapter, I will discuss some real-world examples of how performance issues can impact the concept and realization of SOA. Most of the examples are taken from an international phone company with hundreds of services running in its day-to-day business. For example, whenever a customer calls in for support, several services are called even before the conversation with a call center agent begins. In this environment, performance (especially runtime performance) matters.

13.1 Where Performance Matters

There are different places where performance comes into play in the context of services and SOA infrastructures. If performance becomes critical, it is usually because of the running time of a service. Let's explore this by following one successful synchronous service call that includes one requesting message from the consumer to the provider and one response message from the provider back to the consumer (see Figure 13-1).

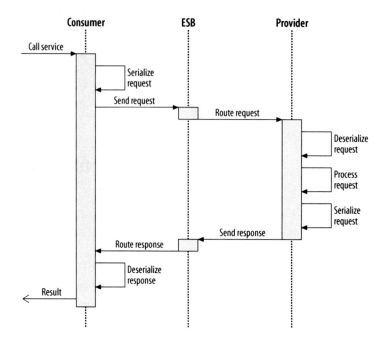

FIGURE 13-1. Sequence diagram of a service call

As this diagram shows, first you have to serialize the service call into the protocol format of the enterprise service bus. Then you send the request over the ESB to the provider. The provider in turn has to deserialize the request so that it can process it. For the response, the steps are the same, but in the opposite direction.

The following steps can be critical:

- Sending the request and response over the ESB
- Deserializing the request or response
- Processing the request

Note that SOA is a concept for heterogeneous system landscapes. For this reason, you can't simply send binary data between systems (COBOL assembler code does not match Java bytecode, and even C++ assembler code from different compilers does not necessarily match). You need an intermediate protocol that the consumer and provider can use to exchange data.

These days, such a format typically is XML-based (e.g., SOAP for a Web Services infra-structure). But XML is pretty chatty, resulting in the essential data increasing in size by a factor of between 4 and 20. This can have a significant impact on bandwidth in environments where it is limited (although this shouldn't usually be a problem).

The use of an intermediate protocol can also have performance effects for deserialization. This might (but usually shouldn't) be critical, because it can take time to translate a byte sequence to complex data. Of course, your perception of acceptable versus unacceptable delays depends on your requirements and tools. For this reason you should validate your concrete behavior to be sure, because each additional mapping takes some time and there still might be deserializers around that are badly implemented.

There is one case where bandwidth and deserialization are more likely to become issues: if you have to process the data while it is being transferred in your ESB. For example, if you have to map data between different protocols or you want to verify inside your ESB whether service calls are well formed, this can significantly slow down the running time of a service call. Adding message-level security aspects (see Section 14.3.2) can also impact running times.

In practice, the primary reason for slow services is that their implementation takes time. That is, the service provider needs time to process the request and provide the response. In this case, you have to look at the usual answering time for one service call and consider how well this answering time scales. If the service provider has limited resources or bottlenecks, processing multiple service calls at the same time might lead to significant performance penalties. For this reason, a service contract should include a service-level agreement (SLA) specifying both the average answering time and the number of calls to be answered in a certain period of time (the so-called "time service factor," TSF).

If the response time of a service is too slow for a consumer and you can't improve performance by adding more system power or bandwidth, you usually have to decouple things on the consumer's side. That is, the service consumer might not have to synchronously wait for an answer to its service call. Note, however, that asynchronous communications can significantly raise the complexity of your system. See Section 4.2.1 for details.

Note, in addition, that unreliable networks and protocols may also have an impact on the performance of your system. Although you might not see it in your service APIs, a service request might be sent over the ESB more than once before it is successfully delivered. See Section 10.4 for details.

In general, it's a good idea to gather statistics about the running times of different service requests and monitor the numbers over time. This can help you identify near-term problems and long-term tendencies.

However, even when in general performance seems to be okay, it can become an issue. The following sections will discuss some examples.

13.2   From Remote Stored Procedures to Services

Even if the average time a service request takes is fine, you can still run into trouble. Let's look at an example that occurred at one company when it started to introduce basic services (see Section 6.2).

Before introducing services, the company had lost control over which systems were accessing certain backends. Growth over the past few years had been rapid, and it turned out that several systems spread over the whole company were now directly accessing the database data using remote stored procedures* (see Figure 13-2).

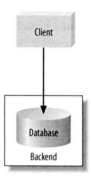

FIGURE 13-2. Direct backend data access using remote stored procedures

As a consequence, the departments maintaining the backends couldn't modify the database schema without breaking several other systems. For this reason, useful database modifications became risky and costly. Even finding out whether and how a modification would influence other systems' behavior became more and more of an effort. And from time to time it happened that modifications wound up breaking systems the departments in question didn't even know about (at least they knew about the systems then).

By introducing basic services, the company hoped to reduce these dependencies and regain control over the technical aspects of the backend systems. The idea was that instead of directly accessing database data, the other systems should use services, which encapsulate technical details of the service implementations from the outside world (see Figure 13-3).

Of course, performance was an issue from the beginning of the project, but initial measurements showed that the expected service calls would be fast enough. A service call usually took between 100 and 300 ms, provided that there was no significant overhead due to the service implementation. The consumers could usually live with these numbers, because there were graphical frontends (for human users, any feedback or result given in less than half a second is perceived as an immediate effect).

---

* Stored procedures are database scripts that directly operate on the native technical data of the database.

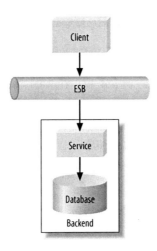

F I G U R E 1 3 - 3 . Basic services separate technical backend details from clients

The company started the project by forcing existing clients to switch from remote procedure calls to services. But it turned out that this didn't work. The problem was that, on
average, the service calls were slower than the remote stored procedure calls by a factor of
between 5 and 10. One or two consecutive service calls could be made without the user
perceiving any delay, but the existing clients were implemented under the assumption
that 10 or more consecutive remote stored procedure calls could be made without any
delay being noticed (because they took only 10 to 30 ms each). Simply replacing each
stored procedure call with a service call introduced unacceptable delays: 10 remote stored
procedure calls taking 30 ms each took only 300 ms, but 10 service calls took something
like 3 seconds, which was too long for the frontend.

As a result, the company had to reimplement existing clients in a way far more complicated than just switching from remote stored procedure calls to service calls. Acceptable
performance was achieved by combining some remote procedure calls into single service
calls and by sending some services requests in parallel, but these modifications took far
more effort than was initially planned. In addition, the client code became more complicated, because it had to be able to deal with asynchronous replies to different parallel
service calls. Still, after this reconstruction, service providers were finally able to modify
their internal technical data structures without breaking external systems.

After reading this, you might think that because of the inherent overhead of each service
call it is a good idea to have coarse-grained services. But although it is often written that
services (in general) should be coarse-grained, again, performance can become a problem
here. The next section explores this topic.

13.3 Performance and Reusability

It's often recommended that services be coarse-grained. However, aside from the problem of defining when a service's granularity becomes "coarse" (see Section 3.3.2), this recommendation is highly influenced by its link to performance:

- When the overhead of many fine-grained service calls compared to one coarse-grained service call becomes too high (as discussed in the previous section), performance concerns may lead to coarser-grained services.

- On the other hand, when the price for processing more data becomes too high, performance concerns may lead to finer-grained services.

The latter topic will be discussed in this section.

The example I'll use here is that of a service provided by a company's CRM system.* One of the first services this system provided was a service returning all customer data. Of course, "all customer data" could include several hundred attributes—besides data such as the customer ID and associated addresses and payment methods on record, the information returned could include all contracts and even all invoices and payments on record. In this example the company was a phone company that returned all phone contracts as part of the customer portfolio.

As discussed in the first section of this chapter, processing a service request can result in a significant performance penalty. And indeed, loading all customer data could take a significant amount of time (especially when the customer was a good customer with many contracts).

One day, a new system came along and asked for some customer data. According to the ideal of reusability, the CRM team recommended the reuse of the existing service returning all customer data. But the new consumer immediately complained because the service took too long. The CRM team asked them to mark the attributes they really needed. The result is shown in Figure 13-4—only five attributes out of several hundred were needed.

Of course, processing a result that returned just the desired attributes would be a lot faster than processing the usual response containing the complete customer portfolio. But how could this be achieved in the context of the original service? In the figure, you can see the pretty complex data model of the original service result, which contains several different data structures (records) and arrays of structures. Because the five attributes of interest appear in different structures and are not grouped together, it would not help to simply return only one or a few of these structures and skip the rest. In other words, having an input attribute forcing the service not to return the contracts, for example, would not solve the problem.

---

* A customer relationship management (CRM) system has the task of managing customer data.

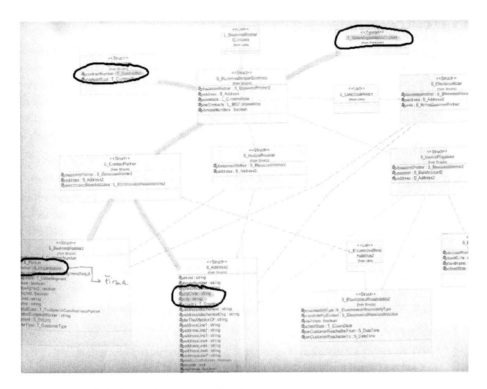

FIGURE 13-4. Marked selection of a coarse-grained service

We see this same situation when we analyze how different systems attach to the same database. Each system has its own view, and therefore we often introduce different views to databases. It seems we need a "view" concept for services as well, because there is no such thing as one typical view a service can provide.

The question is, how do you deal with different views in services? There is an obvious answer to this question: you can think of each view as a separate service, because it represents a specific business functionality. This means that to solve the problem we've been looking at, a different service had to be provided.

This is exactly what the company decided to do, and in fact the CRM system in question now has several different services to return customer data. A few are coarse-grained, but several others are fine-grained services providing different views of the customer data.

Is this a problem? It does mean that the general idea of reusability of services does not work as expected. If somebody computes a business case for a service and claims that this service will suit all consumers' needs, this business case will probably be broken because of performance issues. But this does not mean that the goal of reusability can never be met. Of course, there are services returning customer data that are consumed by multiple systems.

13.3.1 Call Constraints

One problem with performance is that it is hard to predict. You always have to measure. But to measure, you need the software to be in place and in use. When you implement a service that should be provided for two different consumers, you might find out at a very late stage of development that you have to split this new service into two services due to performance reasons. However, adding a new service at a late stage of distributed system development can be a problem in itself (interfaces change, and you have to go through all the steps of the lifecycle for services under development; see Chapter 11).

To avoid this overhead, in one project I worked on we introduced a concept called "call constraints." When a new service gets designed, it always gets an additional string attribute called `callConstraints`. Then, if problems are discovered at runtime and it is too late to fix them in the service interface, the provider and consumer(s) can agree on a special flag that is passed in this attribute to handle special cases or to perform some optimizations. This is a very useful feature, but note that you should consider it a workaround that gives you some time to fix the problem in future releases (although, as we all know, temporary workarounds often have the longest lifetimes in practice).

> **NOTE**
>
> Introducing a flag such as `skipContractData` or `specialOptimizationForSystemX` helps to signal that this is an exception or workaround and will help you find the corresponding code in both the provider's and consumers' source.

Now, you might be thinking that an even better approach would be to introduce a special notation so that each consumer can specify which data it really needs. That is, by passing something like `address.zipCode & contract[1].phoneNumer`, the consumer could specify that it only needs the zip code and the phone number of the customer's first contract. This, however, introduces too much flexibility. You would have to verify whether the argument is well formed, and as an implementer you would have to parse this attribute and process it with each attribute access. In addition, maintenance would become far more complicated, and what the service really did would be controlled by a pretty complicated format. For example, think about orchestration. It would be very hard to orchestrate such a service in an orchestration engine.

According to my experience, as a rule of thumb, a service or a service operation should not be so generic that it returns different structures. Or, from a business point of view, a service should perform one concrete business functionality. Usually, the limit for coarse granularity is when the service becomes generic (without having a business requirement for generic interfaces, such as when structures frequently change).

13.3.2 Customized Services

As discussed previously, different systems often need different views of the same data, which leads to different services being created when performance comes into play. However, it is sometimes necessary to go even further and create *consumer-specific* services. Again, I'll demonstrate this issue using real-world experience with a phone company's CRM system.

When a customer calls a large company, the call is usually handled by a CTI system[*] that routes the call to a call center agent. Ideally, during the routing the customer data gets loaded to the call center agent's desktop so that she can welcome the customer by name, verify a password, and so on. Unfortunately, you usually don't know in advance why a customer is calling, so ideally you should have all the customer's data available; this enables you to handle any type of question or request. For this reason, all customer data should be loaded to the desktop of the call center agent before the conversation begins (see Figure 13-5).

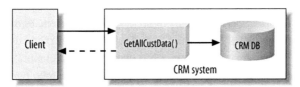

FIGURE 13-5. Loading all customer data takes time

However, loading all the customer data (especially for good customers with a lot of data) may take too long. Ideally, all of the data should be loaded on the call center agent's display while the phone call is being routed. That means all the customer data should be loaded in less than a second.

Technically, there is an easy solution for this dilemma: just load the data in two steps (see Figure 13-6). That is, when the customer calls in, the CTI system calls the first service, which loads all the data necessary for the call center agent to welcome the customer (name, password, etc.). Then, as the conversations starts, a second service call is made to request and load all additional customer data. As a further optimization, the first request can have the effect of "preloading" all the additional data into a local cache after the response is returned. In effect, the second call then only has to transfer the data in the cache to the client (see Figure 13-6).

This trick isn't particularly innovative, but it's important for SOA for one reason: it demonstrates that there can be services that are individually designed for one specific consumer. This specific split of customer data doesn't make sense in any other circumstances. In fact, in a situation such as this, it's best to bring together the system architect of the

---

[*] A computer telephony integration (CTI) system simplifies processing of telephone calls by allowing computers to process the calls (partially) or route them to the right destinations.

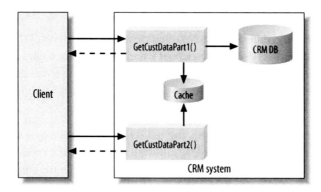

FIGURE 13-6. Loading customer data in two steps

consuming system and the system architect of the provider to discuss the exact design of the service. In other words, this is a *customized* service, which again demonstrates that not all services fall into the category of *reusable* services (see Section 3.3.6).

This example also demonstrates the limits of orchestrating services. Returning the customer data for an incoming call is only the first of several steps in the business process as a whole. Splitting this step into two service calls is usually an implementation detail and not something you worry about when designing the process as a whole. For this reason, different process models are involved and the important question is when and how the fact that this step consists of multiple service calls comes into play.

13.3.3 Reusability in Practice

The examples in this section have demonstrated that performance concerns can lead to decreased reusability of services. While in theory you may need only one service that returns all customer data, in practice you are likely to end up needing several services providing different (even customized) views of the customer data.

Figure 13-7 show a possible graph of the average number of consumers services might have over a five-year period. The ratio of implemented services to (re)used services is often smaller than you might expect. In my experience, for a system with a large number of services in production, you have done a good job if after one or two years of working on establishing a SOA landscape, each service is used by, on average, one consumer. For SOA landscapes that are three or four years old and that have hundreds of services, you might expect each service to be used by, on average, between two and four consumers.

You might be surprised by the fact that the average number of consumers for services can be below one. Shouldn't each service have at least one consumer? In practice this is not always the case, for three primary reasons:

- In large systems, a lot of implemented software never gets into production. This is also true (although possibly less so) for services. Requirements may change, implementations may turn out to be impractical, or it may turn out not to be in the interest of systems to consume services that you expected them to.

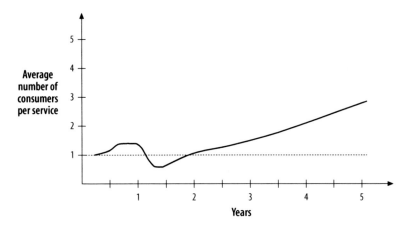

FIGURE 13-7. Possible service (re)usage graph

- If services are provided according to the portfolio management approach (see Chapter 7), there is only ever an assumption that the services will be consumed. They might be used eventually or following the YAGNI ("You Ain't Gonna Need It") principle, they might never be used.

- Services might be not in use any longer because the consumers have switched to other services (which, logically, are newer versions).

13.4 Performance and Backward Compatibility

Performance concerns can also impact the backward compatibility of a modified system. To explore this issue, let's again consider a service returning customer data for a phone company.

Almost all large enterprises that have thousands or millions of customers categorize these customers into different groups. The best customers gain certain privileges: there might be special bonus programs to bind them to the company, or they might be routed to more experienced call center agents because their problems tend to be more complicated or they required better service. Historically, a typical categorization of customers was whether they were business clients or private customers. But this distinction didn't work well for the company in question, because some private customers generated high call volumes while some business clients generated very low volumes. In addition, it was not clear how to treat freelancers and self-employed customers.

For these reasons, the company started to introduce a more specific categorization based on the volume of calls generated by each customer. In accordance with this volume each customer was assigned a value between 1 and 10, which in a sense represented the customer's value to the company. The plan was to extend the usual services that returned customer data by a simple integer attribute so that external systems could process the new customer values.

All the analysts, designers, and solution managers expected that the extensions of the existing services would be backward compatible; just adding a simple attribute independent from the other attributes was not anticipated to affect the behavior of the existing services. However, it turned out that the new versions of the services caused trouble. For certain scenarios, the new version raised the running time by a factor of two or more. The new attribute ended up causing existing applications to complain that the new version of the service was not usable anymore.

But why did this happen?

Consider the computer telephony integration (CTI) system. When a user called in, the CTI system started a service request to get the customer data so that when a call center agent answered the phone, she had all the customer data on her screen. The input parameter of the service was the calling customer's phone number.

This seemed straightforward, but the situation was complicated by the fact that individual customers could have multiple phone contracts. Therefore, we couldn't simply look at the sales volume for the phone contract associated with the number the customer happened to be using for that phone call, because the customer might be using a low-volume number but have other numbers that generated very high volumes. For this reason, we decided to rate customers by processing the *total* volume of all of their phone contracts.

Unfortunately, this processing was done at runtime. Thus, when the service was called, suddenly we had to load all of the customer's phone contracts to process the rating. And because loading and processing all the contracts took time, the service took dramatically longer than before (especially for good customers that had many contracts).

In other words, the simple integer attribute caused a very high performance penalty because it was processed at runtime, and its processing could take a pretty long time.

So, what does this have to do with backward compatibility? Well, the signature of the service remained backward compatible, but the contract was broken. That is, the nonfunctional service-level agreements of this service (stating, for example, that 90 percent of all calls would be answered in under 500 ms) were broken.

Now, you might object that this is a bad example, because it demonstrates only one thing: bad design always leads to trouble. Of course, processing this simple attribute at runtime wasn't a good idea, and we should have known that. The obvious alternative would have been to start a batch job that processed the current customer values each night and to return those values when the customer data was requested the following day.

However, the mistake wasn't that silly, and the fix wasn't that obvious. This case illustrates some important lessons to learn for SOA and large distributed systems:

- First, in large, complicated systems, it's impossible to know or anticipate everything. The involvement of different people, departments, and systems can obscure obvious things.

- Second, no one solution may prove to be a magic bullet. In this case, the approach of processing the customer values nightly would not really have been better, because processing millions of customer values each night would have required a lot more resources than processing tens of thousands of customer values (i.e., only the values for those customers who placed a call) each day at runtime.

- Third, even if you recognize the problem and decide that a different solution (such as processing the customer values each night) would be a better approach, you might have trouble realizing it. Again, the reason is different owners of different domains: the people or department responsible for maintaining the database, including providing batch jobs for it, might not be the same as the people or department responsible for providing customer services. Reprioritizing resources in different departments to fix this design immediately might prove difficult (even if collaboration, in principle, works).

Note that it doesn't matter which solution is right in this particular scenario. What I wanted to demonstrate here is the impact performance can have on services and system design. From a business process point of view, the way the customer value gets processed is a technical detail, but this detail can break the whole business process. In general, this example demonstrates that there are some risks when you think that it is enough to design distributed processes by breaking them down into different steps and implementing these steps.

Note, in addition, that current standards for composing (orchestrating) services, such as BPEL (see Chapter 7), don't deal with nonfunctional attributes. This does not mean that the whole approach doesn't ever work, but you should know its limits.

As a side note, I want to mention an important tie-in of this experience to the versioning concept of services. It turned out that having a versioning policy that defined each modification of a service running in production as, technically, a new service helped us to minimize the impact of this problem. Consumers were able to choose which version to use, as existing business processes were not broken by the problem with the new version of the service (which would have been the case if there had been mechanisms in place to force consumers to switch to new versions of existing services). See Section 12.2.1 for details.

13.5 Summary

- For services, performance (especially running time) is an issue.

- Switching from proprietary remote data access to services can have a significant impact on running times.

- There can be a tradeoff between reusability and performance.

- Performance can have an impact on service granularity, in both directions: services tend to become more coarse-grained if the overhead of multiple service calls is too high, and more fine-grained if the overhead of processing unnecessary data is too high. In addition, coarse granularity should be considered to have reached its limit when services become generic silver bullets.

- Call constraints might help to (temporarily) implement special service behavior without breaking the service's formal interface (signature).

- Nonfunctional attributes (SLAs) are part of a service contract. For this reason, additional attributes that cause runtime penalties can break the backward compatibility of a service.

- Performance aspects can break business process and system designs, which introduces some risks when using business-process-modeling standards like BPEL that ignore nonfunctional attributes.

CHAPTER FOURTEEN

SOA and Security

WHEN INTEGRATING DISTRIBUTED SYSTEMS, SOONER OR LATER SECURITY COMES INTO PLAY. **P**ROBLEMS can arise because many people have access to the system landscape, while not all of these people are allowed to see and manipulate all the data.

This chapter gives a brief overview of security aspects for SOA.*

14.1 Security Requirements

When talking about security in distributed systems many different aspects come into play, and as usual, there are many different ways to categorize them. Generally speaking, the following categories are key:

Authentication

Authentication has to do with verifying an identity. An identity may be a user, a physical device, or a foreign service requestor. Regarding SOA, this means finding out who is calling the service.

---

* Thanks to Bruce Sams of OPTIMA (*http://www.optimabit.com*), who, as a leading expert on security in distributed systems (including SOA and Web Services system landscapes), gave me a lot of input while writing this chapter.

Authorization

Authorization has to do with determining what an identity is allowed to do. Regarding SOA, this means checking whether the caller is allowed to call the service and/or see the result.

Confidentiality

Whether data remains confidential while in transit or in storage is another key aspect of security. Regarding services, this means ensuring that no one besides the service caller can see service data while it is being transferred between the provider and the consumer.

Integrity

The key here is guaranteeing that data can't get manipulated or counterfeited, such that either the data is simply wrong or, even worse, authentication and authorization credentials are faked so that someone can get access to data she is not supposed to see.

Availability

It is possible to attack ("flood") a system in such a way that, while data is not lost or corrupted, the system simply becomes inoperable. A typical form of flooding is a "denial of service" (DoS) attack.

Accounting

The key here is to keep track of the consumption of resources. Regarding SOA, this means tracking service calls for management, planning, billing, or other purposes.

Auditing

The key here is to evaluate a security concept and its application, with the aim of improving its reliability. Auditing might involve recording all security-relevant information, so that you can detect or analyze security holes and attacks. So, it also includes monitoring, logging, and tracing of all security-relevant data flow. In addition, auditing may be a functional component: when services are manipulating data, this manipulation has to be "audited" (e.g., for legal reasons).

In the context of security, "AAA" is often used to refer to authentication, authorization, and accounting.

14.2 Dealing with Security Requirements

Dealing with security is nothing new. For all the aspects I've just laid out, SOA uses the same approaches typically used by distributed systems:

- For authentication and authorization, you usually need the concept of user IDs and passwords (although there are other authentication standards, such as Kerberos, certificates, hardware tokens, etc.). For user IDs, typically there is some form of indirection so that users can be assigned roles; privileges, such as the ability to call a service or the ability to see a result, are associated with these roles. If there is a central service to manage users and user profiles, this is often called an identity provider (see Section 14.3.3 for more on this subject).

- For confidentiality and integrity, the usual concepts such as encryption and digital signatures are used.

Regarding these concepts, SOA security is no different from security in any other form of distributed computing. However, there are some aspects special to SOA, which I will discuss in the following sections.

14.2.1 Interoperability Versus Security

One key concept of SOA is high interoperability (see Section 2.3.2). Following the concepts of enterprise application integration (EAI), it should be easy to connect to other systems. In SOA, the idea is to replace individual connectivity solutions for each pair of systems with a common ESB, so that any system connected to this ESB is connected to each other system that is also connected to it.

As a consequence of this approach, "natural" firewalls introduced by using different communication channels and different protocols are not available. When connected to an ESB, by default your system is open. Bruce Sams shared with me the analogy of a castle: in the old times we had multiple walls, moats, arrows, and hot tar to protect the castle, but high interoperability requires that the drawbridge is lowered.

Consequently, to protect sensitive data, we have to restrict consumers' abilities to call all services and see all the results. This is usually a motivation for introducing security concepts into an ESB.

14.2.2 Heterogeneity and Security

SOA is a concept for dealing with business processes distributed over different heterogeneous systems. The existing security mechanisms and policies for these systems are likely to differ. Thus, you face the challenge of introducing a general security concept over many different existing security concepts. The process starts with having different user IDs for the same people and results in having different abstractions and processes to introduce roles and user profiles.

14.2.3 Distributed Processes and Many Layers of Abstraction

The most important problem is that SOA leads to many different layers of abstraction. When each service abstracts business functionality of a lower layer, it also has to abstract the user identity context from the underlying application.

Combined with the heterogeneous security concepts of the individual backends, this leads to the fact that it's a long way from the initial request for a business process to the systems that deal with this request.

Figure 14-1 shows a possible example: a customer might start a process using a service portal, and that process might run over different layers (process services, composed services, basic services) and different backends; in addition, a call center or back office agent might be involved in performing some steps of the process.

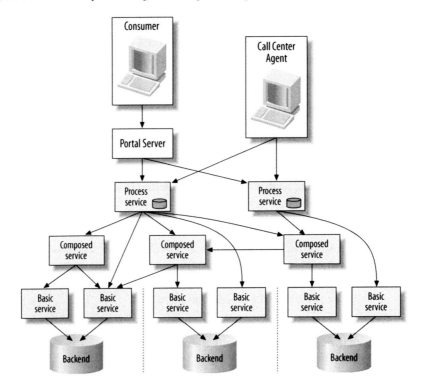

FIGURE 14-1. Many hops between the end user and the backends

These many layers lead to two important problems:

- It is not clear which system authenticates and authorizes a user.

- Confidentiality must be assured across not one but multiple connections and nodes in between.

Let's first discuss why it is not clear which system authenticates a user and authorizes her activities. Is this the responsibility of the backend, the frontend, or both? On the one hand, it is in the interest of the backend to decide which users are allowed to perform certain functions and retrieve certain data. The reason is that each backend is responsible for its data, and usually not all users are allowed to perform all modifications or to see all data. On the other hand, however, it is the interest of the frontend to authorize user abilities, to provide overall consistency and avoid users starting business processes whose services they are not allowed to call.

To be able to cover both interests, ideally both the frontend and the backend must share the same identities (such as user IDs) and their associated profiles and roles. This implies that identities and/or profiles have to be passed to the backends.

Now we come to the second problem, which has to do with confidentiality and integrity. If multiple systems are involved between the frontend and the backend, it is not enough to make the physical connection between the two systems secure. When you have multiple connections with nodes involved, you need to guarantee the end-to-end security of specific data. For example, if you transfer data such as passwords, credit card numbers, or account details or limits, usually only the frontend and the backend should be allowed to see this information. Any processes dealing with this data can pass it on but shouldn't actually see it.

For this reason, security mechanisms dealing with the transport layer are usually not enough. In fact, the usual Internet approach—the Secure Sockets Layer (SSL), which is also available for Web Services—is not sufficient. It provides point-to-point security, which is different from end-to-end security, which is necessary when multiple layers are involved. As a result, you usually need message-layer security, which means dealing with security inside the messages that are sent around. Transport-layer security and message-layer security are discussed in Section 14.3.2.

14.2.4 Multiclient Capabilities

You might have noticed that I always write about users being allowed to call a service *and/or to see the result*, and you might wonder why I don't just talk about being allowed to call a service. This is because distributed systems often have multiclient capabilities. That is, they use the same backend to manage the data of multiple clients, and it must not happen that one specific client gets access to the data of another client.

For example, a data processing center might manage the data of several different banks. In general, the banks may be allowed to call the same services, but they should only be allowed to see data for their own customers. For example, if the service returns customer data associated with a specific bank account, the calling bank should be able to see the result only if the account number identifies a customer of that bank. If an account number from another bank is used, the calling bank shouldn't see any customer data.

You might argue that this problem is easy to deal with: the bank service simply has to require that a bank can only ask for data with its own bank code, and this rule can simply apply to all services called. However, this approach doesn't work in all situations. With mobile phone companies, for example, there are only a few network providers, but there are several more companies that sell mobile phone contracts. The companies that sell contracts for the networks are called "service providers." Some of the data associated with these service providers must be kept private, but some of it should be accessible by the systems of all the companies in the network. For example, because end users are allowed to transfer phone numbers from one service provider to another, it might not be appropriate to restrict access to the customer data associated with a mobile phone number to a particular service provider. The backend might not know ahead of time which provider the customer is associated with, so it will need to allow access to all of the companies affiliated with the customer's network.

When multiclient capabilities are involved, therefore, you may need to perform runtime security checks. That is, usually it is not enough to statically allow or deny certain service calls for certain systems.

14.3   SOA Security in Practice

In practice, security is very often neglected, for several reasons:

- Security requires effort.
- It is impossible to achieve absolute security (except by disconnecting distributed systems).
- You might assume that the usual security mechanisms for the Internet (firewalls and special protocols such as SSL) are enough.
- You might assume that SOA infrastructures usually provide enough security.
- It is not clear whether security is an issue for the infrastructure team or the business teams.

The following subsections will discuss these topics, directly or indirectly.

14.3.1 Infrastructures Don't Provide Sufficient Security

In general, you should not assume that infrastructures (the Internet, Web Services, or any other middleware) deal with security in such a way that you don't have to think about it any longer.

The first problem is that there might be a lack of conceptual support. For example, the fundamental Web Services protocol doesn't deal with security: it was designed to provide connectivity. As [PulierTaylor06] claims about Web Services standards:

> The new standards were also developed without security in mind....None of these Open Standards (XML, SOAP, WSDL, and UDDI) contain any inherent security aspects of their own. If left alone, they are completely nonsecure. In fact, web services were designed to move efficiently through firewalls.

Similarly, process-modeling standards such as BPEL so far have no concept for composing and aggregating security concepts when they compose services.

In addition, even if an infrastructure provides some security support, you have to consider whether it covers all aspects of security (authorization, authentication, confidentiality, integrity, availability, accounting, and auditing), and the quality of the support.

If security is an issue (and it usually is), you should always deal with it explicitly. If an examination shows that the security solutions provided by your infrastructure are enough, that's fine; however, don't assume that this will be the case.

14.3.2 Dealing with Confidentiality and Integrity

In practice, you can deal with the confidentiality and integrity of the data transferred by your services on either the transport layer or the message layer:

Transport-layer security

Here, you use the underlying protocol of your infrastructure to introduce security. A typical example is encryption of Web Services calls via SSL (that is, using the HTTPS protocol instead of HTTP).

While this is typically easy and cheap, the problem is that it only helps when data gets transferred from system to system (or node to node). That is, this is a point-to-point encryption instead of an end-to-end encryption. Inside the nodes and between different layers, the data is still readable.

Message-layer security

Here, you introduce security within the actual messages being sent. That is, you use the protocol of your infrastructure in such a way that nobody is able to read the messages or modify them without being detected. For this approach, you have to define some special constraints in the format of your messages so that all endpoints are able to communicate with each other. While the sender of a message might encrypt or certify all of the data or parts of it, the receiver decrypts the message or verifies the certificate. A typical example is encryption of Web Services with additional attributes defined by standards such as WS-Security.

Note that you still have to be able to send the messages around. For this reason, you usually encrypt only the business data of a message (its payload). Any information to do with sending the message inside the infrastructure is included in such a way that it can be processed separately from the payload. Such information is typically located in a message header (see Section 15.4).

As discussed earlier, message-layer security is usually preferable because it leads to end-to-end security, while transport-layer security leads only to point-to-point security. The drawback, however, is that the transport layer often is better supported and has better performance. In addition, maintaining, distributing, and signing certificates can become an organizational challenge.

Note that it is possible not to provide any security inside the ESB, either on the transport layer or on the message layer. Does this mean you have no security? Not necessarily. Security then becomes an issue of the business layer. That means both providers and consumers have to deal with security aspects in the business APIs. That is, you define service parameters to exchange tokens or encrypted data (of course, the exact format must be specified in the service contract). The problem with this approach is that multiple parties must expend effort to fulfill the same requirement.

In any case, it should be clear to all service participants how to deal with security. This is a good example of the fact that the infrastructure and architecture of SOA have to match. Providing only the infrastructure, which might leave participants alone with security questions, is a very poor and risky approach.

14.3.3 Security as a Service

Because security has impacts in many different places, it is usually necessary to have an overall strategy to deal with security in a systematic way. Otherwise, sooner or later you lose control.

Systematic authentication and authorization of identities requires you to separate the decision to authorize an identity and the enforcement of that authorization. That is, you must distinguish between a *policy decision point* (PDP), which is the place where a decision is made (in [ISO10181-3] this is called an "access control decision function," or ADF), and a *policy enforcement point* (PEP), which is the place where a decision is enforced (in [ISO 10181-3] this is called an "access control enforcement function," or AEF).

This type of separation allows you to centrally define which kinds of decisions can be made and to ensure that these decisions are consistent over the whole system. Whenever in a local application you need some security decision, in effect what happens is a PEP asks a PDP for a decision. A PDP is a perfect example of a service that is called by different consumers to determine whether something is allowed or available.*

In other words, the best way to deal with security in SOA is to provide security as a service. For example, [HintonHondoHutchison05] introduces "security enforcement services" that, from within an ESB or an application (or wherever data gets processed), call a "security decision service" (see Figure 14-2).

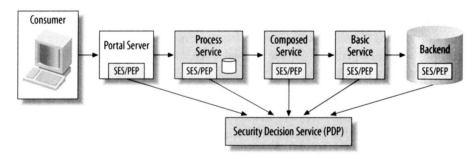

FIGURE 14-2. Security as a service

Whatever terminology you use, the idea is to introduce some central component or system that manages identities and their associated roles and profiles. This is often called an

---

* Distinguishing between PDPs and PEPs is a general concept to deal with consistent common behavior. See Section 9.2.2 for another example.

identity provider (IdP). As discussed earlier, if it provides services to make security decisions, it has the role of a security decision point, policy decision point, or access control decision function.

The IdP is a central manager for identities and their profiles. Because central security servers introduce bottlenecks, technically and organizationally you might need some special techniques to deal with this problem. Usually, you need to cache to local IdPs or even services so that user authentication and authorization scales.

In practice, though, integrating all systems of a distributed process is not always possible. For this reason, it is pretty common to work with technical users, which are IT representations of bail bondsmen or sureties. Another approach to provide single sign-on for different backends is to allow an identity provider to map different identities to each other (this is called an *identity federation*). Then, switching between different local user profiles is also possible.

> **NOTE**
> The Liberty Alliance Project has the aim of introducing a central IdP for users/people and other identities across the globe, which can be used by different companies to provide single sign-on and share user profiles all over the world. See [ProjectLiberty] for details.

14.3.4 Security, Performance, and State

Security costs. Calling additional functions or services for decisions, encrypting and decrypting data, validating integrity, and checking for availability takes time and resources. However, usually there is no alternative except putting your system at risk. In essence, to deal with security you have to find the right balance of risk and performance.

Because security impacts performance, it might also have an impact on the statefulness of services (see Section 15.1). From a business point of view, you might say that services are stateless. However, for each service call you have to find out whether the caller is allowed to perform the call and/or see the result. To make this decision you need some data, which is often not transferred with each service call. As a consequence, a backend might take the identifying input data and use it to load the user profile and/or roles associated with that data. This might take some time. Furthermore, if the services are routed to different providing systems, you'll have to load the profile and/or roles with each call, or at least with the first call into each physical providing system. The profile and/or roles can be cached so that if the request is routed to the same physical system again, the data must be loaded only with the first call. In this case, the system might return a token that is used with each further request. However, then the issue of how long the data cached remains valid (i.e., how quickly barriers and profile modifications can be distributed) will come into play.

Note that there are different ways to deal with state and services. For example, you might deal with the state in backends only and use a session ID that is returned with the first service call and sent with all additional calls. See Section 15.1.2 for details.

14.3.5 Security in Reality

If I had to describe the security concepts I have seen in reality, all I would be able to say is that they are heterogeneous: they involve some central user management, some technical users, some encryption on different layers, and so on. A wild mixture of different security concepts, identity providers, technical users, and other security solutions are in use today.

In addition, often there is, at least partially, no security. Conceptually, this is possible and sometimes makes sense. Consider, for example, a demilitarized zone (DMZ), which is a zone where each system trusts each other system and security plays a role only when data crosses the border of the zone. This means that all backends inside the zone trust all applications on the border, which behave like company firewalls (such as portal servers, fat call center applications, and so on). Of course, this means that all these border-crossing applications have to share common security policies and implement them correctly.

For example, instead of dealing with multiclient capabilities in each backend, all consumers within a DMZ might be allowed to retrieve all data. Then it is up to them to ensure that outside the DMZ, consumers only see data relevant to their own domain or company. Unfortunately, the service provider (as the responsible owner of the data) can't actually guarantee the business rules regarding data access, because the implementation of these rules requires the cooperation of all service consumers. This might make auditing pretty complicated, if not impossible.

I have seen the DMZ approach used even for very sensitive data. For example, say a service returns customer data to each consumer. Because the data of top managers or VIPs should be visible only to a few special people, this approach is risky. To diminish the risk, in such a situation I have seen a policy to "encrypt" the data itself by assigning these customers fake names and giving only a few people the list mapping the fake names to real names. This is an interesting example of dealing with security on the business layer.

I haven't written much about auditing, but it plays an interesting role regarding security. As long as you are able to trace and correlate the flow of data flow so that you can find out later who or what was the reason for a security attack or a security hole, the threat of being caught might bolster the security of your system. In other words, by logging, monitoring, and auditing message traffic, you might encourage programmers to be more responsible with or vigilant about security aspects and deter delinquents from possible security violations. And if you cannot avoid all security violations, you might at least be able to throw light on ones that do occur. Whether or not the risk of relying solely on this approach is too high is your decision.

14.4   Security with XML and Web Services

Next, I'd like to give you some hints regarding security with XML and Web Services. Note that Web Services are discussed in detail in Chapter 16; you might want to read that chapter first before reading this section.

In principle, you can use different types of standards, including the following:

- General security standards
- XML security standards
- Web Services security standards

Figure 14-3 illustrates the options in more detail.

FIGURE 14-3. Security stack for XML and Web Services

The general security standards include the well-known algorithms, such as RSA, AES, and DES, as well as basic security standards for encryption and secure conversation, such as SSL, Kerberos, and so on. There are also special standards that deal with XML documents. Their advantage is that they read and write XML files, so the result of an encryption or signature can be processed using the usual XML processing chain. Finally, at the top of the diagram there are general XML-based security standards, such as SAML, and standards with special Web Services aspects, such as WS-Security.

Let's briefly discuss some the most important standards.

14.4.1 SAML

One important general standard, maintained by OASIS, is the Security Assertion Markup Language (SAML). SAML is an XML-based language for the management and exchange of security information between different systems. It allows for one party to assert security information about a *subject* (an identity that is often a human user, but may also be a technical user, system, or company). Other attributes may also be asserted in addition to the subject's identity, such as the customer's email address or the user's role. For example, an assertion might state "This is Nicolai Josuttis, having the email address *nicolai.josuttis@somedomain.de*, who is allowed to modify the contents of this book."

Assertions may be managed and exchanged in a distributed environment. For example, protocols allow an identity provider to identify a subject, pass around assertions, map between different identities, and perform distributed logouts (also called single logouts, or

SLO). As a result, you can manage and combine different user profiles using (different) identity providers over distributed processes. This includes the support of single sign-on (SSO).

See [SAML] for details.

14.4.2 XML and Web Services Security Standards

For XML and Web Services, several specific standards exist. These standards don't introduce new security technologies or procedures, but rather define how to apply existing technologies and procedures when exchanging data in XML files or via Web Services.

For example, for XML the following standards exist:

XML Signature (XML DSig)
> Allows XML documents to be signed to guarantee the integrity (and authenticity) of some of their data. This is similar to PGP, but for data having an XML format. See [XMLSignature] for details.

XML Encryption (XML Enc)
> Allows XML documents to be (perhaps partially) encrypted. For example, you can encrypt a whole XML document, or only some data in the document, such as a credit card number or "all except the username." See [XMLEncryption] for details.

XML Key Management
> Supports key management for the XML Signature standard. See [XMLKeyMan] for details.

For Web Services, the most important standards are:

WS-Security
> Defines how to apply different security techniques for authorization, integrity, and privacy with Web Services (SOAP). Describes a standard way of embedding security information such as tokens, encryption, signatures, SAML, Kerberos, and so on into a SOAP header. See [WS-Security] for details.

WS-SecurityPolicy
> Enables you to find out which security standard a service provider requires and/or supports. As part of a Web Services definition in WSDL or UDDI, a provider can define that it, for example, accepts X.509 and Kerberos (while preferring Kerberos) and requires some specific signature. See [WS-SecurityPolicy] for details.

WS-Trust
> Enables you to issue, renew, and validate security tokens. See [WS-Trust] for details.

WS-SecureConversation
> Establishes a shared security context across multiple message exchanges. The primary motivation for this is to improve performance by reducing the number of time-consuming requests sent to an IdP. See [WS-SecureConversation] for details.

WS-Federation

Defines mechanisms, enabling integration and federation of different security realms by allowing and brokering trust of identities, attributes, and authentication. See [WS-Federation] for details.

As usual with Web Services, these standards don't necessarily lead to interoperability, because there are just too many versions and too many ways to interpret the standards. Consequently, similar to the WS-I Basic Profile (see Section 16.3.1) there is a WS-I Basic Security Profile, which restricts certain versions of security standards to guarantee interoperability. See [WSI-SecurityProfile] for details.

For additional information see, for example, [KannegantiChodavarapu07] and also [NewcomerLomow05].

14.4.3 XML and Web Services Attacks

In all distributed systems there is a risk of attacks from the outside, such as flooding (DoS) attacks. Too many requests, legitimate or not, can break a service provider, and when malicious attacks are launched you will need to be able to detect these attacks and react accordingly. However, some other types of attacks are also possible with XML and Web Services.* Let's look at a few examples (these examples are very concrete, to give you an impression of how easily they can occur and how realistic these problems might be in your day-to-day work):

XML bombs

XML is a primitive recursive language, and in certain situations XML parsers may expand even very small XML documents to huge documents. Consider the following example:

```
<?xml version="1.0"?>
<!DOCTYPE xmlbomb [
<!ELEMENT data (#PCDATA)>
<!ENTITY a "&b;&b;&b; ">
<!ENTITY b "&c;&c;&c; ">
<!ENTITY c "&d;&d;&d; ">
<!ENTITY d "foo ">
]>
<data>&a;</data>
```

The problem is that the referenced entity a here expands to multiple other entities. Here, this leads to 3^3 (three times an entity is expanded to three other entities), which might be visible in a browser as follows:

```
<data>foo foo foo foo foo foo foo foo foo foo foo foo foo foo foo foo foo foo foo
foo foo foo foo foo foo foo foo</data>
```

Now, say you have 10 expansions to 10 entities each. Not much code is required, but this results in the XML parser attempting to expand this to a sequence of

---

* Thanks to Bruce Sams for providing these examples.

10,000,000,000 occurrences of foo, which uses up a lot of time and memory. Usually processes running into this problem simply crash.

Note that this is a kind of denial-of-service attack that can't be detected by a firewall, because the problem is not in the number of messages, but in the contents.

If this is a risk for your application and availability is important, you might need some way to restrict XML parsers or detect these situations before they get parsed.

XPath injections

XPath injection is a kind of code injection. As with SQL injection, the trick is to misuse the implementation technique of mapping user input directly to code so that the original meaning of the code gets modified.

Let's first demonstrate the concept of code injection by looking at an example where user input maps directly to a SQL request, which is defined as follows:

```
SELECT city, zip, street FROM customers WHERE ID=input
```

Now, if the user input (which might be input data of a service request) is 42, the resulting SQL request is as follows:

```
SELECT city, zip, street FROM customers WHERE ID=42
```

This is fine—you return the city, zip code, and street for all database entries for which the ID is 42.

Now consider the following input:

```
42 UNION SELECT login, password,'x' FROM user
```

If you simply map this input to the SQL request, it becomes:

```
SELECT city, zip, street FROM customers WHERE ID=42 UNION
SELECT login, password,'x' FROM user
```

As a result, in addition you get all the logins and passwords from a table called user (the 'x' is necessary to also have three columns; otherwise the union is not possible).

When using XML, the same technique is possible. With XPath, you can navigate through XML documents. If the input directly maps to such a path, you can manipulate the path so that it leads to another place in the XML document, allowing you to retrieve or manipulate other data.

Consider, for example, some source code that uses the following XPath expression:

```
string(//user[name/text( )='user' and password/text( )='pw']/account/text( ))
```

to find account data in an XML database or file such as the following:

```
<user>
  <name>josuttis</name>
    <password>secret77</password>
    <account>admin</account>
  </name>
  <name>
    ...
  </name>
```

LIBERTY ALLIANCE PROJECT

The Web Services standards mentioned here are not the only standards regarding identity management in conjunction with SOA. In 2001, the Liberty Alliance Project (LAP; see [ProjectLiberty]) was founded by a group of more than 30 organizations, with the aim of establishing common standards for federated identity management. Today, LAP is supported by more than 150 members, including major software vendors, consumer-oriented companies (e.g., telcos), and government and public sector organizations.

The *Identity Federation Framework* (ID-FF) was LAP's first release, which enabled users to participate in an Internet-wide single sign-on (SSO) based on federated identities. These specifications were later contributed to OASIS, and they formed the basis for the SAML 2.0 specifications. The next major step was made in 2003, with the publication of the *Identity Web Services Framework* (ID-WSF), an open framework to support identity-based Web Services as part of a SOA. ID-WSF supports protocols for identity propagation as well as service discovery between Web Service providers and clients, all based on standard protocols. Regarding SOA, the ID-WSF standard can be considered a long-term solution because it brings SSO from browsers to the level of Web Services and backend systems.

The current focus of LAP is on establishing standards for Web Service applications (ID-SIS) related to identity management. The Geo-Location, Presence, Liberty People Service, and other specifications may prove to be central components for social applications like blogs, bookmarks, and instant messaging applications.

The Liberty Alliance has adopted a lot of common Web Services standards (e.g., SOAP, XML Enc, XML DSig, and WS-Security), and it has contributed to new and existing OASIS standards (such as SAML and Metadata). Some of the LAP standards are now competitive approaches to Web Services standards such as WS-Federation.

To deal with interoperability, heterogeneous environments require deep knowledge of the Liberty standards and protocols and their implementation quirks. Therefore, the Liberty Alliance has introduced a certification program wherein different vendors and tools prove interoperability in large-scale heterogeneous environments during formally organized interoperability tests.

Liberty Alliance protocols are supported by major software vendors, through both commercial products and open source implementations (such as Sun's OpenSSO). To simplify the adoption of Liberty protocols into applications and security infrastructures, an open source project called openLiberty.org was set up at the beginning of 2007. Unfortunately, it has not yet made any implementation publicly available.

The overall architecture and protocols of the Liberty Alliance are complex, and can best be handled by large organizations. For smaller scenarios, we currently see a convergence with upcoming lightweight standards such as OpenID and XRI, which lower the barrier for simple integration of web applications.

—Jochen Hiller (*http://www.jochen-hiller.org*)

Now, if the username is as follows:

```
' or 1=1 or ''='
```

the XPath expression becomes (with newlines inserted to clarify the meaning):

```
string(//user[name/text( )=''
          or 1=1
          or ''='' and password/text( )='pw']/account/text( ))
```

Because the second of the three expressions combined with or always yields true, the whole constraint inside the [and] becomes worthless. As a result, the expression yields the account of the first user.

See, for example, [Sanctum04] for more on this.

SOAP attachments

Because SOAP allows attachments of any type, as with emails, this can become another door for viruses, worms, etc. Consequently, you might have to integrate the usual anti-virus software as part of your SOA infrastructure.

14.5   When Security Comes into Play

Finally, some words regarding the question of when security comes into play. SOA is a pretty complex strategy, which only works if you introduce it step-by-step. One reason is that you can't anticipate all the requirements and the effects of some implementations (both technology and processes) ahead of time. Thus, you can't solve all security aspects before you start to live SOA. This means you will introduce and change some security concepts as the landscape evolves.

Security is a fundamental part of the whole system, which means it might impact *all* services. For this reason, in addition to building it in at the beginning, you have to be able to improve security for existing services.

You should have security in mind from the beginning. You don't need to try to provide techniques for all possible requirements and situations, but you should provide extension points for introducing security aspects later. That means you should introduce hooks for security enforcement, introduce a generic field in service headers so that future fields don't break the compatibility of APIs, and so on.

Think large, but start small.

14.6   Summary

- In SOA, the usual security aspects and techniques of distributed systems apply, together with some supplementary threads:

  — SOA forces high interoperability, which lowers default security.

  — SOA has to deal with the heterogeneous security concepts of existing systems.

— Distributed processes transfer data over multiple services, so point-to-point solutions are not enough for end-to-end security.

— Multiclient capabilities force runtime security checks.

- You must define and implement a strategic security approach that covers infrastructure, architecture, and applications. The best approach is to introduce security as a service.

- Security influences performance, and it might force stateless services to be able to deal with state.

- XML and Web Services might introduce special security problems, such as the danger of XML bombs and XPATH injections.

- Keep security in mind from the beginning (which does not mean that you need to try to deal with all aspects of security immediately).

CHAPTER FIFTEEN

Technical Details

IN EACH **SOA,** THERE ARE SOME TECHNICAL ASPECTS TO IMPLEMENT (OR AT LEAST TO THINK ABOUT). This chapter presents and discusses those that are fundamental enough that you should be familiar with them, because sooner or later you will have to deal with them.

15.1 Services and State

Often descriptions of SOA claim that services should (ideally) be stateless. However, what is meant by "stateless" or "stateful" in the context of services can be a source of confusion. One reason is that there is always some state involved, even with stateless services. The key questions are where and for how long this state is kept. In addition, whether a service is stateful is a matter of perspective. Services may be stateless from a business point of view and stateful from a technical point of view, and vice versa. This section looks closely at the issue of "state" in the context of services, clarifying the terminology and discussing different approaches used in practice.

15.1.1 Stateless Services

Conceptually, a stateless service is a service that does not maintain any state between different service calls. That is, after the service call is over, all local variables and objects that have been created temporarily to run the service are thrown away. Note that we're talking about the data of the service itself, which is neither the process or application that calls the service nor the backend system(s) on which the service operates. The service is stateless when all the data of the service instance (process or thread) that performs the call is thrown away after the call. In other words, it must not matter whether the next service call is performed using the same or a different service thread or service process.

According to this definition, even a stateless service can change state. However, it is only the state of the backend or frontend that gets modified. For example, if a service adds some money to a bank account and returns the new balance, this is a stateless service. If you add $30 twice, you can use two different service threads or processes to add the money. Provided the initial balance is $100, the first call will add $30 and return a new balance of $130 while the second call will add another $30 and return a new balance of $160 (see Figure 15-1).

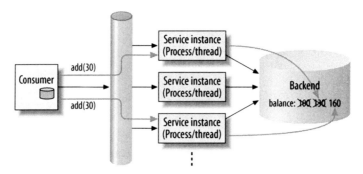

FIGURE 15-1. Adding $30 via two different stateless service calls

You might say that in this example it is obvious that no service state is involved, because you don't even need any data to be kept in the service implementation while running it. But let's look at another stateless service that does internally keep a state. Say you have a service that modifies an address on two different backends. A loosely coupled implementation of the service using compensation instead of transaction contexts (see Section 4.2.8) could be written using the following pseudocode:

```
string changeAddress (custID, newAddress)
{
    oldAddress = backend_1.getAddress(custID);

    status = backend_1.changeAddress(custID, newAddress);
```

```
    if (status == failure) {
        return "couldn't modify address in backend 1";
    }

    status = backend_2.changeAddress(custID, newAddress);
    if (status == failure) {
        // compensation: restore old address to keep consistency
        status = backend_1.changeAddress(custID, oldAddress);
        if (status == failure) {
            fatalError(...);
        }
        return "couldn't modify address in backend 2";
    }
    return "OK";
}
```

As you can see, this implementation needs some state information, such as `oldAddress`. Before the address is modified in the first backend, the old address in this backend is stored in `oldAddress`. This is done so that, in the event that backend 1 is modified successfully but backend 2 is not, you can restore the old address on backend 1 to maintain overall consistency. While running, this service has a state, and at the end, the state of the associated backends might be modified (see Figure 15-2).

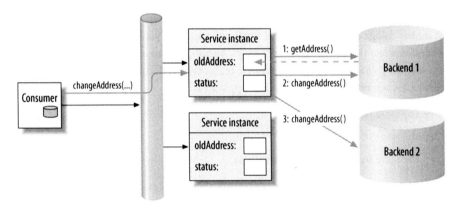

FIGURE 15-2. Running a stateless service that has an internal temporary state

The service as a whole is stateless, however, because at the end of the call you can throw away all the internal data. A second call of this service could run using a totally different service instance.

15.1.2 Stateful Services

So, what's a *stateful service*, then? A stateful service is a service that maintains state over multiple service calls.

The typical example of a stateful service is a shopping cart. If you shop online at, say, Amazon.com, each time you select a book and add it to your shopping cart, the number of items in your cart grows.

And if you order and pay for the items in your shopping cart, they'll be delivered to you (see Figure 15-3).

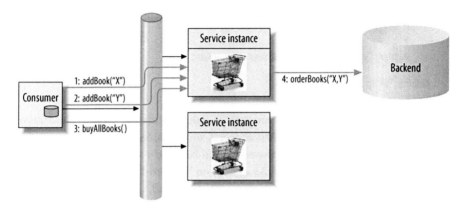

FIGURE 15-3. Running a stateful service

What makes things complicated is that having the state of your shopping cart as part of your service is not the only possible solution. Although from a business point of view you might consider this service a stateful service, technically it doesn't have to be. In fact, there are three possible ways to implement a shopping cart:

- Keep the state in a service.
- Keep the state in the backend.
- Keep the state in the frontend/consumer.

Probably the most intuitive way to implement a shopping cart is to keep the state in a stateful service (as shown in Figure 15-3). That means the backend doesn't know anything about the cart until the user orders the items it contains. To fill the shopping cart you have to ensure that subsequent service calls get routed to the same service instance. That is, with the first service call you are establishing a *session*. Usually, each service call returns a session ID that the consumer sends with each following request so that the ESB can route the request to the corresponding service instance. When you use a browser to shop at *Amazon.com*, this state is usually stored as a cookie or as part of your URLs. Depending on your browser policy, your shopping cart will be emptied when your cookies are deleted, or if you visit the site using another web browser (e.g., if you switch from Firefox to Internet Explorer).

Now let's look at another way of implementing the shopping cart application. The second solution is to keep the state in the backend. Again, you need a way to identify the user's shopping cart (or session) in the backend. As in the previous example, the backend might create a session ID, which the service transfers to the consumer, where it can again be stored as a cookie or as part of the URLs. Now, when a new service call is performed, the consumer sends the session data to a stateless service, which transfers it to the backend to identify the session.

Both solutions need some way to locate the correct session. With stateful services this is a task of the ESB, and when the state is kept in the backend it is a task of the backend.

The third solution is to store the state in the frontend or consumer. In this case, the service returns the complete state, not just a session ID, to the consumer (in a form that might or might not be readable by the consumer). Again, the state is stored as a cookie or as part of the URLs. When another item is added to the shopping cart, the consumer sends the whole state to the service. Because the complete state is stored in the client, the service can be stateless, and again, the backend doesn't know anything about the shopping cart until the user orders the items or makes the shopping cart persistent for later use.

Note that all three options (summarized in Table 15-1) have different advantages and drawbacks:

- Putting the state in the frontend/consumer means that the services can be stateless and the backend is not involved. However, you can't change the frontend while the session is running (which is a drawback if multifrontend channel support is required or you want to be able to transfer a session to another desktop).

- Putting the state in stateful services requires more resources in the service layer and some way to route service requests to the same service instance. However, you can change frontends, and the backend is not involved.

- Putting the state in the backend allows you to use stateless services, and the frontend doesn't have to provide storage. However, the backend is involved in each session.

TABLE 15-1. Comparisons of dealing with state

	State in frontend	State in service	State in backend
Storage in frontend	All state	ID	ID
Services	Stateless	Stateful	Stateless
Storage in backend	None	None	All state
Multichannel support	No	Yes	Yes

Note that from a consumer's point of view, all three policies result in the same interface. The service returns some data that has to be sent with the next request(s). The only difference is in the size and meaning of the data stored in the frontend. For this reason, your service interface should use a generic data type (a binary or string type) to leave open the choice of which policy to use. You might even be able to change the policy if different priorities apply.

15.1.3 Why Stateless Services Are Better

Although we have discussed the difference between stateless and stateful services, we have not discussed whether one policy is better than the other. There are some recommendations in favor of stateless services, but why?

First of all, with stateless services load balancing and failover for the service layer are pretty simple. The ESB only has to get implemented in such a way that the next best available service instance (process or thread on some hardware) is used. It can even be a thread that other consumers were using earlier (if pooling mechanisms are implemented). This means that if a system fails, others can easily continue to perform the work. If the throughput of the service layer is not high enough, you can double the number of service instances to double the throughput. That means the solution scales linearly, and if a service instance dies others can jump in.

Stateful services, on the other hand, have the drawback that they are bound to sessions. Thus, the resources allocated for them are bound to one specific consumer session until the consumer session ends (or the connection is disabled). In addition, you have to be able to enable the ESB to route consecutive service calls to the same service instance.

Note, however, that stateful services can still scale linearly. Using a policy called *sticky routing*, you find your service instance when the first service call is performed, according to the available resources. Thus, doubling the number of service instances will again double the number of sessions possible. However, you don't have the advantage that service resources can be shared among different consumers, and if a service instance dies, the session state is lost.

Note also that stateful services can have failover mechanisms (and still scale linearly). Each server then returns not only its own session ID, but also an ID of a failover session. Provided that this failover session is not at a central server but at a neighbor (and each server uses a different neighbor), this does not lead to bottlenecks.

Some application servers support this feature. However, in practice it is often acceptable for a server's session data to be lost if the server fails (provided this scenario is relatively rare). If the data is important or even "juristically relevant" for the business, it is always recommended to use the solid backup strategies of backends. If you put such data in stateful services, your service layer (silently) gets the role of a backend system, which usually leads to confusing architectures (roles and responsibilities). See Section 6.4.2 in for more on this topic.

15.1.4 Stateless Services in Practice

In practice, services may become stateful for very different reasons:

Shopping cart implementations and process services with multichannel support

As discussed earlier, there might be a business requirement to preserve the combined state of multiple service calls before this state gets further processed or persisted in a backend. In this case, a stateful service can be used to avoid keeping the state in the client and to enable you to change the frontend while the service is running.

Bulk services

Sometimes a service processes bulk data and/or calls hundreds of other services. For example, a CRM service might assign all customers of a certain kind (working for the same company, having the same existing contract, etc.) a new contract or option. Usually, you can't be sure that all of the hundreds or thousands of modifications were successful. But you also can't see ahead of time what problems might occur, so you can't provide rules or implementations to solve them. How you handle errors depends on the type of the error and how often it occurs, and you can't wait until the service ends to decide how to proceed. In this case, you need some ability to interact with this "long-running" service, which means that you have to have access to its state.

Performance

Performance can be a very important reason to introduce stateful services. One typical example is services that allow you to iterate over lists of results. Processing the results might take a significant amount of time. If you return the first 100 result items and then throw away the state, you'll have to process 200 results when the consumer asks for the 101st to 200th items (returning the first 100 items is necessary to find out where the second 100 items start). In database terminology, you need a place where you can store the complete result and a corresponding cursor that can iterate over it. However, again there is an alternative: you might keep the results in a backend and transfer the state of the cursor/iterator to the consumer using stateless services.

In general, stateful services will always be useful when caching inside the service layer is useful or necessary. From a consumer's point of view this is an implementation detail, so it should not change the service interface. However, you need some way to connect to the same service instance again. If this is not handled inside the ESB, you might need a general attribute (binary or string) that the first service call can return as a kind of session ID and subsequent service calls can send.

Security

Security can be another important reason to switch to stateful services. It might be necessary to keep the state of a session inside a service so that you don't have to identify the consumer and load its user profile with each service call. See Section 14.3.4 for details.

Because stateful services are so useful, it's a good idea to provide some way of implementing and dealing with them. As stated earlier, stateful services may require more resources, but they don't prevent linear scalability (provided there is not one session or stateful service that creates 30 percent of the calls).

Nevertheless, it is still a good idea conceptually to recommend that services should be stateless. From a business point of view, services should be self-contained and atomic. However, as you've just seen, there can be many reasons to make services stateful.

15.2   Idempotency

Idempotency is a possible attribute of services (see Section 3.3.5). In the context of services, it means that multiple deliveries/processings of identical service calls cause no problems. Say you have a service that adds money to a bank account. If a consumer calls this service (for example, to deal with a bank transfer) and gets no response, the consumer won't know whether it was the service request or the response that failed (see Figure 15-4).

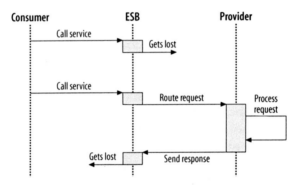

FIGURE 15-4. Service messages might get lost before or after a request is processed

In the latter case, from the provider's point of view the service was successful, and the specified amount of money was added to the bank account. In the first case, the service had no effect (i.e., no money was added).

When the service consumer does not get a response, it doesn't know whether the service was successful or not. To be sure, it might retry the service call, sending the same request again. As a result, the service request might arrive at the provider for either the first or the second time. If the service is idempotent, it makes no difference how often the service request arrives: multiple requests of the same service call have only one effect.

The banking service just described is *not* idempotent, because depending on when the failure occurred in the first call, the sum may end up being added to the customer's balance twice, not the one time that the consumer intended. To avoid such problems, it is usually a good idea to make services idempotent if possible.

15.2.1 Idempotent Services

All reading services are idempotent, because it doesn't matter how often a service provider performs a request to return data. Note, however, that reading services become writing services when you enable things such as writing a protocol entry for each request. If this protocol is of some relevance for the business, this might become an issue (for example, you might end up with multiple contact entries for the same contact).

Writing services can be either idempotent or not. They are not idempotent when the effect of a service call depends on the existing state of the backend. For instance, in the previous example, the resulting balance of the bank account depends on the initial balance. If the balance was $500 and the service call added $100, the result would be $600. If a second request then arrived and got processed because the initial response was lost, the resulting balance would be $700.

An example of an idempotent writing service would be a service that sets the address of a customer by sending all address data. It doesn't matter how often the provider processes the request; the result will be the same.

Note that you can often avoid having services that are not idempotent. For example, we could make our banking service idempotent by modifying its semantics so that the new value is sent instead of the amount to add. That is, instead of calling:

```
addToBalance(100)
```

we could call:

```
setBalanceTo(600);
```

This call could be sent and processed repeatedly, and the result would still be a balance of $600. Of course, this might lead to problems if other services could add or subtract funds in the same account. How would you know what the resulting balance should be? As you can see, from a business point of view, making services idempotent can become complicated.

In addition, from a business point of view there are some services that are inherently not idempotent. All services that create something new have no state to compare with (unless you know the state of the factory that creates new resources). For example, if you have a service that creates a new bank account, you create it and that's it.

15.2.2 Implementing Idempotency

If introducing idempotency is a problem from a business point of view, you need some technical support for idempotency. The general way to implement idempotency is pretty simple. The consumer has to send data in such a way that the provider can see that two technical requests are the same. For this purpose, the consumer can send a unique ID with each new request. If the consumer gets no response, it uses the same ID for each retry. This is illustrated in Figure 15-5.

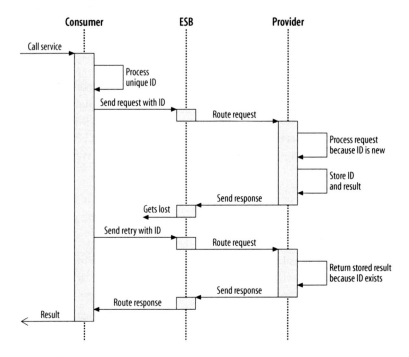

FIGURE 15-5. Making services technically idempotent

Before it processes each incoming request, the provider stores the request and its associated unique ID in a central repository. If it receives a request whose ID is already in the repository, the provider knows that the request has already been processed. So, instead of processing it, it resends the initial response (which it has also stored prior to sending it out the first time) to the consumer. If a second request arrives while the service implementation is still running, the provider can return a response saying that the service call is running, or it can wait and send the response again when it has been processed.

As an optimization, a consumer can send a flag with a request so that the provider knows whether it is a retry. This can improve performance, because then the provider doesn't have to verify whether the request ID is already in its repository, if the call is not tagged as a retry.

Of course, idempotency doesn't have to do only with request messages and doesn't affect only service providers. If a consumer resends a request because the response takes too long to arrive, it might end up receiving multiple responses. However, for the consumer this situation is easier to deal with, because it knows that two requests were sent.

Note that communications protocols—including, notably, the Web Services protocol HTTP—often are not reliable. That is, messages can get lost. In this case idempotency is a common requirement for better reliability: to become more reliable, any component should resend a message if it is not sure that it was delivered successfully. However, this means that multiple copies of a message might be delivered, and it's important that this does not cause unintended effects. In effect, the protocol guarantees only that messages will be delivered *at least* once. Guaranteeing that a message will be delivered *once and only once* requires even more effort (i.e., implementing the technical workarounds we just discussed as a general approach inside the infrastructure). Chapter 10 provides a general discussion of message exchange patterns.

15.3 Testing and Debugging

Distributed processes are a fundamental part of your business. Therefore, you must ensure that they behave correctly before you bring them into production. In addition, you must have mechanisms in place to track problems and fix bugs in the event that problems arise.

15.3.1 Unit Tests

Services are a natural fit for unit testing. For each individual service, it should be relatively easy to implement unit tests. Because services should be self-contained, unit tests that test the interfaces will usually also be self-contained. The only problem is providing test data so that the service running in test mode can be semantically validated.

For a basic service, you need some way to provide test data for the backend only, which should be relatively easy (you may already have such data available). However, as you'll see in the next section, for more complicated services testing can be more difficult.

Note that if you generate service code, test code may also be generated. This minimizes the effort required to write unit tests (see Section 18.1).

15.3.2 Distributed Testing

Testing composed or process services can become a real problem. Because these services use multiple backends, you need consistent test data distributed over all the backends. In systems with different owners and interests, this can become a nightmare. If this is not possible, you will have to simulate other services that are used (which lowers the quality of the test).

One option that I've seen is to replace service calls to other systems with local dummy implementations. However, then the unit test will test only *some* behavior of the service, not its full distributed behavior. For the company in question, this approach helped for local testing, but it turned out that a lot of problems were not found until integration tests over all the backends began.

Another option to consider is introducing the ability to label service calls as being in test mode. Because providing distributed test data can be very complicated, sooner or later you'll end up testing in production environments. If only one backend is involved you might be able to roll back some modifications, but if distribution comes into play, it's useful to be able to signal that a service call is a test and that writing services should not commit any modifications to the backends. Otherwise, the test data will be overwritten again and again and will have to be restored regularly. If the ESB can mark service calls as being in test mode, this will facilitate the testing of connectivity and process flow in production mode.

Still, for complicated distributed business processes, I have never seen a case where no final manual tests were necessary to validate the exact behavior over all the distributed systems (including dealing with errors in an appropriate fashion).

15.3.3 Correlation IDs

In distributed environments, it is very important to be able to monitor process and data flow so that you can understand system behavior and analyze bugs. Distributing business logic doesn't make the logic simpler. As with local processing, you need the ability to trace and monitor distributed processing. The problem is that in distributed environments you are not in a single process or on a single system where you can just use your favorite debugger. To debug, you need the support of your infrastructure. In other words, your infrastructure becomes your debugger for distributed processes.

In fact, there is a significant difference between local and distributed debugging in terms of tool support and effort required, especially if heterogeneity comes into play. This can be a major drawback of distributed processing. Distribution looks great when everything runs smoothly, but when problems occur, it can become a nightmare.

For this reason, it is a vital requirement for your infrastructure (ESB) to be able to correlate the messages that make up a service call or a complete business process. In addition, you have to be able to correlate the data flow outside of the ESB with the data flow inside it. For this reason, you usually need to be able to tag the data in different systems and processes with one or more IDs. Such IDs are called *correlation IDs*.

Correlation IDs can be used either to correlate all the data and processings that belong to *one service call* (including service calls inside that service call), or all the data and processings that belong to *one business process* (including all service calls).

It's up to you (or your infrastructure provider) to decide how many correlation IDs to use. Usually, the ESB has internal (message) IDs, but often this is not enough. Thus, you might end up using as many as four different IDs with each service call:

- A local ID for the message, provided by your infrastructure (tool)
- An ID that correlates a message with all other messages related to the same service call
- An ID that correlates a message or service with all other messages and service calls related to the same business process
- A technical ID to deal with idempotency (see Section 15.2.1 earlier in this chapter)

In practice, of course, IDs might serve different purposes, and there are ways to correlate different IDs. Nevertheless, you should take the semantics of the different IDs into account.

Your correlation ID policy may evolve as your ESB grows, but you should decide one thing up front: the data type of an ID. There is no doubt that it should be a readable string, so that it is easy to track, filter, view, and process, and so that it can have any size (to accommodate future requirements).

NOTE

One customer of mine initially defined the correlation ID as a combination of two integers (one for the system and one unique ID computed by the system). Tracking these IDs became a nightmare, because the string representations of the integers differed (some systems interpreted them as signed and others as unsigned values; one even merged both IDs to one value). In addition, the IDs were hard to read, so looking at log files and trying to filter log entries for a certain period of time was a huge effort. Unfortunately, we couldn't introduce a better format because this was binary data used by each service and each system, and we couldn't replace the format in all systems at once. Finally, we decided to "abuse" another string attribute that all services had but was not being used anymore.

15.4 Dealing with Technical Data (Header Data)

Correlation IDs are only one example of technical data that is used to deal with messages inside the ESB at runtime. Besides the business data ("payload"), you need some data to route messages, check security aspects, trace and monitor messages, and so on. How all of this is handled depends on your middleware and ESB technology, but usually this information is kept in a kind of header (for example, a SOAP header; see Section 16.2.3). Regarding this header data, there is one general hint I'd like to give: never assume you know all the technical attributes ahead of time.

When your SOA landscapes runs, you will inevitably find that you need some additional data for other or new ways to deal with messages from an infrastructure point of view. For this reason, you must provide some way to add new technical attributes without breaking interfaces generated for a service. That means binary compatibility is a must. It is almost impossible to change the fundamental technical format of a message in a way that requires all associated systems to recompile and deploy at the same time. Therefore, the recommended approach is for your technical header to include a generic list (such as a key/value list), which might grow over time.

15.5 Data Types

Another fundamental technical detail you have to decide upon is which data types and programming paradigms to use to exchange data via services. As discussed in Chapter 4, this issue is influenced by concerns about loose coupling. The more complex data types and programming models you introduce, the more tightly coupled the systems will be.

Harmonizing data types over distributed systems is a common and natural goal, because it simplifies data sharing. Be careful, though—once you have introduced a new fundamental type, you will probably never be able to get rid of it.

> **NOTE**
> In one project, we defined the generic list for future technical data having a key, a value, a type information for the value, and some additional attributes that allow giving additional hints on dealing with this value (e.g., one attribute allowed to define that service providers should pass this data through when they call other services while processing a service call).

15.5.1 Fundamental Data Types

You should clearly differentiate between fundamental data types (FDTs) and common data types:

- Fundamental data types are simple and stable, so no versioning is provided for them. For these types, code generators and adapters have native behavior and implementations.

- Common data types might change over time, so versioning is required.

In practice, being conservative when specifying fundamental types usually pays off. But don't be too extreme and provide only a string type. I recommend starting with these fundamental data types:

- Strings
- Numeric types (integers, floats, etc.)
- Booleans

- Some fundamental general business types, such as date/time

- Some fundamental domain-specific types, such as phone numbers for telecommunications companies and bank numbers for financial domains

- A type to exchange binary data

As Section 4.2.2 suggested, be careful with fundamental domain-specific types. Because consumers' requirements for something like an address type or a bank account type might vary widely and change over time, specifying such a type as a fundamental data type would be too risky. In addition, agreeing on such a type across all systems often turns out to be pretty complicated. If you are able to agree on such a type, you can define it as a "common" data type that can have different versions, just like any other domain-specific data type (see Section 12.3).

Note that you also have to define the exact semantics of the fundamental data types. One important question is whether these data types provide reference semantics (discussed in the following section). In addition, you should make clear whether strings can contain binary and/or wide characters, the range of numeric values, and so on.

The fundamental data types should be part of your meta model (see Section 18.3).

15.5.2 Reference Semantics

Enabling reference semantics (sometimes also called "null semantics") means that defined values exist that represent the state "not set" (in programming languages, values such as null or NIL are used for this purpose). This has an important impact on service interfaces.

For example, with reference semantics you can provide an interface with the following signature:

```
changeContactData (string customerID,   // customer ID
                    string phoneNumber, // null: no change, empty: delete
                    string faxNumber,   // null: no change, empty: delete
                    string email);      // null: no change, empty: delete
```

For all three parameters—phoneNumber, faxNumber, and email—you can pass a string containing the new value. However, passing null means that there is no change, and the existing customer properties remain valid. This is different from passing an empty string, which results in the existing value being deleted. Without reference semantics, you could not specify the difference between "no change" and "delete." This means that the consumer either always has to pass all three values (because they all replace the existing settings) or that an empty string means no change, which means that you need an additional interface to delete existing settings.

Of course, if you enable reference semantics, the infrastructure protocols and programming languages you use must support it. While Web Services does support reference semantics (with the attribute nillable), as does Java (using types such as Integer instead of int), you might need workarounds for other programming languages. For example, in

C++ you can't use the standard string type, because it only has value semantics. As a consequence, in that particular language binding you will need to use a special string type or you won't be able to deal with the difference between "not set" and empty.

15.5.3 Higher Data Types

You should be able to create new types based on your fundamental data types. Note that in accordance with the principles of loose coupling, each provider usually has its own types (see Section 4.2.2), which usually leads to some namespace conventions being adopted in order to avoid conflicts. For example, as mentioned previously, you might have a common namespace for versioned data types common to all systems.

In principle, I recommend providing the ability to define data types, as is possible in structured programming languages. That means:

- You should be able to compose structures and records containing multiple attributes or members of different types.
- You should be able to define lists/arrays of a specific data type.

In addition, you might think about being able to define type aliases (typedefs). This allows you to semantically use a type name like CustomerNumber while technically it is processed as a string.

You might also think about value constraints such as specific value ranges for numeric values or formats for strings. However, don't fall into the trap of expecting that your interface will be able to formulate all semantic constraints. There will always be a limit, and for large systems it is often better to have simple interfaces. For everything else, runtime exceptions and error messages can be used.

Be very careful with anything else. You should not use enumeration types (integers that represent sets of possible values). Strings (with value constraints) are easier to read and are supported on more platforms. In addition, avoid inheritance and polymorphism. You might have problems providing appropriate interfaces to languages that are not object-oriented.

> **NOTE**
> Web Services allow a lot of the possibilities that I've suggested you should be careful with or avoid: inheritance (called extensions), complex value constraints (called restrictions), and choices (some kind of unions). Note that Web Services use XSD types, and that XSD serves more purposes than just Web Services. This might be one reason why it is so difficult to provide interoperability with Web Services (see Section 16.3.1). Although my recommendations place constraints on the abilities Web Services provide, following them will make your life easier.

When defining your fundamental data types, you have to find the right balance between powerfulness, complexity, and portability. As Albert Einstein recommended, "Make everything as simple as possible, but not simpler." Keep in mind that you'll often need your own code to deal with all of these features, and that all complexity has an impact on maintenance and debugging.

15.6 Error Handling

Unfortunately, things can go wrong. Therefore, you need some way to deal with errors. Exceptions are the usual way to deal with unexpected behavior without having to deal with any errors inside the normal interface. So, services that return something (such as those using the request/response message exchange pattern, discussed in Chapter 10) should not only have a return type but also one or more types for errors and exceptions (take a look at the meta model in Section 18.3). With Web Services, for example, you can specify fault messages that serve this purpose.

Although you might be able to define specific exception types for each service, you should consider introducing a common type for all services.* This has the advantage that it is possible to deal with exceptions in a generic way. Otherwise, for example, a generic router or gateway will not be able to return a valid error message when it has to process a service it doesn't know.

The common error or exception type should, of course, provide enough information that individual error handling still is possible. For this reason, it should contain an individual error ID and a key/value list for specific details. Table 15-2 gives an example of the attributes a generic exception type might have.

TABLE 15-2. Attributes of a generic service exception type

Attribute	Data type	Meaning
message	String	A (default) error message
errorCode	String	An ID that allows you to deal with this type of error programmatically
errorClass	String	The type of error (fatal, technical, logical)
time	Date/time	The date/time when the error occurred
source	String	The system where the error was found
context	String	Some context information (such as a stack trace)
params	Key/value list	Additional error-specific information
correlationID	String	The correlation ID (which identifies the process)
innerException	Service exception type	The exception that caused this exception (allows you to deal with exceptions that are wrapped by or mapped to other exceptions)

Note that warnings are not errors. They have to be part of the return type of a service.

---

* The common exception type might also serve as base type for all exception types, but remember that I just recommended avoiding inheritance in service interfaces.

15.7 Summary

- There are several valid reasons for introducing stateful services. Note, however, that there are different ways to deal with state, depending on the view. Dealing with state can be pretty complicated and confusing.

- Prefer stateless services, but use stateful services if necessary. Note that stateful services need more resources but usually do not prevent linear scalability.

- The way state is handled should be transparent to service consumers.

- Try to make your services idempotent. If this is not possible, think about a common way (policy) to deal with services that are not idempotent.

- Support unit tests for services. Note, however, that for non-basic services unit testing can become very complicated, because of the task of providing consistent distributed test data.

- Distribution looks great when everything runs smoothly, but when problems occur it can become a nightmare. It's important to provide support for debugging and monitoring.

- Use correlation IDs, and use a string data type for these IDs.

- Provide the ability to extend message headers later without breaking the binary compatibility of interfaces (via key and value lists).

- Be careful when defining the fundamental data types and programming models for your service infrastructure (ESB). I recommend using common structured data types.

- Consider defining a common exception type that is used by all services. This allows you to deal with errors in a generic way.

CHAPTER SIXTEEN

Web Services

MOST ANALYSTS, VENDORS, AND AUTHORS THESE DAYS RECOMMEND ONLY ONE APPROPRIATE WAY TO realize a SOA landscape: with Web Services.

In this chapter, I will discuss Web Services from a conceptual point of view, provide an overview of their current state, and discuss how to use them in practice. My aim will be to improve your understanding of Web Services and to clarify some of the tasks and efforts that are necessary when using them.

16.1 Motivation for Using Web Services

Web Services are widely regarded as *the* way SOA should be realized in practice. For example, [Erl05] states that "Contemporary SOA represents an...architecture that promotes service-orientation and is comprised of...services, implemented as Web services" (see "Thomas Erl's Definition of SOA in 'Service-Oriented Architecture'" in Chapter 2 for the complete quote). And [Gartner05] predicted:

> By 2006, more than 60 percent of the $527 billion IT professional services market will be based on the exploitation of Web services standards and technology.

Of course, as is so often the case with SOA, what all of this means is not very clear. What are Web Services, in practice? Let's take a look at the definition given in an interview between Kirk McKusick (KM), former head of the UC Berkeley Computer Systems Research Group, and Adam Bosworth (AB), a senior manager at Microsoft in the late 1990s who was one of the people most central to the effort to define Web Services. This interview was published in the first edition of *ACM Queue* in March 2003 (see [McKusickBosworth03]):

> KM: People sure talk a lot about Web Services, but it's not clear they're all talking about the same thing. How would you define "Web Services"?
>
> AB: The term Web Services refers to an architecture that allows applications to talk to each other. Period. End of statement.
>
> KM: Fair enough. So what can we say Web Services aren't?
>
> AB: Well, they aren't super-efficient. But that may not be such a big deal since we're talking about self-describing messages that are easy to route and control and massage along the way. And that's something that wasn't true under previous message infrastructures.

For you as a reader, that's probably not enough. So, let's go into some of the details of the history and terminology of Web Services.

16.1.1 What Are Web Services?

Web Services refers to a collection of standards that cover interoperability. In fact, these standards define both the protocols that are used to communicate and the format of the interfaces that are used to specify services and service contracts.

16.1.2 History of Web Services

Microsoft coined the term Web Services in 2000, to describe a set of standards that allow computers to communicate with each other via a network (typically, but not limited to, the Internet). One of the core standards is the eXtensible Markup Language (XML); another is HTTP (the core protocol of the Internet).

Together with some others, Microsoft had already begun working on a protocol called SOAP that used XML to exchange data over a native connection based on HTTP and TCP/IP. Then IBM jumped in, and as a result in autumn 2000, two other standards were announced: the Web Services Description Language (WSDL) and Universal Description, Discovery, and Integration (UDDI). At the end of 2000, Oracle, HP, and Sun also announced their intention to support and deploy the Web Services standards in their products (see [Levitt01] for more details of the history of Web Services).

Nowadays, Web Services is a major movement based on several standards and driven by many companies and standardization organizations. The names of the standards usually start with WS. Based on about 10 low-level standards for XML and HTTP, there are more than 50 Web Services standards, plus about 10 profiles specified by different standards bodies, such as the World Wide Web Consortium (W3C), OASIS, and the Web Services Interoperability Organization (WS-I). These Web Services standards cover almost all areas of distributed computing and remote procedure/function/service calls, such as security (see Section 14.4), transactionality, reliability, process modeling (e.g., BPEL; see Section 7.4.2), and service management (see Chapter 17); there are also several minor standards for technical details such as error handling, addressing, and so on.

16.2 Fundamental Web Services Standards

There are five fundamental Web Services standards. Two of them are general standards that existed beforehand and were used to realize the Web Services approach:

- *XML* is used as the general format to describe models, formats, and data types. Most other standards are XML standards. In fact, all Web Services standards are based on XML 1.0, XSD (XML Schema Definition), and XML namespaces.

- *HTTP* (including HTTPS) is the low-level protocol used by the Internet. HTTP(S) is one possible protocol that can be used to send Web Services over networks, using Internet technology.

The other three fundamental standards are specific to Web Services and were the first standards specified for them:

- *WSDL* is used to define service interfaces. In fact, it can describe two different aspects of a service: its signature (name and parameters) and its binding and deployment details (protocol and location).

- *SOAP* is a standard that defines the Web Services protocol. While HTTP is the low-level protocol, also used by the Internet, SOAP is the specific format for exchanging Web Services data over this protocol.

- *UDDI* is a standard for managing Web Services (i.e., registering and finding services).

Using the WSDL standard is usually the key characteristic of Web Services. Everything else is optional. For example, you don't have to use SOAP and HTTP to send service requests around; you can use other protocols and still be using Web Services. In addition, UDDI plays only a subsidiary role, which is not required and often not used in practice (see Section 16.2.4 and Chapter 17 for details).

Let's look at these three standards in a bit more detail.

16.2.1 WSDL

To help you understand what WSDL files are all about, let's begin by looking at the general structure of a WSDL file. Note that there are different versions of the WSDL standard. At the time this book was written, in 2007, WSDL 1.1 was the version generally in use, but WSDL 2.0 was underway (with the status of a Candidate Recommendation).

Figure 16-1 shows the general structures for both versions, which are similar, but not the same.

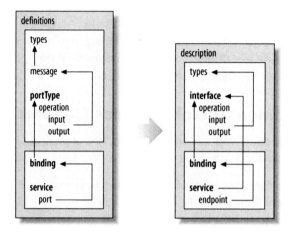

FIGURE 16-1. General structure of WSDL 1.1 and 2.0 files

WSDL files describe services from the bottom up. That is, they start with the data types used and end with the location (address) of the service. In addition, they have three layers of description:

- The first layer describes the interface of a service. This interface (called the "port type" in WSDL 1.1) can consist of one or more operations with input and output parameters that use types specified in the first section of the WSDL file. In WSDL 1.1 the service parameters were defined in <message> sections, while in WSDL 2.0 they are defined just like any other type in the <types> section.

- The second layer defines the "binding" of a Web Service; that is, the protocol and format for which the Web Service operations are provided.

- The third layer defines the physical location (address, URL) where the Web Service is available.

Note that due to the different layers inside WSDL files, different teams modify the contents of WSDL files at different times. See Section 16.3.3 for details.

16.2.2 WSDL by Example

Let's look at a simple example of a WSDL file. This WSDL file defines a service called CustomerService, which provides one operation called getCustomerAddress(). Its input parameter is a customer ID of type long, and the output is a structure of three string attributes: the street, the city, and the zip code.

Here is the WSDL 1.1 version:

```
1  <?xml version="1.0" encoding="utf-8" ?>
2  <definitions name="CustomerService"
```

```
3      targetNamespace="http://soa-in-practice.com/wsdl"
4      xmlns:tns="http://soa-in-practice.com/wsdl"
5      xmlns:xsd1="http://soa-in-practice.com/xsd"
6      xmlns:xsd="http://www.w3.org/2001/XMLSchema"
7      xmlns:soap="http://schemas.xmlsoap.org/wsdl/soap/"
8      xmlns="http://schemas.xmlsoap.org/wsdl/">
9
10   <types>
11     <xsd:schema
12         targetNamespace="http://soa-in-practice.com/xsd"
13         xmlns="http://soa-in-practice.com/xsd">
14
15       <xsd:element name="getCustomerAddress">
16         <xsd:complexType>
17           <xsd:sequence>
18             <xsd:element name="customerID" type="xsd:long"/>
19           </xsd:sequence>
20         </xsd:complexType>
21       </xsd:element>
22
23       <xsd:element name="getCustomerAddressResponse" type="Address"/>
24       <xsd:complexType name="Address">
25         <xsd:sequence>
26           <xsd:element name="street" type="xsd:string"/>
27           <xsd:element name="city" type="xsd:string"/>
28           <xsd:element name="zipCode" type="xsd:string"/>
29         </xsd:sequence>
30       </xsd:complexType>
31
32     </xsd:schema>
33   </types>
34
35   <message name="getCustomerAddressInput">
36     <part name="params" element="xsd1:getCustomerAddress"/>
37   </message>
38   <message name="getCustomerAddressOutput">
39     <part name="params" element="xsd1:getCustomerAddressResponse"/>
40   </message>
41
42   <portType name="CustomerInterface" >
43     <operation name="getCustomerAddress">
44       <input message="tns:getCustomerAddressInput" />
45       <output message="tns:getCustomerAddressOutput" />
46     </operation>
47   </portType>
48
49   <binding name="CustomerSOAPBinding"
50             type="tns:CustomerInterface" >
51     <soap:binding style="document"
52         transport="http://schemas.xmlsoap.org/soap/http" />
53     <operation name="getCustomerAddress">
54       <soap:operation
55           soapAction="http://soa-in-practice.com/getCustomerAddress" />
56       <input>
57         <soap:body use="literal" />
58       </input>
```

```
59        <output>
60          <soap:body use="literal" />
61        </output>
62      </operation>
63    </binding>
64
65    <service name="CustomerService" >
66      <port name="CustomerPort"
67            binding="tns:CustomerSOAPBinding">
68        <soap:address
69            location="http://soa-in-practice.com/customer11"/>
70      </port>
71    </service>
72
73  </definitions>
```

Let's go through it from the bottom up:

- The <service> section at the end defines a service named CustomerService, available at the URL http://soa-in-practice.com/customer11, which is provided with a binding called CustomerSOAPBinding. The prefix tns: is the namespace where we can find details about this identifier. It is defined at the beginning of the document and is the same as the target namespace, which is the namespace all identifiers identified in this file belong to (see lines 3 and 4). That means CustomerSOAPBinding is an identifier defined in this file.

- The <binding> section defines the protocol and format that are used to provide the service. Here, we see the definition of the CustomerSOAPBinding. It starts by specifying which interface type this binding is for (CustomerInterface). Without going into details, the binding specified here is a SOAP binding based on the low-level protocol HTTP (see lines 51 and 52). This section also defines which style of SOAP is used (yes, more than one SOAP binding is possible!).

- The <portType> section defines the interface, CustomerInterface. It consists of one operation, called getCustomerAddress, and specifies the messages that will be sent over the service bus when this operation is called. This service sends a request and gets a response (see Chapter 10 for a discussion of message exchange patterns), which is defined by specifying an input message (getCustomerAddressInput) and an output message (getCustomerAddressOutput). Other messages could be error messages.

- The <message> sections define the individual messages, using the identifiers referred to in the <portType> section. Both getCustomerAddressInput and getCustomerAddressOutput use a data type defined in the <types> section.

- The <types> section defines the data types used: in this case, the input parameter customerID of type long and the output parameter address, which is a structure/record of three string attributes. All types have their own namespace, xsd1.

The <binding> section states that the SOAP style used here is document/literal, which is a combination of the style attribute in line 51 and the body definitions in lines 57 and 60. In fact the style is document/literal wrapped, because it uses some additional conventions (the input message has a single part that refers to an element; this element has the same name as the operation, and the element's complex type has no attributes). Over the years, this has evolved as the prevalent SOAP binding.

> **NOTE**
> For details on WSDL 1.1, see [WSDL 1.1]. For details about the different SOAP styles, see [Butek03].

Here is the corresponding WSDL file for version 2.0 (using SOAP 1.2):

```
1   <?xml version="1.0" encoding="utf-8" ?>
2   <description
3       targetNamespace="http://soa-in-practice.com/wsdl"
4       xmlns:tns="http://soa-in-practice.com/wsdl"
5       xmlns:xsd1="http://soa-in-practice.com/xsd"
6       xmlns:xsd="http://www.w3.org/2001/XMLSchema"
7       xmlns:wsoap="http://www.w3.org/2006/01/wsdl/soap"
8       xmlns:wsdlx="http://www.w3.org/2006/01/wsdl-extensions"
9       xmlns="http://www.w3.org/2006/01/wsdl">
10
11    <types>
12     <xsd:schema
13         targetNamespace="http://soa-in-practice.com/xsd"
14         xmlns="http://soa-in-practice.com/xsd">
15
16      <xsd:element name="getCustomerAddress">
17        <xsd:complexType>
18          <xsd:sequence>
19            <xsd:element name="customerID" type="xsd:long"/>
20          </xsd:sequence>
21        </xsd:complexType>
22      </xsd:element>
23
24      <xsd:element name="getCustomerAddressResponse" type="Address"/>
25      <xsd:complexType name="Address">
26        <xsd:sequence>
27          <xsd:element name="street" type="xsd:string"/>
28          <xsd:element name="city" type="xsd:string"/>
29          <xsd:element name="zipCode" type="xsd:string"/>
30        </xsd:sequence>
31      </xsd:complexType>
32
33     </xsd:schema>
34    </types>
35
36    <interface name = "CustomerInterface" >
37
38     <operation name="getCustomerAddress"
39                pattern="http://www.w3.org/2006/01/wsdl/in-out"
40                style="http://www.w3.org/2006/01/wsdl/style/iri"
41                wsdlx:safe = "true">
42       <input messageLabel="In"
43              element="xsd1:getCustomerAddress" />
```

```
44        <output messageLabel="Out"
45                element="xsd1:getCustomerAddressResponse" />
46      </operation>
47
48    </interface>
49
50    <binding name="CustomerSOAPBinding"
51             interface="tns:CustomerInterface"
52             type="http://www.w3.org/2006/01/wsdl/soap"
53             wsoap:protocol="http://www.w3.org/2003/05/soap/bindings/HTTP">
54
55      <operation ref="tns:getCustomerAddress"
56                 wsoap:mep="http://www.w3.org/2003/05/soap/mep/soap-response"/>
57
58    </binding>
59
60    <service name="CustomerService"
61             interface="tns:CustomerInterface">
62
63      <endpoint name="CustomerEndpoint"
64               binding="tns:CustomerSOAPBinding"
65               address="http://soa-in-practice.com/customer20"/>
66
67    </service>
68
69  </description>
```

The major differences are:

- The root XML element is named <description> instead of <definitions>.

- The <service> section uses "endpoint" instead of "port."

- Inside the <binding> section, lines 52, 53, and 56 define the specific protocol (SOAP 1.2, based on HTTP, using HTTP GET).

- The <portType> section is replaced by an <interface> section. It uses more specific message exchange patterns, which define the low-level ordering of messages (see Chapter 10).

- The <message> section is not available anymore. Instead, the operations directly refer to data types (defined in the <types> section). Which messages are sent follow from the MEP and the types specified in the <interface> section.

- Different namespaces are used to identify WSDL 2.0 and SOAP 1.2.

For details, see [WSDL 2.0].

Note again that the first layer (types, messages, and portTypes for WSDL 1.1 and types and interfaces for WSDL 2.0) is the syntactic interface of the Web Service, specifying the signature of the service. The other layers define technical details, such as the binding and the location of the service.

Note also that these examples skip error handling (which is usually done by providing fault messages similar to input and output messages).

16.2.3 SOAP

As stated earlier, SOAP was the first real Web Services standard that was developed. Originally, SOAP was an acronym for "Simple Object Access Protocol." However, it turned out that SOAP wasn't simple, and it didn't deal with object access. As a consequence, since version 1.2 the acronym has stood for itself.

Current SOAP versions are 1.1 and 1.2, but they don't differ as much as the WSDL versions. The specifications are primarily relevant for SOAP adapters and are not visible to ordinary Web Services programmers.

Here is an example of a SOAP request according to the WSDL file specified above (using the document/literal wrapped style):

```
<?xml version='1.0' ?>
<soap:Envelope xmlns:soap="http://schemas.xmlsoap.org/soap/envelope/">
  <soap:Header>
    ...
  </soap:Header>
  <soap:Body>
    <getCustomerAddress xmlns="http://soa-in-practice.com/xsd">
      <customerID>12345678</customerID>
    </getCustomerAddress >
  </soap:Body>
</soap:Envelope>
```

A corresponding reply message might have the following contents:

```
<?xml version='1.0' ?>
<soap:Envelope xmlns:soap="http://schemas.xmlsoap.org/soap/envelope/">
  <soap:Header>
    ...
  </soap:Header>
  <soap:Body>
    <getCustomerAddressResponse xmlns="http://soa-in-practice.com/xsd">
      <address>
        <street>Gaussstr. 29</street>
        <city>Braunschweig</city>
        <zipCode>D-38106</zipCode>
      </address>
    </getCustomerAddressResponse>
  </soap:Body>
</soap:Envelope>
```

You can see that the SOAP messages have an XML format containing a root element called <Envelope>. It might contain an optional <Header> and a mandatory <Body> element. While the body element contains the payload (request, response, or fault data), the header can contain additional information to help the infrastructure deal with the messages (such as routing hints, security hints, and so on).

Note that the style documented here (document/literal wrapped) starts the body with the service name (for the response extended with the string "Response") and transfers data without any format information. There are other SOAP styles that allow you to pass data including data types. The good thing about not having type-encoding information is that this approach is more generic regarding (backward-compatible) modifications of interface types, which can be helpful when dealing with different service versions (see Chapter 12).

When sending SOAP requests via HTTP, the usual HTTP headings are used. For example, the request might look as follows (SOAP 1.1):

```
POST /customer11 HTTP/1.1
Host: soa-in-practice.com
Content-Type: text/xml; charset="utf-8"
Content-Length: nnnn
SOAPAction: " http://soa-in-practice.com/getCustomerAddress"

<?xml version='1.0' ?>
<soap:Envelope xmlns:soap="http://schemas.xmlsoap.org/soap/envelope/">
  ...
</soap:Envelope>
```

A corresponding response might have the following format:

```
HTTP/1.1 200 OK
Content-Type: text/xml; charset="utf-8"
Content-Length: nnnn

<?xml version='1.0' ?>
<soap:Envelope xmlns:soap="http://schemas.xmlsoap.org/soap/envelope/">
  ...
</soap:Envelope>
```

16.2.4 UDDI

"Universal Description, Discovery, and Integration" was initially itself part of an even broader term, "Universal Description, Discovery, and Integration Business Registry" (or, in short, UDDI Business Registry, or the even shorter UBR). The original idea was to introduce all three roles of a working marketplace: providers that offer services, consumers that need services, and brokers that bring them together by advertising and locating services. This resulted in the famous triangle that is often shown when explaining Web Services (see Figure 16-2).

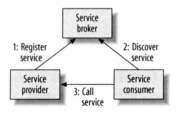

FIGURE 16-2. Provider, consumer, and broker

The intention behind the UBR was that it would be the central broker for a worldwide marketplace of Web Services (like a worldwide yellow pages for Web Services). Providers could put any new Web Services into the UBR, and consumers could search the UBR to find any services they desired. UDDI was intended to be the protocol used to register and find Web Services.

It turned out, however, that the UBR didn't work, and in January 2006, it was turned off. The official reason was announced as follows (see [UBR]):

> IBM, Microsoft, and SAP have evaluated the status of the UDDI Business Registry and determined that the goals for the project have been achieved. Given this, the UDDI Business Registry will be discontinued as of 12 January 2006.

This was a remarkable example of a falsification of history. Instead of admitting that the idea of a worldwide yellow pages for Web Services didn't work (yet), the providers of the UBR redefined the initial motivation behind the UBR, claiming that it was intended as a prototype that could be used to learn about how to design an appropriate interface for a true central services broker.

The failure of the UBR does not necessarily mean that UDDI also failed, but there are doubts about how important UDDI is in practice. Part of the reason is that service management requires a significant service portfolio to be useful. But another part is just insufficient homework. To quote [NewcomerLomow05]:

> However, for various reasons including the difficulty of creating meaningful categorization information for the Web, UDDI did not achieve its goal of becoming the registry for all Web Services metadata and did not become useful in a majority of Web Services interactions over the Web.

Still, for technical reasons Web Services usually do need a broker. They are inherently point-to-point connections, and some mechanisms and/or processes are needed to avoid hardcoded addressing in Web Services consumers (see Section 5.3). So, other solutions appeared. To quote [NewcomerLomow05] again:

> In general, it seems that some companies are using UDDI, but others are extending registry solutions already in place such as LDAP, Java Naming and Directory Interface (JNDI), relational databases, or the CORBA Trader. Still another alternative in some limited use is the ebXML Registry.

There are now multiple versions of UDDI, and other upcoming Web Services standards that partially overlap with it. According to [NewcomerLomow05]:

> These overlaps between specifications highlight yet another reason Web Services standardization needs leadership and architecture.

After all, the whole situation with UDDI looks like a mess. Time will show how things evolve.

16.3 Web Services in Practice

I've already introduced some aspects of Web Services that make them more complicated than they initially look. In this section, I will discuss them in detail.

16.3.1 Open Standardization

The first problem with Web Services is that it is not just one standard defined by one standardization organization. As stated earlier, there are more than 50 different Web Services specifications, specified by three different standardization organizations (W3C, OASIS, and WS-I). Figure 16-3 gives a brief overview.*

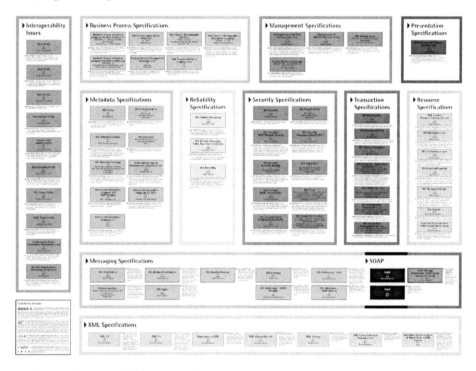

FIGURE 16-3. Overview of Web Services standards

Say you're a tool vendor, and you want to provide tooling for Web Services. Which of these standards should you follow? And once you've determined that, which versions of the specific standards should you follow? It's a mess, and as a consequence interoperability is still a real problem.

Even for the five fundamental standards mentioned previously (XML, HTTP, WSDL, SOAP, and UDDI), the goal of interoperability has traditionally been hard to attain. Even if you chose the same versions of these standards, the specifications were too sloppy or too

---

* Thanks to innoQ for allowing me to reprint this overview. You can find the original poster and a description of Web Services at [WSStandards].

broad. For this reason, something interesting happened: in 2002, several vendors (Accenture, BEA, Fujitsu, HP, IBM, Intel, Microsoft, Oracle, and SAP) got together and founded a standardization organization for standardizing the standards. This organization is called the Web Services Interoperability Organization (WS-I). In 2006, WS-I had more than 130 members, including Sun.* (For more details about WS-I, see [WS-I].)

One important thing WS-I creates is "profiles," which are defined sets of standards, each of specific versions, combined with guidelines and conventions for using these standards together in ways that ensure interoperability. In 2004, the WS-I Basic Profile 1.1 was specified (for the five fundamental Web Services: XML 1.0, WSDL 1.1, SOAP 1.1, HTTP 1.1, and UDDI version 2) to provide interoperability for calling Web Services. This Basic Profile contained 150 additional Conformance Requirements and 24 Extensibility Points that provided additional constraints and extensions for the fundamental five standards. See [WSI-BasicProfile] for details.

Note that the Basic Profile 1.1 covers only 5 of the more than 50 standards. So, for the other standards (which cover aspects such as security, reliability, process modeling and orchestration, dealing with service-level agreements, and service management), interoperability is still an issue. Future versions of the Basic Profile covering more standards will follow, and other profiles will cover topics such as security and reliability. In fact, there is already a WS-I Basic Security Profile (see Section 14.4.2). In practice, you should always follow these profiles, if they're available. But in general for Web Services, interoperability is still an issue you should take into account.

16.3.2 Protocol Aspects

The next aspect of Web Services that I want to mention is the fact that Web Services are inherently point-to-point and protocol-driven.

As explained in Section 5.3.3, a protocol-driven ESB has the advantage that each consumer and provider can use individual tools to call and implement Web Services. The only thing that must be assured is that the protocol's requirements are properly met. Unfortunately, as just discussed, interoperability is still an issue for Web Services. As a consequence, just because consumers A and B can interoperate with provider P and consumer A can interoperate with provider Q, you can't assume that consumer B can also interoperate with provider Q. In other words, you have to verify each combination of provider and consumer. That means instead of verifying one interface for each system, you have to verify $n \times (n-1)$ combinations of interfaces.

An important aspect of point-to-point protocols is that you need to ensure that the location of the service provider is not hard-coded in the consumer code (see Section 5.3.1). You might use UDDI (which has the flaws discussed previously) for this purpose, or you might use another solution, but for scalability and fault tolerance, you need *some* solution.

---

* Sun's absence from the list of founders of WS-I was a deliberate choice, because the Microsoft's commitment was bound to "Sun not being one of the movers/announcers/founding members" (see [Wong02]).

In essence, I strongly recommend that you incorporate appropriate solutions for these problems when you establish your Web Services SOA landscape. The best solution is to make the fact that the ESB uses Web Services an implementation detail of the infrastructure and give consumers and providers everything they need to call and implement services. That is, from the providers' and consumers' points of view, the ESB should be API-driven. Any modifications, such as introducing interceptors, changing the WSDL or SOAP version, and so on, then become transparent. (See Section 5.3 for details about API-driven ESBs and interceptors.)

A typical scalable approach for Web Services might look like Figure 16-4.

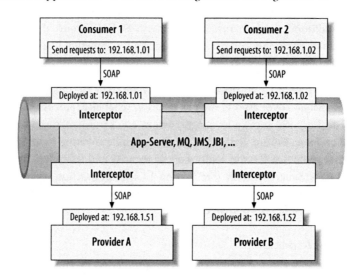

FIGURE 16-4. A Web Services ESB might internally use different protocols

Outside the ESB, interceptors (see Section 5.3.2) provide a Web Services interface (using the SOAP protocol). However, internally the ESB is implemented by some other standard or proprietary technology. For example, a set of application servers might serve as central hub-and-spoke servers connected via a specific JMS protocol. Each application server provides connectivity to a specific set of providers and consumers and routes service messages either internally or to another server (each application server might, for example, be responsible for one physical location).

With such an approach, you might also solve the inherent problems of security (see Chapter 14) and reliability (see Chapter 10). Each provider and consumer uses a specific HTTPS channel, and inside the bus, the reliability of the protocol used might provide better guarantees than those provided by HTTP.

Note that you can take an incremental approach. When starting with Web Services, you require only that there be some indirection, so that the consumer does not use the endpoint specified by a particular provider. To this end, you should instead define a location where the consumer can find the actual endpoint to use. At the beginning, you can put the provider's endpoint at that location (so that the service calls go directly to the provider). Later, when you introduce interceptors, you can instead put their endpoints at that location, so they can route service calls accordingly. As time goes on, you can specify more details about how you implement your ESB and provide more and more value-added ESB services (see Section 5.4). Providing value-added ESB services incrementally allows everyone to learn from experience what is necessary and appropriate.

16.3.3 The WSDL Lifecycle

As stated earlier in this chapter, due to the different layers inside WSDL files, different teams may modify the contents of those files at different times. That means that, from a development perspective, there is no *one* WSDL file describing a Web Service. From a consumer's perspective, you might see the final version of a WSDL file, which contains all the information needed to call a Web Service when it is in production (but even then endpoints might differ when using different interceptors, as just discussed). So, at least from a development perspective, WSDL files have a lifecycle, consisting of the steps shown in Table 16-1. This lifecycle corresponds to the service lifecycle discussed in Chapter 11.

TABLE 16-1. The WSDL lifecycle

Layer	WSDL 1.1	WSDL 2.0	Contents clear at	Defined by
Service interface	`<types>`, `<message>`, `<portType>`	`<types>`, `<interface>`	Solution design time	Solution managers, business process managers, service portfolio managers…
Service interface with namespaces and other details	`<types>`, `<message>`, `<portType>`	`<types>`, `<interface>`	Service design and/or implementation time	Service designers and/or implementers
Protocol	`<binding>`	`<binding>`	Configuration time	Infrastructure (ESB) team
Location	`<service>`	`<service>`	Deployment time, runtime	Operators

The steps can be elaborated as follows:

- Initially, you can use a WSDL file to specify the interface of a service by using only the first layer of the file (the `<types>` section and `<message>`/`<portType>` or `<interface>` section). This is typically done when a service gets identified as part of a business process or solution, by solution managers or other high-level designers responsible for service design (see Chapter 7 and Section 11.1.2). Note, however, that WSDL may not cover the whole service contract (see the next section, "WSDL Deficits").

- To integrate a service as part of a SOA landscape, you might have to deal with conventions and requirements that apply to your specific infrastructure. That is, you might need to introduce namespaces, use specific data types, and so on. This refinement of the initial first design is usually done at design and/or implementation time, by service designers and/or service implementers (see Section 11.1.1).

- The protocol that is used to provide and call the service depends on the infrastructure being used. For this reason, the <binding> section comes into play when the infrastructure details of the service are clear. Typically, this is at implementation or configuration time (depending on whether the implementers fill out the corresponding data or a configuration tool does it right before deployment).

- Finally, you have to define where the service is available. This is typically specified at deployment time and/or runtime (i.e., when it is clear whether you are using a test environment or the production environment).

Because a WSDL file for a service goes through different stages, you should set up your processes, documentation, and configuration management procedures so that you can't easily confuse these stages. Part of this might be supported by generators and might be a step of the model-driven development process (see Chapter 18).

Figure 16-5 gives an example of what a WSDL lifecycle might look like in practice. At design time, somebody defines a first version of the file describing a new service. While internal teams should follow usual naming conventions, external teams might not follow them, so you may need some mapping to integrate externally created files into your SOA infrastructure. This might also be the moment at which you define the binding, according to your infrastructure and policies. Different teams can then generate code out of these landscape-conforming WSDL files and implement against the resulting APIs. However, at deployment time (which might be during integration tests or when the service enters production), WSDL files supplemented with deployment details are used to provide connectivity. Note that if you use interceptors, different consumers might use different WSDL files to call a service. Note also that some effort may be required to map your internal technical requirements and conventions to external service providers that do not follow them. This shouldn't be too big a deal.

16.3.4 WSDL Deficits

You should also understand that a WSDL file does not contain the full interface of a service. That is, it doesn't contain any semantic information. That means a WSDL file is not provided to manage the whole service contract. WSDL is simply a format for specifying the technical aspects of calling Web Services. For this reason, it makes no sense to use this format for service repositories. It's provided only for registries (see Chapter 17 for more on registries and repositories).

Surprisingly, WSDL also has deficits regarding the technical attributes of services. One important constraint (at least up to WSDL 1.1) is the lack of nonfunctional attributes and attributes for service-level agreements. A WSDL file does not specify how long a service usually runs, who is allowed to call it, how much a service call costs, and so on. All these aspects must usually be known in order to manage a service in a large SOA landscape.

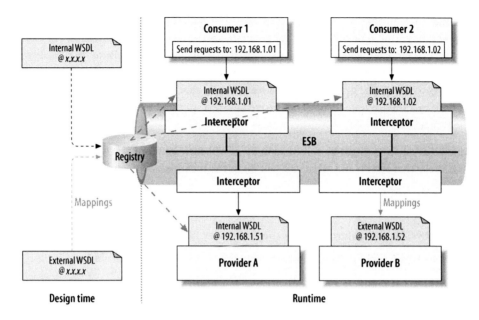

Consumer 1
Send requests to: 192.168.1.01

Consumer 2
Send requests to: 192.168.1.02

Internal WSDL
@ x.x.x.x

Internal WSDL
@ 192.168.1.01

Internal WSDL
@ 192.168.1.02

Interceptor

Interceptor

ESB

Registry

Interceptor

Interceptor

Mappings

Mappings

Internal WSDL
@ 192.168.1.51

External WSDL
@ 192.168.1.52

External WSDL
@ x.x.x.x

Provider A

Provider B

Design time

Runtime

FIGURE 16-5. Example for a WSDL lifecycle

With future WSDL versions, this might change. For example, WSDL 2.0 provides the ability to extend WSDL files. One possible extension was shown in the WSDL 2.0 file we looked at earlier in the chapter. The WSDL extension safe defines whether a service call is "safe" for a consumer, in the sense that the consumer does not incur any obligation beyond the interaction with the provider:

```
<?xml version="1.0" encoding="utf-8" ?>
<description
    ...
    xmlns:wsdlx="http://www.w3.org/2006/01/wsdl-extensions"
    ...>
  ...
  <interface name = "CustomerInterface" >

    <operation name="getCustomerAddress"
               pattern="http://www.w3.org/2006/01/wsdl/in-out"
               style="http://www.w3.org/2006/01/wsdl/style/iri"
               wsdlx:safe = "true">
        <input messageLabel="In"
               element="xsd1:getCustomerAddress" />
        <output messageLabel="Out"
                element="xsd1:getCustomerAddressResponse" />
    </operation>

  </interface>
```

A typical "unsafe" service call would be an order or a booking.

This is only one example, but it demonstrates the concept.

Note that such attributes are not just semantic information provided for documentation purposes only. Different code might get generated according to these attributes. For example, for "unsafe" calls, code might get generated that makes service calls more reliable or writes a protocol entry. As another example, in one project I know of, code is generated according to SLAs. The generated code automatically cancels a service call when the response to a service request does not arrive before a specified maximum service running time is reached.

Some WSDL deficits might be solved soon by new WSDL standard versions. But what about those that aren't, and what can you do in the meantime? You have three options:

- Use your own format for service descriptions and generate WSDL out of it when and where necessary.
- Extend WSDL files externally with supplementary files that specify missing attributes.
- Extend WSDL files internally with additional XML elements and attributes.

Note that the last option is a problem, because it leads to WSDL files that are not well defined. Although the result has correct XML syntax, it isn't valid according to the corresponding format description of WSDL (in general, adding new attributes breaks the validity of XML files for which the format is specified).

In principle, I recommend the first option, because it has the advantage that infrastructure-specific aspects don't come into play too early. Also, it enables you to generate additional information for WSDL files as necessary, as WSDL and Web Services standards improve. See Section 18.3 for more about defining your own service model and notation.

16.3.5 So, Should You Use Web Services?

You have read now about several problems (or "challenges") involved in the application of Web Services:

- WSDL files have a lifecycle for which you need a process.
- WSDL files lack attributes.
- Too many standards hinder interoperability.
- Lack of interoperability necessitates verifications for each new combination of provider and consumer.
- The inherent point-to-point nature of Web Services protocols necessitates interceptors.
- The effort required for individual verifications and interceptors leads to an ESB that is API-based.

So, does this mean you should abstain from using Web Services?

Well, let's look at the alternatives:

- You can use a proprietary SOA infrastructure solution that is more consistent and mature and has solved the inherent problems of Web Services. But as with all proprietary solutions, this might lead you to lose control and freedom of choice and to become dependent on a specific vendor.

- You can create everything on your own, which means reinventing the wheel and making the same mistakes again.

Of course, your decision will depend on your specific situation, but setting priorities on an emerging standard is probably not a bad idea. Note also that it's up to you how much you get involved in Web Services standards. For example:

- You might use WSDL only as a format for service interfaces (with or without additional attributes), but use your own specific protocol.

- You might use a process engine using BPEL, with your own ESB protocol.

- You might extend Web Services files with SLA attributes.

- You might put further constraints on Web Services to provide better interoperability.

The important lesson of this chapter is that using Web Services will not automatically solve all your problems. You'll need to provide people, time, and money to make Web Services a working infrastructure in your SOA landscape.

And, please, do your homework. If the infrastructure team provides half-baked solutions, this will only lead to frustration and ignorance. If people don't want to use the infrastructure provided, it is always the fault of the infrastructure team. You want to make them excited about your SOA infrastructure (see also Section 19.2.2).

This chapter has focused on using Web Services as your technical infrastructure, but of course, this is only one option. Knuckling down the whole SOA strategy under the Web Services standard is a very risky and shortsighted approach. Web Services are only one possible infrastructure, and even if you don't start out with multiple infrastructures for your SOA (see Section 5.2), you can't expect that Web Services will be the only infrastructure (standard) you ever implement.

For this reason, you should be wary of using Web Services standards on layers that are infrastructure-independent. In fact, service contracts (the whole descriptions of services) should be described and managed in a format that is independent from any specific infrastructure. That means service repositories (unlike registries—see Section 17.2) should not just be tools that manage WSDL files.

Note also that using Web Services doesn't automatically mean that you are implementing SOA. It might be just a way to let some systems interact, without all the other aspects SOA provides and requires. Recently, a nice acronym has evolved for such an application of Web Services: *JaBoWS*, which stands for "Just another Bunch of Web Services."

16.4   Closing Notes

After all that, let's come back to the question of what Web Services really are. The important point I want to make here is that Web Services standards play two different roles:

- On the one hand, they specify standards for abstract descriptions of services. These might be interface descriptions, as in the first layer of a WSDL file, or service orchestrations and workflows, as in the first layer of BPEL (see Chapter 7).

- On the other hand, they specify protocols for a particular implementation of a SOA infrastructure (ESB).

Be sure to distinguish between these two roles. You can use BPEL to model workflows without using any specific Web Services protocol, and you can specify service interfaces (with the limitations discussed previously) with WSDL without saying anything about how to call these services.

Again, in general I recommend not using any Web Services infrastructure-specific aspects until infrastructure details really come into play. In other words, you should always know what it would mean to change the technical infrastructure of your SOA landscape and try to minimize the effort that would be involved.

REPRESENTATIONAL STATE TRANSFER (REST)

Recently, an alternative to Web Services, called *Representational State Transfer* (REST) came to public attention. It refers to a collection of network architecture principles that focus on simple and stateless access to resources (which could be considered as key design principles to help the Internet scale and grow).

RESTful HTTP (what is often used as a synonym for REST) uses the four fundamental HTTP methods: GET, PUT, POST, and DELETE, to stateless read, write, create/perform, and delete resources identified by URLs. Because this native usage of the HTTP protocol is simple and fast, this can be a good way to provide access to data or resources provided by (web) servers, including inherent technical support for typical requirements, such as caching.

However, because of its lack of support for security aspects, nonfunctional attributes, composability, and so on, it can hardly be used as a core protocol for a full-blown sophisticated SOA infrastructure with process services, orchestration, and scenarios where read services have different granularity than write services.

So, if you just want to provide access for external systems to your data or resources, REST is definitely a principle or technology to consider, but, if you plan to establish a SOA landscape running distributed business processes, REST is not an option (yet).

16.5 Summary

- Web Services are (evolving as) the de facto standard for SOA infrastructures.

- Based on the core protocols XML and HTTP, the most important protocols are WSDL, for the description of Web Services interfaces, and SOAP, as a protocol format for Web Services communications.

- WSDL files have different layers for the service interface, bindings, and deployment details. For this reason, you usually need processes to deal with the lifecycle of WSDL files.

- WSDL is not bound to SOAP. You can use other bindings, so the interface descriptions can (in principle) be used with any technology.

- WSDL as a standard defines only core properties for interoperability. Additional attributes for security, SLAs, and so on are not provided or are provided by other standards.

- A lot of different Web Services standards and versions are specified by different standardization organizations. For this reason, interoperability can be a problem. The Web Services Interoperability Organization (WS-I) tries to solve this issue by providing different profiles for certain sets of standards.

- In practice, to be interoperable you should usually use the WS-I Basic Profile and the SOAP document/literal wrapped binding.

- Web Services is a protocol-driven ESB standard with inherent point-to-point communications. For this reason, you might have to introduce interceptors. This also gives you the opportunity to use a different protocol or technology inside the ESB.

- For better synergy, you might consider implementing an API-driven ESB.

CHAPTER SEVENTEEN

Service Management

As a SOA GROWS, SOONER OR LATER THE QUESTION OF HOW TO MANAGE ALL THE EXISTING SERVICES arises. How does a consumer find out whether and where a service exists? Where can further information about a service be found, so the consumer can understand it and use it correctly? Dealing with such questions often leads to the concept of a service repository and/or a service registry. This chapter introduces these concepts and discusses when and how to manage services.

17.1   The History of Service Brokers

Almost every introduction to Web Services introduces three major roles: the role of a service provider, the role of a service consumer (requestor), and the role of a service broker. They interact as shown in the famous Web Services triangle depicted in Figure 17-1.

This triangle recognizes that there is a need for some way to bring providers and consumers together. For this reason, as soon as a provider starts to provide a service, it registers the service at a well-known place (i.e., with the service broker). Then, when a consumer needs a service, the consumer can use the broker to find providers of this service.

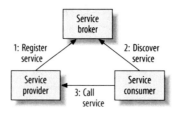

FIGURE 17-1. Provider, consumer, and broker

In 2000, when Web Services began to take off, a broker called the "Universal Description, Discovery, and Integration Business Registry" (also known as the UDDI Business Registry, or UBR) was announced as the worldwide yellow pages for Web Services. The UBR was intended to act as a global broker, with providers all over the world registering the Web Services they provided and consumers searching the UBR to find any services they required.

As Section 16.2.4 noted, this concept ultimately failed. So, what does this prove? Primarily, only that the approach taken by the backing companies at that time didn't work. Maybe the timing wasn't right, maybe the idea wasn't right, or maybe they didn't do their homework.

One important reason for the failure of the UBR may have been that establishing a central broker is not the first step in realizing a SOA. As I heard once at a conference, "Those who have friends don't need yellow pages." That is, before we look in the yellow pages to find a dentist, we ask our friends for recommendations. Likewise, when services are provided as part of a solution that uses distributed business processes, the providers and consumers will already know each other. Therefore, in the early stages, a broker won't (yet) be necessary.

The topic becomes relevant when a SOA grows. Then the need to list all the existing services in one place might arise, so that consumers can easily find them by asking a broker (or, to use the current terminology, by looking into a service *repository*). In other words, the need for a broker that helps consumers find the right services arises only when the SOA landscape has reached a certain size.

However, there was another reason for introducing UDDI and the UBR: because Web Services calls are inherently point-to-point calls (that is, the caller has to send the message to a physical address; see Section 16.3.2), it usually makes sense to introduce some form of loose coupling here. Instead of hard-coding the address of the receiving system into the calling system, the address of the providing system can be requested from the broker at runtime.

This approach enables load balancing and failover, because it is possible to give callers different addresses. Note, however, that this is not the only way to introduce loose coupling to deal with the point-to-point nature of Web Services calls: another approach is to use proxies or interceptors that delegate each call to a specific provider system, according to their routing policies (see Section 5.3.2 for details).

In other words, a broker might be used for different purposes, such as finding services at design time and finding the right provider at runtime. This means that we can differentiate between the roles a broker can fulfill. The two primary roles are discussed in the following section.

17.2 Repositories and Registries

The most common terms used for brokers these days are *repository* and *registry*. Often, these terms are used interchangeably, as general terms referring to the concept of a service broker from all points of view. However, they are increasingly being used to indicate distinct roles. The difference is as follows:

- Repositories manage services and their artifacts from a business point of view. That is, they manage interfaces, contracts, SLAs, dependencies, etc. to help to identify, design, and develop services. From a business point of view, a repository should contain all the information about the behavior and interface of a service. This information should be independent from technical details and infrastructure aspects. That is, it should not be necessary to change the repository when a company switches to a new infrastructure (ESB).

- Registries manage services from a technical point of view. That is, they manage interfaces, but not all of the contract details: they manage all the technical details necessary to use a service at runtime (i.e., deployment information) and might be used to route service calls to different systems that provide corresponding services. A registry, if necessary, can be part of the infrastructure (ESB).

Both repositories and registries might exist in a SOA landscape. One system might even be used for both purposes. This case, however, raises the danger of making the repository dependent on the infrastructure, which means changing that infrastructure is not as easy as it would be if the repository were infrastructure-independent.

If the repository and registry are distinct entities, it is usually a good idea to have a reference from the registry to the repository. Then, if people want to know about the semantic details of the running system, they'll know where to look. As registries are typically generated out of repositories (and enhanced with deployment information), referencing a repository from a registry should be no problem.

You might also think about referencing a registry from a repository. However, this goes in the opposite direction of the normal data (or generator) flow, so it might introduce some additional dependencies. In general, such references should be soft (such as URLs).

17.2.1 Designing Repositories and Registries

As I mentioned previously, repositories and registries can be used for different purposes. For this reason, you should be clear on the role and responsibility a repository and/or registry has in your concrete SOA landscape. The specific roles and responsibilities lead to different kinds of solutions and different processes to deal with these entities.

Here are some important topics and questions to consider:

Internal coordination or marketplace

Is the repository/registry provided for internal use, to optimize processes and force reuse, or is it provided to support the idea of a marketplace? The latter leads to a requirement for multiple providers to provide the same service (which is usually not the case internally, where you try to avoid redundancy).

Amount of information

Does the repository/registry manage all service information (i.e., the contract, including all semantic information and nonfunctional attributes), or only technically relevant information?

Role in the development process

Is the repository/registry provided to help solution managers and designers to find existing services when designing new business processes and solutions, and/or to find necessary information to provide interoperability at runtime? That is, does it include technical infrastructure-specific data and/or deployment information?

User interface

Does the repository/registry provide support for (graphically) designing or modeling new services, or does it "only" provide an interface to insert, update, and retrieve services designed with different tools?

Amount of centralization

Is there only one central repository/registry, or is the whole repository/registry a collection of several decentralized chunks of information? If the former, how do you prevent it from becoming a bottleneck in development processes? If the latter, how do you deal with and avoid redundancy?

Offline ability

Is it possible to work with the repository/registry without being online inside the development environment?

Versioning and configuration management support

How does the repository deal with having different versions of a service and different configurations under development? (For example, a service interface in test might be different from a service interface under development, because something has changed recently—see Chapter 12 for details.)

In practice, the answers to these questions can be very different, and as a result repositories can look very different. Figure 17-2 shows a possible example for dealing with different repositories and registries. Here, each department or business unit has its own way of designing and modeling services. A general requirement is that these models are transformed into the input format of the central registry, which provides interfaces for consumers and providers and deploys service information into the ESB. For this reason, in the registry deployment details come into play. The repositories are also required to provide HTML files for their service descriptions. The corresponding URLs are part of the intermediate format that is used to transfer data into the central registry so that it also can display URLs with detailed specifications.

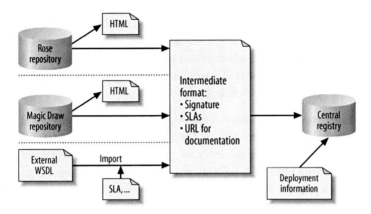

FIGURE 17-2. Possible combination of repositories and a central registry

For services provided by external systems (representing B2B connections), there is an import mechanism that transfers the service descriptions (which usually have the WSDL format) into the intermediate format, adding missing information such as SLAs and URLs to the service documentation.

17.2.2   Establishing Repositories and Registries

Repositories and registries usually evolve over time. As mentioned earlier in this chapter, you don't need them right from the beginning, except if your technical infrastructure requires you to have a registry for loose coupling. Therefore, you might start with no repository, or just a simple Excel worksheet describing your first services.

As your SOA grows, you might think about general ways to design processes and model services. However, it might also happen that different teams, departments, or business units will prefer different ways to design and model services. Synergy is better when everyone uses the same tools, but the organizational effort required might be too high, and dealing with half-working solutions can easily lead to frustration in the business teams. Therefore, a situation like the one shown in Figure 17-2 might easily occur.

There is nothing wrong with this approach. Integrating services later might be an issue, but remember that there will always be some kind of heterogeneity regarding service design, because you're likely to join with other companies and introduce new B2B connections with other companies, which will probably use different tools and processes.

As long as the descriptions of your services are stored in a well-formed fashion (such as using XML files), you should always be able to transfer this information to any other format required or introduced.

Note that tool vendors can provide solutions for repositories and registries. These solutions might integrate repositories and registries, or integrate technical components of the ESB with repositories. In fact, technical solutions for a whole infrastructure, including repositories, might be offered using different terminology than I've used here. This is probably fine, as long as these solutions don't lead you to become too dependent on one vendor. Note that there are no real standards yet, except for the emerging standard of using Web Services to interchange interface information (and Web Services have their flaws, as discussed in Section 16.3). You should also beware of making yourself too dependent on a specific technology, such as Web Services.

Note also that not having a repository at the beginning of a SOA project does not mean that it doesn't make sense to have a clear idea of which aspects and attributes should be defined for services. For this purpose, early on you might define a *meta model* (see Chapter 18). You might even have an XML notation for this meta model right from the beginning (this can play the role of the intermediate format in Figure 17-2). Strictly speaking, a set of files using this notation can be considered as your first service repository. As discussed in Section 18.3, such an approach can be extended as your policies regarding repositories and registries develop and mature.

17.3   Summary

- Repositories and registries help to manage services, both from an organizational and a technical point of view.

- Repositories manage services from a business point of view, dealing with the whole contract but no infrastructure-specific information. Registries manage services from a technical point of view and contain all the information required to deploy and run those services in a specific infrastructure.

- There are multiple aspects to take into account when defining the roles and responsibilities of repositories and registries.

- If you change your infrastructure, you should be able to keep your repository.

- Repositories and registries are not typically needed when you begin establishing a SOA. It is usually fine to introduce them when they become useful or necessary.

CHAPTER EIGHTEEN

Model-Driven Service Development

SERVICE INTERFACES IN HETEROGENEOUS ENVIRONMENTS REQUIRE A LOT OF CODE. MOST OF THIS CODE often has the same structure, differing only according to the different parameters, exceptions, and other configuration data. This is a perfect situation for the application of code generators, or, to use a term that is more hype, *model-driven service development* (MDSD). (The S in MDSD more typically stands for "software," but as we're talking about services here I'll use the alternative "service.") Model-driven service development encompasses code both for the provider and for the consumers.

18.1   Generated Service Code

Because SOA is a concept for heterogeneous environments, you might need a lot of different code to implement and call a service. However, aside from the implementation details, the structure of the code is usually pretty much the same for any given platform. Thus, code for two different services will differ only in the specific data transferred, including aspects such as message exchange patterns (see Chapter 10).

The code that deals with this data conceptually (code to map the middleware protocol to an API, code to deal with security and reliability, and so on) will be pretty much the same. You could use libraries and frameworks to deal with the commonalities, but this approach has limits. Somewhere, the specific behavior of a specific service must come into play, and unless you provide full generic solutions, you'll need code that operates on different attributes and different data types. It makes sense to generate such code based on a given service description.

Code generated for a service might include (but is not limited to):

- Code that provides the framework for implementation details of the service. Its purpose is to provide an API for the service provider so that all common aspects of service implementations are solved and the service implementer can concentrate on the specific business functionality. Such code often is called a *skeleton*, because the generated code is a, well, skeleton that is manually extended with the code of a specific implementation.

- Code that provides the ability to call a service. Its purpose is to provide an API for a service consumer so that it is easy to call a service from a business point of view. All technical details of calling a service (which are required by the ESB) should be covered. Such code often is called a *stub* or a *proxy*.

- Code that allows you to deal with the service inside the infrastructure, such as code for business activity monitoring (see Section 5.4.7).

- Code that provides a framework for tests. For example, the code might provide a very easy and intuitive way to specify different test cases, just using descriptive configuration files.

- Documentation, which is strictly not code but a result of a generator working on a service description. For example, you might generate HTML pages or plain Word files that describe one or all of a system's services.

- Scripts for the processing of generated artifacts during build and deployment.

Figure 18-1 demonstrates a possible MDSD approach. While some teams design their services in a Rational Rose Repository, others use Web Services tools to create initial WSDL files. Because the Rose Repository includes the whole contract, a generator exists to create Word documentation out of it. Both Rose and WSDL can also be transformed into an intermediate format that serves as a base for code generators for specific platforms (Java, C, C++). In addition, some registry code for the ESB is generated, and via the Java code an infrastructure-specific WSDL file is generated.*

---

* For those wondering why WSDL is both input and output, remember that WSDL files have a lifecycle. So, even for the same service, input and output WSDL files might differ. See Section 16.3.3 for details.

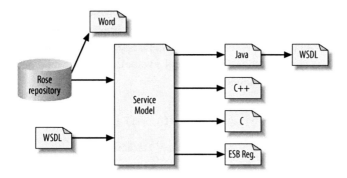

FIGURE 18-1. An example MDSD approach

I don't claim that this is the right process; it's just one example of what a historically grown generation process might look like. In practice, the examples I have seen are much more sophisticated. For example, the platform-specific code generation typically has different modes to control what kind of code is generated (skeletons, stubs, data types, test code, and so on); if the intermediate model specifies which platform will be used to implement a service, skeleton code will be generated only for that platform.

18.2 Modeling Services

The idea of generating code is pretty old. Following the rule "Three Strikes and You Automate" (see [ThreeStrikes]), this is a common mechanism to avoid doing the same work again and again. However, to be a bit more concrete, let's dig deeper into the general concepts of code generation and model-driven software development for services. (For further details on this topic see, for example, [StahlVölter06].)

18.2.1 Terminology

If you compare two hard-coded implementations of a service (or of a service call), you can identify three types of code:

- *Generic code* that is the same for each implementation. For services, this might, for example, be code that logs the service name and processes other common technical data. If it is possible to process parameters in a generic way (using Java reflection, for example), such code also falls into this category.

- *Schematic code* that has the same structure but varies somewhat according to the concrete situation. For example, in order to map all service parameters to an API with specific data types, schematic code would process each parameter using its specific name and type, whereas generic code would loop over the set of all parameters in a generic manner.

- *Code that has no commonalities.* For services, this typically applies to the concrete implementation of the specific functionality of a service.

Frequently, the same task can be performed using either generic code or schematic code. The following example highlights the difference between the implementations. Say you want to log a service name and its parameters. With a generic approach, all input parameters would have the same data type (which has a name and a value), and you would need a loop to log the data. Here's a C++ code example:

```
logName(service.getName( ));
for (int i=0; i<service.getParams( ).getSize( ); ++i) {
    Param param = service.getParam(i);
    logParam (param.getName(), param.getValue( ).asString( ));
}
```

With a schematic approach, you would process each parameter individually while accessing them directly or as members of a data structure:

```
logName("getContractData");
logParam ("contractId", contractId.asString( ));
logParam ("firstName", firstName);
logParam ("lastName", lastName);
logParam ("isActive", isActive ? "true" : "false");
...
```

Both forms have pros and cons. For example, generic code doesn't have to get modified when the number of attributes changes. On the other hand, schematic code might be faster, because it deals with different types at compile time, as well as easier to read and debug. Which solution is preferable depends on the exact circumstances; there is no hard-and-fast rule.

Generic code can usually be part of a framework because it does not have to change for every service instance. In contrast, schematic code is specific to a service instance and has to be generated from a formal description of the service (defining the service name, parameter names, and parameter types). The format of the source can vary; for example, it can be a UML class (see Figure 18-2) or an XML file (see Figure 18-3).

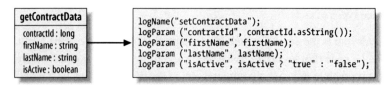

FIGURE 18-2. Generating code out of UML source

Regardless of its format, such a source is called a *model* (because it abstracts implementation details).

Besides the specific notation, a model usually has a specific structure. For example, the preceding figures contain two different notations of a model that allow you to specify a service that has a name as well as different (input and output) parameters that have names and types. The structure of a model is called a *meta model*. In other words, a meta

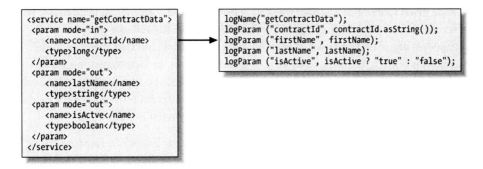

```
<service name="getContractData">            logName("getContractData");
  <param mode="in">                          logParam ("contractId", contractId.asString());
    <name>contractId</name>                  logParam ("firstName", firstName);
    <type>long</type>                        logParam ("lastName", lastName);
  </param>                                    logParam ("isActive", isActive ? "true" : "false");
  <param mode="out">
    <name>lastName</name>
    <type>string</type>
  <param mode="out">
    <name>isActve</name>
    <type>boolean</type>
  </param>
</service>
```

FIGURE 18-3. Generating code out of XML source

model defines the formal structure and elements of a model. It might include formal constraints such as value ranges, but it does not include the semantics. You can decide whether a model is well formed based solely on the meta model, but to generate code from it (or do anything else) you have to know the semantics.

A meta model for the preceding figures might look like Figure 18-4. Using the UML notation, this meta model defines that a service has a name and multiple parameters. Each parameter has a mode ("in" or "out"), a name, and a type to which it refers. Note that only the XML notation in Figure 18-3 defined the mode. The UML notation in Figure 18-2 didn't specify the parameters' modes. In this case, additional information would be required to know whether a parameter is an input or an output parameter.

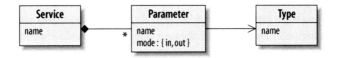

FIGURE 18-4. A trivial meta model

As you have seen, there are very different ways to formulate a model. The concrete notation used to specify a model is called a *modeling language* or *domain-specific language* (DSL). The latter term indicates that the notation used for a model is domain-specific, so the description of a model can concentrate on the essential information. A DSL should be precise, condensed, readable, and complete. As demonstrated in the preceding figures, it can use graphical or textual representations.

NOTE

You can consider the Web Services Description Language (WSDL) as a DSL for Web Services. However, as discussed in Chapter 16, WSDL covers only some aspects of services; it is not complete, so you shouldn't use it to specify all the properties of a service.

The code generated out of a source (model) is usually called a *generation*. In addition, you can transform one model into another model, which is usually called a *transformation*. Some people argue that code is just another form of a model, and that therefore code generation is nothing but a (special) kind of transformation. In fact, some tools for model transformations can also be used for code generation (XSLT, the transformation language for XML files, has this ability). On the other hand, using different terminology for model transformations and code generation might help to clarify what is meant.

Some model-driven approaches distinguish between *platform-independent models* (PIMs) and *platform-specific models* (PSMs). The idea is that the generations might pass through different intermediate formats before the final code is generated, and to some extent the source model is more independent from platform details than the destination model of a model transformation. However, in practice it's difficult to make a black-and-white distinction between PIMs and PSMs, because models are usually specific to *some* platform aspects while independent from other platform aspects.

Note also that transformations are not necessarily bidirectional. Usually you can't (re)generate the source model out of the destination model of a transformation, because the destination usually contains more details overall, but fewer semantic details. Different source models might cause the same result in the destination, and it's impossible to tell which concept was used in the source. For this reason, MDSD usually is not able to perform round-trip processing. That means you can't change the parameters of a service by manipulating the generated source code for a specific platform; you have to modify the source model and generate again. For this reason, it is key that the generation processes and their associated tools are handy and fast. For the same reason, you should generate only as much (schematic) code as is strictly necessary, and provide libraries and frameworks for everything else.

18.2.2 The Model-Driven Tool Chain

The notation (DSL) that you use for your models will impact your choice of tools, because there are specific tools that allow you to operate directly on the abstraction layer of specific notations.

For example, for WSDL (the modeling language for Web Services, which is discussed in Chapter 16) there are special tools that allow you to create WSDL files using special (even graphical) IDEs. While WSDL itself is a textual DSL (using a specific XML schema), these tools allow you to operate on the corresponding abstraction layer of service design via a visual interface instead of using the DSL notation, which is hard to read and maintain. If you prefer, you can also use your favorite text editor or an XML editor. However, using the special editors and IDEs has the advantage that the tools will assist you in keeping the resulting model well formed (i.e., valid according to the meta model). When you use your favorite text editor, it is up to you to ensure validity.

In general, for services very different tools and views can be appropriate. For example, although a graphical model helps to show structures, dependencies, and data flow, it is usually not appropriate for defining signatures. For this reason, a model should not depend on one specific tool. Ideally there is freedom of choice, and developers can use their favorite text editors, spreadsheet tools, UML tools, XML editors, and IDEs. This contributes to acceptance and development performance.

However, be aware that the models the tools operate on are your primary source code. This is the code that defines your system's behavior. For this reason, the usual rules for source code regarding configuration management apply:

- The tools should have very short startup periods so that users can use them to perform small modifications quickly. If starting the tool takes too long, it should at least be possible to run it for the whole day.

- The tool should have an appropriate human-machine interface (HMI), so that a minimal number of actions (clicks, text input, etc.) are required from the user to get the desired behavior.

- The models must be versionable so that you can maintain and distinguish between different versions under development or in production (i.e., different versions of the same code/module, which are not to be confused with different versions of a service from a business point of view). See Chapter 12 for more on versioning.

- The models should support team development, which means that you can merge multiple modifications in the same model, display differences between different models and versions, and navigate directly to a specific part of a model.

Ideally, models should have a notation that allows you to edit them with an ordinary text editor. That is, they should contain readable characters, have a structure that separates different items of information on different lines, contain different levels of indentation, and so on. The advantage of following this guideline is that all configuration-management tools can then work with the models and even perform merges or comparisons.

The more binary and proprietary the modeling notation is, the more restrictions there will be in your development process. For example, if part of your process is a step where all service descriptions are stored in a central repository (see Chapter 17) and its contents are stored in a database, merges and comparisons might become very complicated (if they are not supported by your tool). See the sidebar "Service Modeling with Rational Rose" for another example of using a source code format that introduces some limitations.

SERVICE MODELING WITH RATIONAL ROSE

One pretty old tool for modeling is IBM's Rational Rose. Using a graphical interface, this tool allows you to work on all the different types of UML diagrams, some of which can be used to define services.

However, Rational Rose has some limitations. First, it takes a long time to start up, and the human-machine interface is very limited, which costs development time and can lead to significant acceptance problems (in one project I worked on, loading the model of all services took between 10 and 30 minutes). In addition, it has no real support for merging multiple modifications or showing differences between models. As a consequence, it is not possible for two different people to work on the same model at the same time. These limitations can be worked around by splitting the model into different CAT files, but the principal problem remains. For example, in the previously mentioned project, new services of an upcoming release were modeled in a separate workspace, and when development began they were added manually to the main model. This meant that bugs in the model had to be fixed in all the different releases.

Another problem was that the graphical diagrams were not appropriate for listing the interfaces of different services and service versions in a condensed form, so that inconsistencies and differences between service versions were hard to spot. For this reason, there were a lot more design mistakes than might usually be expected.

To deal with some of the limitations, the company wrote special scripts (using the built-in Visual Basic scripting language) and designed special GUI elements. But, of course, this took a lot of time and effort.

Nevertheless, as a result, the company wound up with a working repository listing several hundred services in a pretty consistent, complete, and platform-independent fashion. This meant that they could easily fulfill all new requirements of certain platforms and infrastructures by modifying or adding corresponding code generators.

18.3   Meta Models in Practice

In practice, it is a good idea to define an initial meta model pretty early on. This meta model should define the different abilities and properties of specified services in your concrete SOA.

A very trivial meta model was shown in Figure 18-4. More practical meta models might, in addition, do the following:

- Provide the ability to group services and service operations. In fact, it is typical to define that a service consists of different service operations (see Section 18.4.8) and to group different services according to different logical or physical categories.

- Define a type system that defines fundamental data types and the way they can be composed (for structures and lists).

- Provide all information required to manage services (e.g., specifying providers and consumers, contracts, SLAs, and so on).

- Distinguish between abstractions and instances of certain kinds of information.

Let's look at a few (still simplified) examples of what a SOA meta model might look like in practice. Figure 18-5 mainly deals with the type system. It specifies that a service interface has a name and one or more operations. An operation might consist of some parameters, a return type, and exceptions (which are a special kind of type). Every type at least has a name, but there are some more complicated types: lists (arrays) have multiple values of the same element type, while structures and exceptions have attributes, which in turn have names and types. (See Section 15.5 for more about data types of services.)

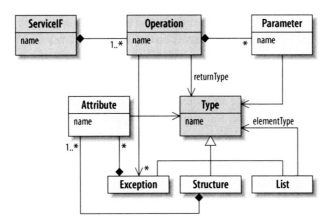

FIGURE 18-5. An example meta model, part 1

In contrast to Figure 18-4, this model defines that a parameter is always an input parameter; there is only one output parameter, which is specified as returnType.

As an example, a concrete model might define a service named CustomerService providing an operation called getCustomerData that has an input parameter contractId of type long and a return type (output parameter) that is a structure of some customer data containing attributes such as firstName and lastName of type string.

Figure 18-6 shows a meta model that represents the relationship between services and systems. First, it distinguishes between a service interface and a service implementation, because there might be multiple implementations of a service interface. Each service implementation is provided by a specific system, which has a name and some contact data. In addition, you can define SLAs that are specified as part of the contract between a specific provider and a specific consumer for a specific service implementation.

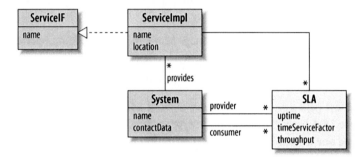

FIGURE 18-6. An example meta model, part 2

In practice, meta models may look quite different from the examples I've shown. For example, you might use other terms, such as service, service instance, or port. You might also divide systems into different components. And if you have requirements such as that services can play different roles and systems can have different instances, things can become really complicated.

To deal with an initial meta model, you don't need very sophisticated tools. At the beginning it is usually enough to have an XML notation for the whole model, from which you generate the corresponding code. Different ways to specify a model can then be transferred into the XML notation. The major benefit of this approach is that it decouples the ways you specify services from transformations to other models and code generation (see Figure 18-7).

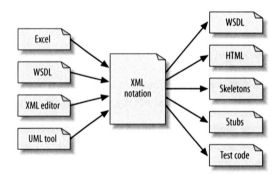

FIGURE 18-7. A meta model notation decouples specifications from generations

If you later introduce different types of service specifications, you only have to provide a way to transfer these specifications into your model notation. If you have modifications in your infrastructure, you only have to define new or modify existing code generators. And if you introduce general repositories and registries (see Chapter 17), you only have to implement a way to read from and write to the model notation to integrate them into your existing system development landscape (see Figure 18-8).

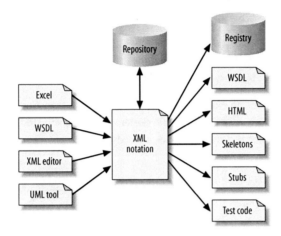

FIGURE 18-8. Integrating repositories and registries into an existing system development landscape

18.4   Setting Up MDSD Processes

Once you've defined which code gets generated out of which model, you might think that your MDSD job is finished. However, an important question remains: who performs transformations and code generations, and when? Conceptually, three different approaches are possible (for simplicity, in the following list and subsequent discussions I use "transformation" as an abbreviation for "model transformation or code generation"):

Consumer-driven transformations
    Those who need the result of a transformation perform it.

Provider-driven transformations
    Those who define the source of a transformation (the source model) perform it.

Third-party-driven transformations
    A separate team performs the transformations.

Let's discuss these approaches in more detail.

18.4.1 Consumer-Driven Transformations

Consumer-driven transformations (where those who need the result of a transformation perform it) are usually the easiest to establish as companywide policies. The consumers only need access to the source (model) and the generator(s). An added benefit is that the consumers have the understanding and the infrastructure to verify the generated result, because the reason they're performing the transformation is that they need the result for their own further processing. However, this approach has some limitations:

- The consumer has to know when a new transformation is necessary. That is, the providers of the source model or of the generator(s) have to inform the consumers when a new transformation is necessary or appropriate.

- There might be a security requirement that a consumer should not see the source model.

- If the transformation is complicated (includes manual steps) or takes a long time, each consumer may have to invest the same significant effort.

Figure 18-9 demonstrates an example of a consumer-driven transformation. The three different providers generate only their specific skeletons for the service implementation, and each consumer generates the stubs/proxies it needs.

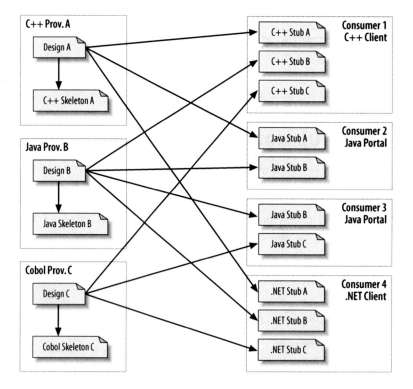

FIGURE 18-9. Consumer-driven transformation

Note that in practice there are more things to generate, and that there can be systems that are both providers and consumers. As a consequence, you might even have cyclic dependencies (for example, if system A calls a service at system B and system B calls a service at system A, which might or might not be a logical response).

18.4.2 Provider-Driven Transformations

Provider-driven transformations (where those who define the source of a transformation perform it) solve the problem of multiple transformations for each consumer. However, they also have some drawbacks:

- Verification of the generated code is difficult (if not impossible), because the provider is generating code for other platforms but is probably only familiar with its own platform.

- Unnecessary transformations might happen.

- If the generators are modified, the provider has to know that a new transformation is necessary.

- If the service interface changes, the consumers have to perform corresponding fixes to avoid breaking the next build.

Figure 18-10 demonstrates what the example in Figure 18-9 would look like if the transformations were provider-driven. All three providers generate both their specific skeletons for the service implementation and all stubs/proxies for possible consumer platforms.

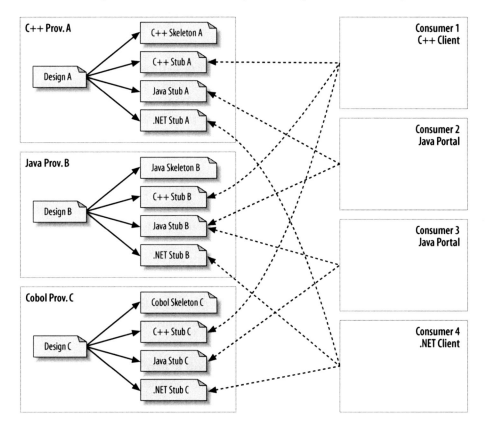

FIGURE 18-10. Provider-driven transformation

Again, note that in practice there are more things to generate, and that there can be systems that are both providers and consumers (possibly with cyclic dependencies).

18.4.3 Third-Party-Driven Transformations

Third-party-driven transformations (where a separate team performs the transformations) are often appropriate when there is a build team that integrates source code from different departments as part of an iterative software development process. The nightly builds might include the necessary code generations. The advantage of this approach is that both source model and generator modifications result in new corresponding code. In addition, the build team should be able to verify the result, because it usually builds the consuming clients that use the generated code. However, this approach also has some drawbacks:

- Consuming systems have to be integrated into the general build process.

- If the service interface changes, the consumers have to perform corresponding fixes to avoid breaking the next build.

- Setting up nightly builds requires effort and time (although this task probably needs to be performed regardless of whether or not you're using this transformation strategy).

18.4.4 MDSD Processes in Practice

In practice, MDSD processes usually involve a mixture of all these approaches. There is no perfect transformation policy. Instead, you have to decide on a case-by-case basis on the corresponding policy to set up the necessary processes. Transformation processes might even be split into two different steps, so that, for example, a service provider generates an intermediate WSDL file that the consumer then uses to generate its platform-specific code.

18.4.5 Labeling

Whatever your process looks like, there is one important thing to consider: in large teams, you need configuration-management support so that you can deal with different versions of the same models and generated artifacts (one version in production, one under test, one under development, and so on).

For this reason, you have to be able to identify all the different artifacts (models, generated code, hand-written code deployment information, and so on) that belong together. Because transformations and generations take time (both technically and organization-ally), you need a very clear way to identify which transformation result (code or model) belongs to which transformation source (model).

That is, a service description that's part of a model needs to have the same (or a corre-sponding) label as the code generated for it. Both should also have the same label as the deployment information added when the code gets deployed into a test or production environment. Ideally, you should be able to identify all the related artifacts with one label or a set of corresponding labels.

Note that in practice labeling should also include the result of a transformation. You might think that this is not necessary, because you can generate the result again out of the labeled source model. However, because generations take time and might happen at different times than modifications of the source model, you need a way to retrieve generated artifacts fast and to know which generated code belongs to which source model.

Alternatively, instead of labeling the results, you might label the generators to provide traceability for all artifacts. This may be a good idea when the generator is a short script or a bunch of configuration files, but labeling and maintaining different versions of complex generators has its limits. Strictly speaking, you might even have to label the operating system the generator uses, because it might influence its behavior. Labeling the result is far easier (and often required anyway, because the result is part of a configuration for further processing).

18.4.6 Debugging

When you generate code, you usually change the abstraction layer. Instead of having one row or entity for each parameter inside the model, you generate code that has many lines that logically operate on each parameter. Now, when you debug your software, you don't step through it step-by-step. For this reason, it is key that the generated code is well formed and readable. This includes generating comments that explain what's happening. Without them, only the implementer of the generator will be able to debug the generated code.

Far too often, concrete code-generation policies are exactly the opposite of what is useful: generators create very condensed code, using no empty lines or comments because readability is not considered to be an issue (the assumption is that once the code is generated, nobody should need to read or maintain it). But even people who implement generators make mistakes, and it's important to be able to follow the data flow of all software (unless code generation includes a form of encryption ;-)).

The only excuse for not having well-structured generated code is when the debuggers operate on the same abstraction layer as the modeling language. BPEL engines (see Section 7.4.2) are good examples of this approach. Most BPEL IDEs that allow you to graphically create high-level services and business processes also provide BPEL engines with visual interfaces, so you can see the state of a process or service at runtime at the same level of abstraction as in the IDE.

18.4.7 Manually Modified Generated Code

Sometimes it is necessary to modify generated code by hand. A skeleton, for example, will contain generated functions or methods whose bodies must be implemented by a programmer. As a result, the file will contain both generated and manually created code.

Initially, this is not a problem. Typically you generate skeleton code only once, so there is no risk of the handwritten modifications being overwritten by a future generation. But what happens when the generated code has to be changed due to a modification of the source model? You have to regenerate the skeleton code, but of course you don't want to lose your hand-coded extensions.

There are many approaches to deal with this problem:

Use different files

> The best approach is to try to organize the generated code in such a way that code provided for modification is physically separated from code that is completely generated. For example, you might generate a base class containing all code not allowed to be modified or containing default behavior and a derived class where you can add hand-coded extensions or modifications.

Use protected areas

> Another typical approach is to use "protected areas" (sometimes also called "protected regions" or "protected zones"). Inside the generated code, you mark the beginning and end of each protected area, indicating where manual modifications are allowed:

```
class
package ...;
public interface CustomerService extends ... {
    public static public java.lang.String getServiceName( ) {
        return "CustomerService";
    }

    public void changeAddress (Address newAddress) {
      //==> Begin Protected Area CustomerService.changeAddress

      //==> End Protected Area CustomerService.changeAddress
    }
    ...
}
```

> Future generations of the skeleton code will update only the code outside of these protected areas; the manually written code inside these areas will remain as it is. Of course, there are limitations to this approach when complicated modifications are made, but for minor modifications it works because you usually identify each protected area with a unique ID that corresponds to a specific item of the source model (of course, this means your model must support these IDs).

Generate once

> A third approach is to avoid regenerating the skeleton code. With this approach, you generate only the first version of the code, which can be manually modified. Any future modifications of the generated code (in accordance with corresponding modifications of the model) must be made by hand. Ideally, necessary changes will be evident because the code won't work or compile. However, you have to understand the impact of all model modifications on generated code.

> In a sense this is similar to the first approach, where you also separate out the code for manual updates, which is generated once (or never).

Merge generated and manual code

I have also seen an approach that tries to merge modifications of the skeleton code with manual extensions using a configuration-management tool's merge tool.

For example, you might have two different versioning branches, one for the generated code and one for the manually extended generated code. When a new version of the skeleton code gets generated, you add it to the skeleton branch and then merge this modification with the branch for the manually extended generated code. You can use this policy for both automatic and manual merges. Of course, how well it works depends on the quality of the merge tool.

None of these approaches is perfect, and you'll have to figure out which one is best for your particular situation. Note that all of the approaches share an important goal: to minimize and isolate manual modifications as much as possible. That is, when it is possible to split generated and handwritten code into different files, do it. Every such split will enhance maintainability.

18.4.8 The Code-Generation Granularity Dilemma

Because services should be self-contained, it is usually a good idea to have separate files for each service. In addition, it might help when the artifacts generated from these files are separated accordingly. This helps to isolate necessary generations when source files change.

Consider, for example, if the result of a code generation for two different services specified in two different WSDL files were *one* Java or C++ file. In this case, any modification of one of these two services will create a new version of the generated file. This creates the risk that a faulty generation due to one service change will bring down both services. In addition, to remove one of the services you have to remove its code from the generated file, instead of just removing a corresponding generated file. Finally, you can't easily perform further processing with only one of the services.

Separating the code for different services is clearly a good idea. In addition, you might want to separate:

• Code for different platforms

• Skeleton from stub code

• Declarations and interfaces from implementations

Following this advice, model-driven processes can easily result in the generation of hundreds or thousands of files. One company I know of creates up to 80 files for each service:

• Skeleton, stub, and test code is created for each platform, as well as a dummy implementation plus common interface files for some of these files.

• A file is created for each data type used in the service.

- Build files (such as makefiles) are generated.

- Additional files may be created for the C++ platform, because the code is separated into header and definition files.

This high number of files, of course, has some drawbacks. It's hard to understand the code organization, and a lot of files must be processed when creating, deploying, and running code. This takes a lot of time (both at compile time and runtime) and space.

Finding the right granularity is not easy. What helps is a good organization of the code, so that your directory structure matches your process structure. This is one reason to separate the sources and results of transformations into different directories. (The other, even more important reason for this separation is that you should be able to see the difference between the source and destination files, so that you can delete the result of a particular generation by deleting the corresponding destination directory.)

18.4.9 Deployment and Robustness

As I've stated throughout this book, SOA is a concept for supporting systems with different owners. Usually, you can't guarantee that all service participants (providers and consumers) will deploy modifications at the same time. Each system may have its own (model-driven) software development process, so it may take varying amounts of time for modifications to be made (see Figure 18-11).

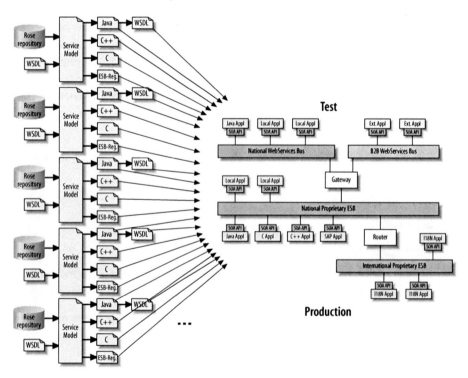

FIGURE 18-11. Many different systems deploying corresponding data

This consideration has two important consequences:

- An enterprise service bus, at least in a test environment, must be able to deal with inconsistencies. If a provider modifies a service under development and deploys it, this should not lead to a situation where all of this provider's services do not work anymore, or where a consumer that uses this service can't call other services where the interfaces still match. That is, it must be possible for the interfaces of an ESB to temporarily not match. This situation, of course, should result in runtime exceptions when a service without a matching interface gets called.

- It is almost impossible to make backward-incompatible modifications that impact *all* services. This includes backward-incompatible modifications of the meta model or of fundamental data types (which might or might not be part of the meta model). For this reason, fundamental data types should be very, very stable (see Section 15.5.1 for more on this topic). In addition to types such as strings, integers, Booleans, and floats, you should be very careful when dealing with other types as common fundamental data types. Be aware that a change such as introducing time zone semantics into a fundamental date type might break the whole system.

18.5 Tools

So far I haven't discussed tools for model-driven development. Because nowadays, almost every modeling language uses XML-based formats, one tool for transformations and/or code generations might be obvious: *eXtensible Stylesheet Language Transformations*, or *XSLT*. XSLT, however, has some limitations, which I will discuss next. I'll then present an alternative.

18.5.1 XSLT

With XSLT, an XSLT processor transforms one or more XML files into one or more result files, which might be in XML or any other text form. The transformations are defined by one or more XSLT stylesheet files. These files provide templates for the resulting code, spiced with control structures to iterate over input tokens and placeholders to fill in certain data derived from the source files (see Figure 18-12).

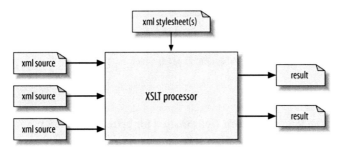

FIGURE 18-12. *XSLT transformations*

For example, say you had the following service description:

```
<service name="getContractData">
  <param mode="in">
    <name>contractId</name>
    <type>long</type>
  </param>
  <param mode="out">
    <name>firstName</name>
    <type>string</type>
  </param>
  <param mode="out">
    <name>lastName</name>
    <type>string</type>
  </param>
  <param mode="out">
    <name>isActive</name>
    <type>boolean</type>
  </param>
</service>
```

A transformation according to the following stylesheet:

```
<?xml version="1.0" encoding="UTF-8"?>
<xsl:stylesheet xmlns:xsl="http://www.w3.org/1999/XSL/Transform" version="1.0">

<xsl:template match="/service">
  <html xmlns="http://www.w3.org/1999/xhtml">
  <head> <title><xsl:value-of select="@name"/>( )</title> </head>
  <body>
    <h1>Service: <xsl:value-of select="@name"/>( )</h1>
    Parameters (sorted):
    <table border="1">
      <tr><td><b>Name</b></td><td><b>Type</b></td>
          <td><b>Mode</b></td></tr>
      <xsl:apply-templates select="param">
        <xsl:sort select="name" />
      </xsl:apply-templates>
    </table>
  </body>
  </html>
</xsl:template>

<xsl:template match="param">
  <tr><td><xsl:value-of select="name"/></td>
      <td><xsl:value-of select="type"/></td
      <td><xsl:value-of select="@mode"/></td></tr>
</xsl:template>

</xsl:stylesheet>
```

would produce the following result (reformatted for better readability):

```
<?xml version="1.0" encoding="UTF-8"?>
<html xmlns="http://www.w3.org/1999/xhtml">
<head> <title>getContractData( )</title> </head>
<body>
```

```
<h1>Service: getContractData( )</h1>
Parameters (sorted):
<table border="1">
  <tr><td><b>Name</b></td><td><b>Type</b></td>
      <td><b>Mode</b></td></tr>
  <tr><td>contractId</td><td>long</td><td>in</td></tr>
  <tr><td>firstName</td><td>string</td><td>out</td></tr>
  <tr><td>isActive</td><td>boolean</td><td>out</td></tr>
  <tr><td>lastName</td><td>string</td><td>out</td></tr>
</table>
</body>
</html>
```

which is an HTML page for the service described in the source model (see Figure 18-13 for a possible screen dump).

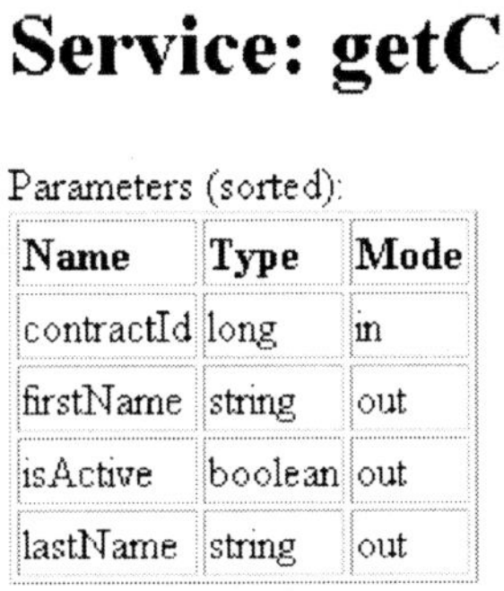

Service: getContractData()

Parameters (sorted):

Name	Type	Mode
contractId	long	in
firstName	string	out
isActive	boolean	out
lastName	string	out

FIGURE 18-13. Possible screen dump for the generated HTML output

XSLT transformations work fine for simple code generations and code transformations. However, experience has shown that they are not ideal for more complicated transformations (such as model transformations and code generations for many files), for the following reasons:

- Stylesheet templates with the transformation rules are hard to read.

- XSLT is not designed for reading complicated data models out of many files and generating hundreds of different results.

- XSLT has no clear separation between reading the input and generating the output. So, often you need XSLT transformations for each combination of a source model and a destination model (or generated code).

- XSLT is difficult to extend with special processing that occurs in many places.

- XSLT is relatively slow.

- XSLT only processes XML input.

XSLT does work, though, and I have seen environments dealing with thousands of files using XSLT (despite some frustration caused by the problems just mentioned).

18.5.2 MDSD Tools

Better alternatives are special tools provided for code generation and/or model transformations, some of which are open source. For example, in one large project we switched from XSLT to a tool called openArchitectureWare (see [oAW]), which resulted in a remarkable improvement in the code generations. The generator code was a lot more maintainable, and generations took significantly less time.

As I wrote in Section 18.3, when setting up an infrastructure for model-driven service development you should ideally start with an initial platform-independent meta model with at least one domain-specific language, such as an XML notation. But how do you create such a model notation for a service, and how do you transfer your model into other models or code? To create a service description using the XML model notation, you can either use a scripting language built into your modeling tool (such as Visual Basic for Rational Rose or Excel), or use a tool such as openArchitectureWare that reads tool-specific output (such as XMI) or specific input formats (such as WSDL) to read a model and write it in XML notation. For the code generation, you can then read the XML notation and create whatever artifact you need.

18.6 Avoiding Bottlenecks

Finally, I'd like to again note that in order to scale, large systems have to avoid technical and organizational bottlenecks. That means whatever you set up as your process, you should avoid tools, process steps, and artifacts that are singletons (i.e., that exist once for the whole system). Don't introduce a model master who has to accept each change before it gets processed (although this does not mean that it doesn't make sense to check modifications independently from the development process). Also, it should be possible to perform all the transformations offline, without being connected to the whole SOA system.

18.7 Summary

- Model-driven service development (MDSD) is a perfect way to generate all necessary service code (including implementation skeletons, call stubs/proxies, test code, and documentation).

- Source models should fulfill all the usual requirements of source code.

- Modeling tools should fulfill all the usual requirements of source code editors.

- You should define your own meta model independent from your specific infrastructure and use a corresponding XML notation to decouple service specifications from generation of infrastructure-specific code and other artifacts.

- It is not enough to provide all the necessary generators. Setting up appropriate processes (defining who generates what, and when) is also part of MDSD.

- It's important to be able to correlate artifacts that belong to the same version of software, even if they are generated (or created) by very different people and at very different times.

- An enterprise service bus should be able to deal with the fact that not all corresponding updates get deployed at the same time.

- XSLT is one, but not necessarily the best, way to generate code. While it works well for transferring small XML files into other formats, XSLT's limitations become apparent when dealing with complex models, complex transformations, and many files.

CHAPTER NINETEEN

Establishing SOA and SOA Governance

SOA IS A STRATEGY. YOU HAVE TO INTRODUCE IT INTO YOUR ENTERPRISE AND ORGANIZATION(S) gradually. This takes time, and as a fully developed SOA requires a lot of modifications and extensions (both technical and organizational), you can't have it all at once. So, how do you get started, and how do you ensure that things go right?

This chapter discusses establishing/implementing SOA, including the topic of "SOA governance." This term is commonly used to describe all you have to do to ensure that a SOA strategy is successful.

19.1   Introducing SOA

As you've seen throughout this book, SOA is a strategy that includes both technical and organizational aspects. Technically, you need some infrastructure (the ESB) to provide interoperability. Organizationally, you need appropriate processes so that it is clear how to design new solutions and identify new services (see Chapter 7), live the service lifecycle (see Chapter 11), and set up corresponding software development processes (e.g., model-driven development, discussed in Chapter 18) and appropriate organizational structures (see Chapter 8).

You also have to make a lot of architectural decisions, such as defining your service data, programming model, and meta model; selecting message exchange patterns; categorizing services; deciding whether the ESB should be protocol- or API-driven; and so on.

All of these aspects influence each other and are influenced by your business and organization. For this reason, two things are clear:

- You can't buy SOA. That is, you can't just buy some particular products (which might inherently make a lot of the architectural decisions and require some specific processes) and put them to use in your organization.

- You can't make all the decisions up front.

The only appropriate approach for introducing SOA is to let it grow, step-by-step. As written in [Spanyi03]:

> Business process performance relies increasingly on enabling technology and process automation. Again it takes iterative work to put this principle into action.

19.2   SOA Governance

Among the SOA hype, recently there have been a lot of articles and recommendations about the need for governance when introducing SOA. For example, Paolo Malinverno, Research VP of Gartner, wrote in [Gartner06]:

> Service-Oriented Architecture governance isn't an option—it's an imperative. The bigger the SOA is, the more governance it needs, and the more complex the governance roles and mechanisms must be. Governance arrangements take a long time to design and install, and are difficult to enforce, but without them, every SOA project out of pilot phase is at risk.

But what exactly does "SOA governance" mean, and who is responsible for it? I will discuss these questions in the following subsections.

19.2.1   Definition of Governance

Regarding the question of what governance in general and SOA governance in particular mean, I like the simple definition Anne Thomas Manes gave at OOP 2007 (see [Manes07]). According to her, governance is:

> Making sure that people do what's "right."

She also gives the supplementary and slightly more concrete hint that governance means:

> Controlling the development and operation of software.

From this point of view, it is always an imperative to have governance. Otherwise, the risk of chaos and/or wasting money and resources is far too high.

Let's try to find a bit more detail about what it means to govern SOA. That is, how do you make sure that people "do what's 'right'" regarding SOA?

In [Manes07], Manes defines the following governance basics:

- *Policies* define what's right.
- *Processes* enforce policies.
- *Metrics* provide visibility and verify policy enforcements.
- *Organization* must establish a culture that supports the governance process.

Of course, there are a lot of other definitions of governance, and trying to formulate a complete list of the issues involved would be almost impossible. However, there is no doubt that SOA governance primarily focuses on nontechnical aspects. Pinning down technical details about the infrastructure (ESB) and tools such as repositories is necessary, but it's worthless if you don't know why to use them, when to use them, and who should use them.

Based on my experience, I usually define SOA governance as a task that deals with the following nontechnical issues:

Visions, objectives, business case, and funding model
> Laying out visions, objectives, and the business case is important in order to answer the question of why to introduce SOA. It's also important to decide on a funding model (see Section 8.2) that determines how the initial overhead of introducing SOA and new services will be paid for.

Reference architecture(s)
> You need a reference that demonstrates your fundamental architectural decisions, including your preferred technology, message exchange patterns, meta model, and so on.

Roles and responsibilities
> You need to define roles and responsibilities to make it clear who drives and cares about the issues. For example, you must clarify who makes architectural SOA decisions, where the responsibility of the ESB ends, and who is in charge of making high-level solution designs that identify new services.

Policies, standards, and formats
> Architectural decisions, artifacts, and technologies lead to policies and requirements, which should be defined using standards and proprietary formats.

Processes and lifecycles
> Along with roles, responsibilities, and policies, you have to define processes and lifecycles for solutions, services, and so on.

In what order should you deal with these issues? While you should always have a vision and an objective to start new things, a reference architecture derived from a first pilot project is a good starting point for introducing SOA. Roles and responsibilities should also be clarified early on. Laying these out together with the objectives will help bring about the supportive organizational culture mentioned earlier. Policies and processes evolve over time and tend to come last (which does not mean that they are less important than other factors for the successful implementation of an enterprise-wide SOA strategy).

THERE IS ALWAYS MORE THAN ONE PROCESS

Although a lot of organizations put a lot of money and effort into defining enterprise-wide processes, thus far in all the companies I've seen these processes are hardly being realized. What I'm seeing instead—and this is true for organizations in completely different domains—is that there are actually three processes in existence:

- First of all, there is the *official process*, often called the enterprise-wide process, which is all too often just not implemented. Most of the time the developers know about this process, but they admit that they have never actually used it on a project. Sometimes it is even worse, and the developers are not even aware of this process.

- Second, there is the *perceived process*, which is the one everyone believes is the one that is being used. Occasionally it happens that the perceived process is the same as the official one, but this is rare. Most often the perceived process is "created" by wishful thinking and misperceptions.

- Third, there is the *actual process*. This is the one that is actually applied, and therefore the one that is really fulfilling its task.

As I mentioned in [Eckstein04], "The important thing to understand is that only the actual process plays a role in practice. All the others exist only theoretically."

Therefore, it is essential to find out which process is actually producing value, and then to make that process explicit. Making the actual process explicit helps in two ways: on the one hand it simplifies the integration of new people into the team, and on the other hand it allows the actual process to be improved in a controlled way. Even if you make the actual process explicit, you have to be aware that each process has a limited lifetime. If people learn a new approach that supports them better, they will make the switch; this will (again) leave you with an unused process, but with a more effective team. Thus, just as you make the actual process explicit, you should explicitly let the teams inspect the process from time to time and reflect on possible improvements. Via these regular inspections and reflections (in the agile world, these are called "retrospectives"), the teams will frequently update the actual (and now hopefully as well the official) process. This of course, means that the official process has to be flexible enough to allow frequent updates.

—Jutta Eckstein

Besides the nontechnical aspects, there are technical governance aspects that, in practice, help to support the nontechnical issues. Technical aspects of governance include:

Documentation
> Documentation plays an important role for *transparency*. That is, it helps to promote all the nontechnical issues of governance (processes, responsibilities, policies, and so on).

Service management
> For the management of services and service contracts, tools like repositories and registries might help.

Monitoring
> Monitoring is an essential task to verify rules, policies, contracts, etc. For example, you might monitor for SLA violations or monitor usage so you can withdraw services that are no longer in use.

Change and configuration management
> The usual configuration-management tools can also help to manage SOA software, SOA artifacts, and SOA documentation.

For these technical aspects of governance, special SOA tools such as repositories (see Chapter 17) and general tools such as configuration-management and monitoring tools usually can help. As a consequence, it is no surprise that tool vendors tend to focus on these technical aspects of SOA governance. Be aware, however, that there is much more to SOA governance than the items mentioned in this list.

19.2.2 Central SOA Teams

For governance, you need people to govern. That is, you need a bunch of people who can pull the strings and coordinate all the steps of implementing the SOA landscape and strategy. Usually, there is a central team responsible for establishing and governing SOA. Such a team may be called a *SOA Competency Center* (SCC), a *SOA Center of Excellence* (SCoE), or an *Integration Competency Center* (ICC), and it might be steered by a *SOA board* or *SOA steering committee* that founds, controls, and decides on the SOA strategy as a whole. This is where the operational aspects of establishing and living SOA come together.

Throughout the rest of this chapter, I will use the acronym *SCC* to refer to the team governing SOA.

The SCC coordinates, consolidates, standardizes, and to some extent even controls the whole SOA strategy, and expertise and pragmatism are required to perform these tasks. Conceptually, the SCC operates centrally. However, don't fall into the trap of establishing a new ivory tower of centralized control.

The SCC should be a virtual team made up of all the different drivers mentioned earlier: developers, business experts, and IT experts. However, bear in mind that establishing SOA is a big task. Once you have brought these experts together, you must ensure that they are given enough time and other resources to solve the tasks involved in establishing and governing SOA.

Between the lines, you might already have read my major message here: introducing and establishing SOA is a task that must be handled appropriately. Far too often, I have seen this task allocated to the wrong people. Introducing services necessitates service-oriented thinking, and the same goes for those establishing and governing SOA.

To support service-oriented thinking, the central team must have enough time to go to the individual business teams and actively help them to use and live SOA. I've had good experiences where the people performing the first pilot project have become "foster parents" for the business teams when the SOA strategy grows. This is one major reason why sufficient resources are required.

Note that an interesting mental experience for the people in the SCC is that, in a sense, they have to aim to make themselves unnecessary. Why? Scalability is key for SOA, but centralization leads to bottlenecks. Such bottlenecks must be avoided. If a provider and a consumer want to exchange data, this has to be a bilateral or multilateral process. Although some central decisions must be made, centralization must be minimized for the day-to-day work. This means that, in theory, if the SCC does its job well it shouldn't be needed any longer. In reality, this never happens because requirements and contexts change and perfectionism is too expensive. Still, the important thing is to have the right mental attitude.

19.3   SOA Step-by-Step

Now let's go into a bit more detail and discuss a possible way to introduce SOA. Be aware that this is just *one* possibility; it is more an example of an iterative establishment process than a guideline for how to adopt SOA. However, it might give you some ideas for how to find your own appropriate procedure.

19.3.1 Step 1: Understand SOA

A necessary first step for introducing SOA is to understand it. SOA is hype, and therefore a lot of stupid things are said about it. Don't introduce SOA because your major business analyst recommends that you do so; do it because *you* see the benefit. Unfortunately, the benefit is not always easy to see. Learning about the differences between small and large systems and between central and distributed control is key (see Chapters 1 and 4, for example).

In addition, before you begin down this path, it's crucial that your management accepts that SOA is a strategy, not an out-of-the-box solution, and knows about the possible consequences of implementing this strategy (especially what it means to have distributed processing; see Chapter 8). Of course, on a management level, you can't necessarily discuss the details of versioning and idempotency. However, it's important that the concept of loose coupling and its consequences be understood.

Another important message is that SOA is not a silver bullet for any kind of system integration: rather, it is a concept for dealing with distributed business processes. Database replication and decoupling frontends from backends are different tasks entirely (although they might use the same patterns and/or technologies).

19.3.2 Step 2: The SOA Pilot

The second step in introducing SOA is usually to try it out. That means you perform a test project that has the goal of bringing into production some functionality that includes some business processing over two or three different systems. Note that this is more than just a prototype. SOA prototypes often suffer from the problem that up to a certain level of complexity the effort required is low and things look fine, but when this level of complexity is surpassed, the effort required suddenly begins to increase much faster than the benefit you gain, until finally things collapse (this is known as the "hockey stick function," introduced at the beginning of Chapter 1).

In this initial project, you will mainly concentrate on technical and architectural decisions. However, it should be driven by business needs. That means the team realizing this pilot should be a mixture of business people and IT people from both the SCC and the business teams.

Be careful with the initial stage of expansion of your SOA landscape. Here are some general guidelines to follow:

- Use only basic services, which means that you start with a fundamental SOA (see Section 6.2).

- Use only one or two message exchange patterns (MEPs). I recommend starting with the synchronous or asynchronous request/response pattern (see Sections 10.2.1 and 10.3.1).

- Define a minimal set of fundamental data types and language constructs to aggregate them (see Section 15.5).

- Choose the middleware technology for your ESB (e.g., Web Services; see Chapter 16).

- Decide about the amount of loose coupling (see Chapter 4). Be conservative here, and watch out for the YAGNI (You Ain't Gonna Need It) principle.

- Think about the amount of security and maintainability you want to provide now and later. Note that I say *think*, which means that you should have these topics in mind even if you don't necessarily realize them in the first pilot ("think big, start small").

The most important focus (besides running the software) should be on providing excellent interfaces between the ESB and the business. You don't have to decide about processes here. First you need working software, then you can see how to create, generate, or implement it in a distributed software development process.

The development of the pilot project itself, of course, should also be an iterative and incremental process, which might include a prototype, a first solution, and a consolidated solution.

From a business point of view, you can't start with a very complicated composed or process service. The aim of this approach is to provide some typical backend functionality with the new SOA infrastructure—maybe you'll replace some existing remote database access with a service. The implemented functionality should have some relevance to the business. Although it would probably be too risky for it to be mission-critical for the company, implementing some useful needed functionality will help focus the SOA approach on pragmatism and usability.

Note that the first solution will not be stable even after it is realized. As later steps are carried out, you will have to refactor it. For this reason, this pilot project should not include code that is part of a fixed-price contract, where you have to commission each little modification.

19.3.3 Step 3: The Second and Third SOA Projects

The second and third projects are very important phases in introducing SOA. Here, you'll start to think about all the important things that lead to synergy effects. Considering the reusability of services, setting up processes for different teams, finding the right balance between centralization and decentralization, and finding the right compromise between theory or concepts and practice all become important.

As more and more projects are introduced, the general approach of multiproject management also comes into play. Figure 19-1 demonstrates this regarding the common infrastructure of three pilots.* The first pilot grows with the infrastructure. The second and third pilots are based on the previous experiences, decisions, and implementation but need and add new features that have an impact on the general infrastructure. As a result, the initial infrastructure changes.

Note that these changes will not just be new feature additions. The majority of the changes will be updates based on consolidations and generalizations. Useful interfaces, processes, and policies evolve by as you use and live with them.

What the Extreme Programming community calls the "Three Strikes" pattern (see [ThreeStrikes]) applies here: whenever some effort is duplicated for the third time, you should do something to automate the process. Note, however, that there are two types of duplication:

- If you do the same thing *at three different times,* you automate it. This is known as the "Three Strikes and You Automate" pattern. This automation leads to more and better model-driven development (see Chapter 18).

---

* This figure is, with friendly permission by the authors, based on Figure 12-7 of [KrafzigBankeSlama04].

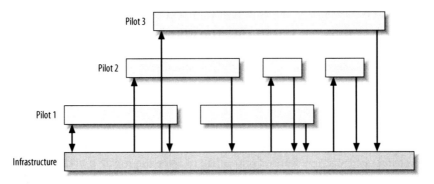

Pilot 3

Pilot 2

Pilot 1

Infrastructure

FIGURE 19-1. Dependencies between the infrastructure and multiple projects

- If you do the same thing *in three different places*, you refactor your code. This is known as the "Three Strikes and You Refactor" pattern. These refactorings lead to changed interfaces, policies, and processes.

Optimizing to avoid doing things repeatedly is the best approach for achieving excellence. The drawback is that you don't have that excellence from the beginning. However, note that the usual programming model in large projects is based on a "copy-and-paste" approach. For this reason, to benefit from improvements, you have to refactor pilot projects that are already finished. Otherwise, people will copy from old, deprecated code and APIs. Refactorings of finished projects require resources, but because implementing SOA is an investment, corresponding resources should be available as part of the SOA strategy.

The "Three Strikes" pattern doesn't just apply to infrastructure aspects. You can replace the word "infrastructure" in Figure 19-1 with "process," "lifecycle," "policies," "architecture," and so on. The important message is that SOA aspects evolve over time, which means that you'd better have the resources to modify existing practices and code in order to achieve better consistency, better maintainability, and (last but not least) better master copies.

19.3.4 Step 4: Grow and Become a General Strategy

Over time, SOA will become a general strategy of your enterprise. Sooner or later, you will have to begin managing your SOA. Repositories (see Chapter 17) will help to manage services and service contracts, and business activity monitoring (see Section 5.4.7) will enable your company to rapidly detect business opportunities and challenges.

It is key at this stage that the usual way to establish new business functionality be completely decentralized and as automated as possible. To achieve this goal, the central service teams will have to do a lot of homework. Again, this requires resources. Don't stop strategic SOA support here.

Although with increasing size, the aspects of your SOA strategy will become more and more stable, there are always new requirements to deal with. These might be technical ("Should we switch to the new protocol standard?") or business-driven ("How do we establish a B2B connection that uses a slightly different protocol?"). It is key here that modifications of the SOA platform and processes be business-driven. Service infrastructures should serve business teams.

In one project I worked on, there was a regular meeting where the different business and infrastructure teams came together to discuss modifications of the SOA infrastructure. If a business team needed a new feature, others had to agree to provide it in the infrastructure. If some effort was required of the different business teams, this helped them to think about the business case for each new improvement. The infrastructure teams themselves could suggest improvements, but the business teams had to accept them to avoid the ivory-tower effect. Of course, this approach requires collaboration and requires that business teams be able and willing to accept work even if they don't benefit directly. As discussed in Section 8.1.3, profit-center approaches and fiefdoms are counterproductive here. All units have to, to some extent, be able to think as a whole company.

19.3.5 Tasks Necessary over All Steps

There are some necessary tasks that cover and grow over all the steps presented here. The most important are documentation and reviews.

There should always be some kind of documentation about the current SOA landscape. This should include the "five most important slides" that explain the concept and major decisions (like the ones I presented in Section 1.5, but usually more concrete). In addition, documentation and slides should exist that introduce the subject to each person involved in the project and explain that all these people have to know to understand their roles and tasks. This documentation should include walkthroughs and cookbooks. However, note that the documentation should not be very voluminous. Nobody reads 1,000-page documents. The important task here (for which some effort is required) is to provide clear, accurate, condensed, and complete documentation.

In addition, I recommend providing time for reviews and retrospectives. A review looks at what you have, whether it is appropriate, what you need, and what you should do next. It can be done internally or externally. Note that internal reviews do not necessarily have to involve experts reviewing novices or ordinary programmers. Reversing the review hierarchy is also important, because it ensures that experts provide appropriate and understandable concepts. External reviews, of course, help ensure that mistakes made in previous projects aren't made again. In addition, even experts sometimes fall into the trap of stewing in their own juices. External reviews deal with this risk.

Retrospectives are reviews on a meta level. That is, they deal with the people and processes involved in fulfilling a task. While a review examines, for example, whether the right technology is being used, a retrospective examines whether the way of choosing the right technology is appropriate.

Both reviews and retrospectives are very important for strategic projects. Making the wrong decisions and choosing inappropriate processes to establish new technologies and concepts can cost an incredible amount of money and introduce big risks. Note that this means that it's not just system architects and programmers who should be involved in reviews and retrospectives; because SOA is a strategy that has an impact on organizations as a whole, all people and "stakeholders" involved should be included.

19.4 Other SOA Approaches

We've just looked at one possible way to introduce SOA, but now I want to mention some other approaches and recommendations I've found in other sources. Of course, this list is neither complete nor perfect. You'll have to find your own appropriate way of establishing SOA, but these examples and views might help.

19.4.1 The "Four Ps," by Pulier and Taylor

[PulierTaylor06] recommends the "four Ps" best practice for the initial steps: people, pilot, plan, and proceed. I like this idea, although I give the elements slightly modified meanings:

- All *people* have to learn about the principles of SOA and their associated technologies.
- A *pilot* project helps to prove the concept.
- A flexible multiphased project *plan* will help to integrate and validate the SOA strategy in a day-to-day business.
- Based on the first three Ps, you *proceed* by establishing SOA via actual developments.

19.4.2 Architectural Roadmap, by Krafzig, Banke, and Slama

In [KrafzigBankeSlama04], the authors define an architectural roadmap with three expansion stages:

- Fundamental SOA (SOA with basic services only)
- Networked SOA (SOA with composed/orchestrated services)
- Process-enabled SOA (SOA with process services)

See Chapter 6 for details.

19.4.3 Top-Down or Bottom-Up, by Krafzig and Slama

In [KrafzigSlama07], the authors discuss different approaches for implementing and governing SOA.[*] A bottom-up approach (see Figure 19-2) starts with a small group of SOA enthusiasts, develops more and more successful projects, and ends with an enterprise-wide rollout.

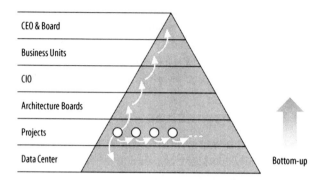

FIGURE 19-2. Bottom-up approach of implementing SOA

An (idealized) top-down approach (see Figure 19-3) is initiated by the top management. Objectives are defined, the business case is calculated, and funding is obtained. Then the SOA strategy is established (including setting up the architecture, organizational structures, and infrastructure). Finally, SOA projects are begun.

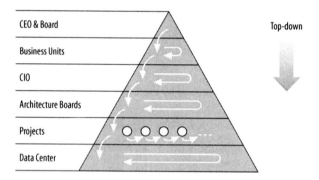

FIGURE 19-3. Top-down approach of implementing SOA

The constraint "idealized" hints that this approach almost never works in practice (remember that decentralization and different owners are properties of large distributed systems). To some extent you need both central resources *and* support from upper management, so that, for example, supporting organizational reorganizations are performed.

---

[*] The figures of the bottom-up and top-down approach of implementing SOA are published with friendly permission from Dirk Krafzig and Dirk Slama, BusinessGlue GmbH, Germany.

As a result, often a combined bottom-up and top-down approach (which might be called a "middle-ground" approach) is appropriate.

There is no doubt that you have to establish SOA step-by-step, but sooner or later you will need management and business unit support. Which comes first is not that important and in a sense only determines whether central service teams such as an SCC and necessary resources are officially established or evolve informally, with more or less unofficial support by CIOs and/or CEOs.

19.4.4 SOA Drivers, by Anne Thomas Manes

Anne Thomas Manes comes to a similar conclusion. According to [Manes07], there are four typical driving forces behind SOA. SOA might be:

Developer-driven (grass roots)
> This approach leads to experience and technology expertise but includes the risk of being uncoordinated and noncollaborative.

Business-project-driven
> This approach usually leads to a proof of concept or pilot, which, if it is successful, encourages further adoption. However, first isolated projects might have limited benefits, so you need some way to expand the SOA approach to cross-organizational collaboration.

IT-driven
> This approach is effective for infrastructure aspects but includes the danger of focusing *only* on those aspects, which often leads to an ivory tower.

Top-management-driven (mega project)
> This approach tries to introduce SOA from the top down, via a highly coordinated effort driven by business priorities. However, an approach based on the idea of making everything right from the beginning is usually expensive, disruptive, and very risky.

Again, none of these approaches usually works alone; in fact, you need a mixture of them all. SOA requires collaboration, right from the beginning. In other words, the best approach is to combine the developer-, business-project, and IT-driven approaches, bearing in mind that this is the first step of a strategy (which is a mega project overall but should not be handled as a mega project from the beginning).

19.4.5 Essence of Different SOA Approaches

If there is an underlying essence of all the different approaches to establishing SOA, it is as follows:

- You have to establish SOA step by step, in an iterative and incremental way.

- Sooner or later, you need management support.

- You need strong operational leadership when establishing a new strategy.

- You should take care with the initial pilot projects. They have to be successful and have some business relevance, but they should not be mission-critical.

- Collaboration is a key factor for success.

19.5 Additional Recommendations

In this section I want to mention some additional aspects regarding the introduction of SOA.

19.5.1 Policies

SOA policies are the rules and guidelines necessary to establish and live SOA. These policies define what's right from both a technical and an organizational point of view.

As written earlier, policies should evolve over time, because they are only useful if they are proven to be appropriate. Nobody can see ahead of time all the different requirements, contextual details, and flavors of a SOA strategy.

Note that there are two kinds of policies: those that are mandatory and those that are goals. Or, as Anne Thomas Manes describes it in [Manes07], a policy might be a "law" or a "guideline":

- A *law* is something that you have to follow. Laws should include all requirements that are key for the SOA objectives. For example, you might require that each service provider has to use a specific protocol (such as the Web Services protocol with the binding `document/literal wrapped`). This should be a law in case all infrastructure components are implemented according to this constraint.

- A *guideline* is something that you recommend, but that it might be possible not to follow. For example, a guideline might be that a service should be stateless or idempotent.

Discussing whether policies are mandatory or just recommended usually leads to several clarifications about processes and tools. Laws lead to simpler solutions, because you can skip other possibilities. On the other hand, laws have the potential drawback that they make development more complicated and may be inappropriate for some requirements.

Take, for example, the discussion about the service versioning policies in Chapter 12. How many versions of a service should or must be available simultaneously, at most? If you make a law about this, you need processes that deal with the case when there are more versions of a service in operation than allowed. If you make it a guideline, you should monitor violations, but you don't have to insist on consequences if they happen. Because in practice withdrawing an old service version is an investment in maintainability without an immediate business value, this example usually is handled as a guideline rather than a law.

As another example, consider how to deal with the policy that all service calls must be logged by a standard logging API. What happens if a service consumer doesn't follow this policy? Is it disallowed from using the service, or are exceptions possible? Of course, the best policies are policies that, once implemented, don't require any effort. For example, if the infrastructure provides standard mechanisms for logging service calls, this can easily be made a law instead of a guideline.

Policies must be defined for different topics, and these policies lead to different consequences. In one project I worked on, we had a *policy table* with columns listing the following information:

- The topic
- The policy (approach) to deal with this topic
- Whether the policy is mandatory (a law or a guideline)
- The consequences for the infrastructure/ESB
- The consequences for service providers
- The consequences for service consumers

Table 19-1 gives an example of what some possible entries in such a table might look like (don't take the contents of the table as recommendations; it contains only fictive examples to demonstrate the concept).

TABLE 19-1. Possible format of a policy table

Topic	Policy	Mandatory	Infrastructure	Provider	Consumer
Privacy	DMZ. Consumers have to ensure that no misuse is possible.	Yes	Provides auditing (monitoring)	Has nothing to do	Has to make sure that service calls and/or processing results is allowed
MEPs	Only synchronous request/reply and asynchronous publish/subscribe patterns are allowed.	Yes	Provides APIs for only these two MEPs	Has to specify MEP for each service	Has to use corresponding API
Number of versions	There should be only three versions of a service in production.	No	Nothing (technically service versions are different services)	Should mark old service versions as deprecated	Should upgrade to newer service versions whenever possible
Idempotency	Services should be idempotent.	No	Provides optional support for making services idempotent	Has to flag services that should become idempotent and provide a way to store data to deal with retries	Has to use a special API/library for idempotent service calls

The exact format of a policy description doesn't matter, as long as you have a form that makes it transparent what the policy for a given topic is, and what this means for the infrastructure, providers, and consumers.

19.5.2 Dealing with People

Introducing a new strategy such as SOA is a change that impacts pretty much everyone in an organization. There can be a wide range of consequences and reactions. There might be people who are keen on it, there might be people who fear and resist it, there might be people who are skeptical, and there might be people who want to keep or gain control. For this reason, change is often hard to initiate and even harder to sustain.

Fearless Change, by Mary Lynn Manns and Linda Rising (Addison-Wesley; see [MannsRising04]), provides several proven techniques, formulated as patterns, for implementing change in organizations or teams of all sizes. I strongly recommend reading it.

19.5.3 SOA Maturity Models

There are different ways to implement SOA, and there are also different expansion stages (see Chapter 6). So, it is no surprise that the concepts of maturity models such as Capability Maturity Model Integration (CMMI) and the Software Capability Maturity Model (SW-CMM; formerly CMM) are being transferred to SOA.

The CMMI (see [CMMI]) deals with five levels of maturity:

- Level 1: Initial
- Level 2: Managed
- Level 3: Defined
- Level 4: Quantitatively managed
- Level 5: Optimizing

Similarly, SOA maturity models deal with different levels of maturity regarding the SOA concept.

For example, Sonic's SOA Maturity Model, which came out in 2005 (see [SOAMM] for details), lists the following levels of maturity (see Figure 19-4):*

- Level 1 is when you provide services that "represent the initial learning and initial project phase of SOA adoption."
- Level 2 is when you provide services using standards that "are set as to the technical governance of SOA implementation."

---

* This figure is printed with friendly permission based on the New SOA Maturity Model © 2005 by Sonic Software Corporation, AmberPoint Inc., BearingPoint Inc., Systinet Corporation. All rights reserved.

- Level 3 is when you provide services "on the partnership between technology and business organizations in order to assure that the use of SOA provides clear business responsiveness."

- Level 4 is when you focus "on the implementation of internal and/or external business processes."

- Level 5 is when you have "optimized business processes SOA," so that "the SOA information systems becomes [sic] the 'enterprise nervous system.'"

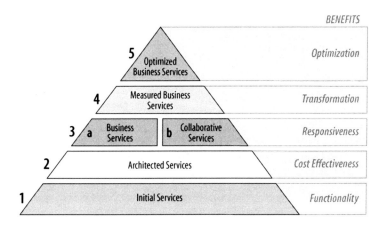

FIGURE 19-4. SOA maturity model by Sonic Software

IBM has developed another model. Here's what the web site has to say about it (see [SIMM]):

> At IBM, we have been working on a maturity model and process for achieving desirable stages of maturity, a model called the Service Integration Maturity Model (SIMM). The level of de-coupling and amount of flexibility achievable at each stage of maturity are what make up the following seven levels of maturity:
>
> 1. Silo (data integration)
>
> 2. Integrated (application integration)
>
> 3. Componentized (functional integration)
>
> 4. Simple services (process integration)
>
> 5. Composite services (supply-chain integration)
>
> 6. Virtualized services (virtual infrastructure)
>
> 7. Dynamically reconfigurable services (eco-system integration)

Based on this, IBM has introduced a model for "the incremental scope of SOA adoption" (see Figure 19-5).*

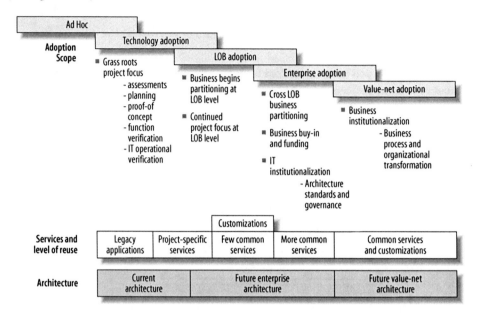

FIGURE 19-5. Scopes of SOA adoption by IBM

You'll have to decide for yourself whether or not the idea of a maturity model for SOA is useful. The good thing is that it again demonstrates that establishing SOA is an incremental process. The problem with the maturity model is that it might lead to the impression that it's important to reach the highest level of maturity, and appropriate to do so in all situations. However, flexibility, loose coupling, and distribution have their drawbacks, so the business case should be carefully monitored for each level of maturity.

19.6 Summary

- You can't buy SOA. You can only buy some tools that will help you implement a SOA strategy.

- Governance is necessary to avoid chaos and/or a waste of money and resources.

- You need a central SOA team to govern the establishment and living of SOA. However, this team has to understand itself as service provider for the business teams and should ideally have the goal of making itself unnecessary.

- Strong leadership and management support are essential for the success of SOA.

- Collaboration is a key success factor.

---

* This figure is printed with friendly permission by Ali Arsanjani, IBM.

- Think big, start small. Be careful with the initial pilot projects, and be aware that your SOA will evolve as you live it.
- Use reviews and retrospectives (both internal and external) to ensure that you have the right decisions, solutions, priorities, and processes.

CHAPTER TWENTY

Epilogue

NOW THAT I'VE PRESENTED AND DISCUSSED SOA IN DEPTH, IT'S TIME TO RETHINK THE ANSWERS TO several questions that are commonly asked about SOA.

20.1 Is SOA Something New?

SOA does not introduce any newly invented concept. It is a paradigm that brings together existing concepts and practices for a specific set of requirements. You might even say that SOA is nothing but the application of brainpower and pragmatism for distributed systems. Look at existing successful integrated large system landscapes, and you will find all the concepts mentioned in this book.

One improvement of SOA might be the fact that Web Services (despite all its flaws) introduces a new standard for interoperability.

Another important aspect of SOA, which represents a revolutionary approach different from what we've typically seen before, is the acceptance of heterogeneity. In the past, far too many solutions were based on the idea of homogenization. Yet in systems beyond a certain size, homogeneity is simply not possible. Homogeneity does not scale, which means that any approach that requires homogeneity will sooner or later fail.* Accepting heterogeneity changes the way we design large system landscapes. This mental shift might be a small step, but it can have dramatic consequences (similar to agile programming, which accepts that requirements change instead of trying to fight against this fact).

20.2   Does SOA Increase Complexity?

There is no doubt that distributed processing is more complicated than nondistributed processing. To deal with large systems and different owners, collaboration and loose coupling are required. But as I've pointed out, any form of loose coupling increases complexity. In addition, distributed debugging and testing requires a lot more effort than debugging and testing in an environment where everything is under central control.

For this reason, SOA should never be an end in itself. If you can avoid distributed processing, avoid it.

However, if you are required to distribute business processes over systems that are under the control of different owners, SOA can help you deal with the complexity of this problem (thereby, in a sense, reducing the complexity).

20.3   What Are the Key Success Factors for SOA?

As with any new strategy, a lot of aspects are important in making SOA a success story. You must begin with an appropriate understanding, realistic expectations, and the right people, and you must work to discover and formulate appropriate technologies and processes. Therefore, my usual answer to this question incorporates the following elements:

Understanding
> You must know up front that SOA is far more than just an infrastructure.

Collaboration
> You must work to create an organizational culture in which people want to help and serve.

Management support
> Management must be persuaded to give enough support (time and money) and be able to make appropriate organizational decisions if necessary.

Careful introduction
> A time frame of three or more years should be permitted for the introduction of SOA, and you must build in the ability to adjust things based on first experiences.

Homework
> Enough care for excellence must be taken that all teams are keen on making (your) SOA.

---

* Failure does not necessarily mean that the resulting systems do not run (although this is what often happens). As Bjarne Stroustrup wrote in [Stroustrup00], "It seems that essentially every approach, however ill conceived and however cruel to the individuals involved, also works for a large project, provided you are willing to throw indecent amounts of time and money at the problem."

As I've stated several times, what all this boils down to is the following four words: you can't buy SOA.

20.4   Where Is SOA Not Appropriate?

You might have the impression or expectation that SOA, as a solution for distributed processes, is appropriate for any form of communication between different systems. But of course, there are limits for SOA. The requirements might be too tough, or the overhead SOA introduces might lead to more problems than it solves.

Database replication, mass data processing, and local clients are not particularly SOAs strengths. You might benefit from concepts and solutions based on the SOA approach, but don't forget that SOA, like any other concept, technology, or paradigm, is no silver bullet.

Note that the question should never be whether or not something is appropriate for SOA; rather, the question is whether or not the solution you're considering is appropriate for your problem(s) and requirements.

I see the counter-hype to SOA coming in a few years. Finding that the price for distribution and loose coupling is too high, we might go back to the roots of software silos (of course, using a new, positive term such as "general-contractor-driven architecture").

20.5   Does SOA Replace OOP?

Another common question has to do with whether SOA replaces object-oriented programming (OOP), or which one is better.

An interesting answer is given in the book *Enterprise SOA*, by Dan Woods and Thomas Mattern (O'Reilly). Under the section titled "Why is service orientation better than object orientation?" two small paragraphs appear. The first explains OOP with the following limitation: "However, the calling application must be written in the same language as the object it is trying to access." The second paragraph consists of only one sentence: "Web Services provide a standard way to communicate between services, which may be written in different languages."

This whole discussion, of course, is rubbish. A comparison of OOP and SOA simply makes no sense, because they serve different purposes.

Neither SOA nor OOP is better than or replaces the other. OOP is a *programming* paradigm for applications, while SOA is an *architectural* paradigm for system landscapes. OOP doesn't scale, because you can control and manage your object model only up to a certain size. SOA is the approach to use to connect systems written in object-oriented or other paradigms. In other words, unless you only have to manage a single program, you need both.

References

THIS APPENDIX LISTS ALL THE REFERENCES MENTIONED OR CITED IN THIS BOOK. I CERTAINLY DO NOT claim that this is a comprehensive list of SOA references, but these references were important for me and my book.

Web sites are typically more volatile than books and articles, so the Internet links listed here may not be valid in the future. For this reason, I will maintain this list on the book's web site (I expect this site to be stable):

http://www.soa-in-practice.com

[ActiveBPEL]
ActiveBPEL Open Source Engine Project. *http://www.activebpel.org*.

[Allen06]
Allen, Paul. 2006. *Service Orientation: Winning Strategies and Best Practices*. Cambridge, UK: Cambridge University Press.

[Bartonitz05]

Bartonitz, Martin. 2005. "BPMS, BPML, BPEL, BPMN, WMS, XPDL,...'Alles so schön bunt hier'" (in German). *http://www.bpm-guide.de/articles/17*.

[Bartonitz06]

Bartonitz, Martin. 2006. "Wachsen die BPM- und Workflow-Lager zusammen?" (in German). *http://www.bpm-guide.de/articles/66*.

[BassClementsKazman03]

Bass, Len, Paul Clements, and Rick Kazman. 2003. *Software Architecture in Practice*, Second Edition. Boston, MA: Addison-Wesley.

[BloombergSchmelzer06]

Bloomberg, Jason and Ronald Schmelzer. 2006. *Service Orient or Be Doomed!: How Service Orientation Will Change Your Business*. Hoboken, NJ: John Wiley & Sons.

[Booch06]

Booch, Grady. 2006. Blog for March 2006, "SOA Best Practices," March 11, 2006. *http://www.booch.com/architecture/blog.jsp?archive=2006-03.html*.

[BPDM]

Business Process Definition Metamodel (BPDM). *http://www.omg.org/bpdm/*.

[BPMN]

Business Process Modeling Notation. *http://www.bpmn.org*.

[Brooks95]

Brooks, Frederick P. 1995. *The Mythical Man-Month: Essays on Software Engineering, Anniversary Edition (2nd Edition)*. Reading, MA: Addison-Wesley.

[BrownEllis04]

Brown, Kyle and Michael Ellis. 2004. "Best practices for Web services versioning." *http://www-128.ibm.com/developerworks/webservices/library/ws-version/*.

[Butek03]

Butek, Russell. 2003. "Which style of WSDL should I use?" *http://www-128.ibm.com/developerworks/webservices/library/ws-whichwsdl/*.

[Chappell04]

Chappell, David A. 2004. *Enterprise Service Bus*. Sebastopol, CA: O'Reilly Media.

[CMMI]

Software Engineering Institute of the Carnegie Mellon University, The Capability Maturity Model Integration Web Site. *http://www.sei.cmu.edu/cmmi/cmmi.html*.

[DesignByContract]

"Building bug-free O-O software: An introduction to Design by Contract." *http://archive.eiffel.com/doc/manuals/technology/contract/*.

[Dreyfus06]
Dreyfus, Paul et al. 2006. "What's the best software to implement as a service if you're just starting SOA?" *http://www-128.ibm.com/developerworks/library/ar-itio4/.*

[ebXML]
Electronic Business using eXtensible Markup Language. *http://www.ebxml.org.*

[Eckstein04]
Eckstein, Jutta. 2004. *Agile Software Development in the Large.* New York: Dorset House.

[Erl05]
Erl, Thomas. 2005. *Service-Oriented Architecture: Concepts, Technology, and Design.* Upper Saddle River, NJ: Prentice Hall.

[ESB Inventor]
"'ESB Inventor' Riddle Solved?" *http://www.businessreviewonline.com/blog/archives/2005/08/ esb_inventor_ri.html* and *http://www.looselycoupled.com/blog/lc00aa00109.html.*

[Gartner96]
Gartner (Roy W. Schulte, Yefim V. Natis). 1996. "'Service Oriented' Architectures," Parts 1 and 2. *http://www.gartner.com/DisplayDocument?id=302868* and *http://www.gartner.com/ DisplayDocument?id=302869.*

[Gartner03]
Gartner (Yefim V. Natis). 2003. "Service-Oriented Architecture Scenario." *http://www. gartner.com/DisplayDocument?doc_cd=114358.*

[Gartner05]
Gartner (D. Cearley, J. Fenn, and D. Plummer). 2005. "Gartner's Positions on the Five Hottest IT Topics and Trends in 2005." *http://www.gartner.com/DisplayDocument?id=480912.*

[Gartner06]
Gartner (Paolo Malinverno). 2006. "Service-Oriented Architecture Craves Governance." *http://www.gartner.com/DisplayDocument?id=488180.*

[GartnerEDA06]
Gartner (Yefim V. Natis and Roy W. Schulte). 2006. "Advanced SOA for Advanced Enterprise Projects." *http://mediaproducts.gartner.com/reprints/oracle/141940.html.*

[GoF95]
Gamma, Erich, Richard Helm, Ralph Johnson, and John Vlissides. 1995. *Design Patterns: Elements of Reusable Object-Oriented Software.* Boston, MA: Addison-Wesley.

[HintonHondoHutchison05]
Hinton, Heather, Maryann Hondo, and Dr. Beth Hutchinson. 2005. "Security Patterns within a Service-Oriented Architecture" (Parts I and II). *http://www.ebizq.net/topics/soa/ features/6535.html* and *http://www.ebizq.net/topics/soa/features/6554.html.*

[HohpeWoolf04]

Hohpe, Gregor and Bobby Woolf. 2004. *Enterprise Integration Patterns*. Boston, MA: Addison-Wesley.

[ISO10181-3]

ISO/IEC 10181-3:1996 – "Security frameworks for open systems: Access control framework." *http://www.iso.org/iso/en/CatalogueDetailPage.CatalogueDetail?CSNUMBER=18199.*

[ITSecCity02]

"Konzeption und Umsetzung von Disaster Recovery-Strategien: Stillstand ist tödlich" (in German). *http://www.itseccity.de/?url=/content/fachbeitraege/grundlagen/020315_fac_gru_veritas.html.*

[KannegantiChodavarapu07]

Kanneganti, Ramarao and Prasad A. Chodavarapu. 2007. *SOA Security in Action*. Greenwich, CT: Manning.

[KrafzigBankeSlama04]

Krafzig, Dirk, Karl Banke, and Dirk Slama. 2004. *Enterprise SOA: Service-Oriented Architecture Best Practices*. Upper Saddle River, NJ: Prentice Hall.

[KrafzigSlama07]

Krafzig, Dirk and Dirk Slama. 2007. Handouts of a talk at the 6th OMG Information Days in Germany. SIGS Datacom.

[Levitt01]

Levitt, Jason. "From EDI To XML And UDDI: A Brief History of Web Services." *InformationWeek*, Oct. 1, 2001. *http://www.informationweek.com/shared/printableArticle.jhtml?articleID=6506480.*

[MagicBus]

Lyrics of the song "Magic Bus" by The Who. *http://www.lyricsdir.com/the-who-magic-bus-lyrics.html* and *http://petetownshend.lyrics.info/themagicbus.html.*

[Manes03]

Manes, Anne Thomas. 2003. *Web Services: A Manager's Guide*. Boston, MA: Addison-Wesley.

[Manes07]

Manes, Anne Thomas. 2007. Handouts of a talk at OOP 2007. SIGS Datacom.

[MannsRising04]

Manns, Mary Lynn and Linda Rising. 2004. *Fearless Change: Patterns for Introducing New Ideas*. Boston, MA: Addison-Wesley.

[McKusickBosworth03]

McKusick, Kirk and Adam Bosworth. "Building Web Services: A Conversation with Adam Bosworth." *ACM Queue* Vol. 1 No. 1, March 2003. *http://www.acmqueue.org/modules.php?name=Content&pa=showpage&pid=29.*

[NewcomerLomow05]
Newcomer, Eric and Greg Lomow. 2005. *Understanding SOA with Web Services*. Boston, MA: Addison-Wesley.

[OasisSoaRM06]
"Reference Model for Service Oriented Architectures," Committee Draft 1.0, February 7, 2006. *http://www.oasis-open.org/committees/download.php/16587/wd-soa-rm-cd1ED.pdf*.

[oAW]
openArchitectureWare. *http://www.openarchitectureware.org*.

[ProjectLiberty]
Liberty Alliance Project. *http://www.projectliberty.org*.

[PulierTaylor06]
Pulier, Eric and Hugh Taylor. 2006. *Understanding Enterprise SOA*. Greenwich, CT: Manning.

[SAML]
The Security Assertion Markup Language. *http://www.oasis-open.org/committees/security/*.

[Sanctum04]
Blind XPath Injection. *http://www.packetstormsecurity.org/papers/bypass/Blind_XPath_Injection_20040518.pdf*.

[SIMM]
Arsanjani, Ali and Kerrie Holley. 2005. "Increase flexibility with the Service Integration Maturity Model (SIMM)." *http://www-128.ibm.com/developerworks/webservices/library/ws-soa-simm*.

[SOAMM]
Sonic Software (Jon Bachman). 2005. "SOA Maturity Model" and "Movin' SOA On Up." *http://www.sonicsoftware.com/soamm* and *http://www.sonicsoftware.com/solutions/learning_center/soa_insights/movin_soa_on_up*.

[Spanyi03]
Spanyi, Andrew. 2003. *Business Process Management is a Team Sport: Play It to Win!* Tampa, FL: Anclote Press.

[StahlVölter06]
Stahl, Thomas and Markus Völter. 2006. *Model-Driven Software Development: Technology, Engineering, Management*. Hoboken, NJ: John Wiley & Sons.

[Stroustrup00]
Stroustrup, Bjarne. 2000. *The C++ Programming Language*, Special Third Edition. Boston, MA: Addison-Wesley.

[ThreeStrikes]
Web Services Federation Language. *http://c2.com/cgi/wiki?ThreeStrikes*.

[UBR]
UDDI Business Registry. *http://www.uddi.org/find.html.*

[WfMC]
Workflow Management Coalition. *http://www.wfmc.org.*

[Wong02]
Wong, Wylie. 2002. "Microsoft ploy to block Sun exposed." *http://news.com.com/2100-1001-912906.html.*

[WS-BPEL]
OASIS Web Services Business Process Execution Language. *http://www.oasis-open.org/committees/wsbpel.*

[WS-BPEL4people]
WS-BPEL Extension for People. *http://www-128.ibm.com/developerworks/webservices/library/specification/ws-bpel4people/.*

[WSDL 1.1]
Web Services Description Language (WSDL) 1.1. *http://www.w3.org/TR/wsdl.*

[WSDL 2.0]
Web Services Description Language (WSDL) Version 2.0 Part 0: Primer. *http://www.w3.org/TR/wsdl20-primer/.*

[WS-Federation]
Web Services Federation Language. *http://www.128.ibm.com/developerworks/library/specification/ws-fed.*

[WSFL]
Web Services Flow Language. *http://www.ibm.com/software/solutions/webservices/pdf/WSFL.pdf.*

[WS-Glossary]
W3C (H. Hass and A. Brown). "Web Services Glossary." *http://www.w3.org/TR/ws-gloss.*

[WS-I]
Web Services Interoperability Organization. *http://www.ws-i.org* and *http://www.ws-i.org/press/pressrelease.aspx?pr=20020206a.*

[WSI-BasicProfile]
WS-I Basic Profile, Version 1.1. *http://www.ws-i.org/Profiles/BasicProfile-1.1.html.*

[WSI-SecurityProfile]
WS-I Basic Security Profile, Version 1.0. *http://www.ws-i.org/Profiles/BasicSecurityProfile-1.0.html.*

[WS-SecureConversation]
Web Services Secure Conversation Language. *http://www-128.ibm.com/developerworks/library/specification/ws-secon/.*

[WS-Security]

Web Services Security v1.1. *http://www.oasis-open.org/committees/download.php/16790/wss-v1.1-spec-os-SOAPMessageSecurity.pdf.*

[WS-SecurityPolicy]

Web Services Security Policy Language. *http://www-128.ibm.com/developerworks/webservices/library/specification/ws-secpol/.*

[WSStandards]

Web Services Standards Overview. *http://www.innoq.com/resources/ws-standards-poster/* and *http://www.innoq.com/soa/ws-standards/.*

[WS-Trust]

Web Services Trust Language. *http://www-128.ibm.com/developerworks/library/specification/ws-trust.*

[XMLEncryption]

W3C (D. Eastlake et al.). XML Encryption Syntax and Processing, World Wide Web Consortium Recommendation, December 2002. *http://www.w3.org/TR/2002/REC-xmlenc-core-20021210.*

[XMLKeyMan]

W3C (Phillip Hallam-Baker, Shivaram H. Mysore). XML Key Management Specification (XKMS 2.0), World Wide Web Consortium Recommendation, June 2005. *http://www.w3.org/TR/xkms2/.*

[XMLSignature]

W3C (D. Eastlake et al.). XML-Signature Syntax and Processing, World Wide Web Consortium Recommendation, February 2002. *http://www.w3.org/TR/xmldsig-core.*

Glossary

This glossary lists the most important specific SOA terms used in this book. Because sometimes there is no common definition of SOA terms it also serves to define my view of terminology used in this book. Terms used in the definitions that are themselves entries in the glossary appear in italics.

See [WS-Glossary] for another glossary of the Web Services community.

Note that this glossary will be maintained on this book's web site:

http://www.soa-in-practice.com.

2PC (two-phase commit)   An approach for maintaining consistency over multiple systems. In the first phase, all backends are asked to confirm a requested change so that in the second phase the commitment of the updates usually succeeds. In accordance with the principles of *loose coupling*, in SOA *compensation* is usually used instead of 2PC.

Activity   Possible term for one step in a *business process*. In the context of SOA, an activity is typically implemented by a *service*.

Agent   A *Web Services* term for *participant*, which is the general term for a *consumer* or *provider*.

Architecture   According to [BassClementsKazman03], the architecture of a computing system is the structure or structures of the system, which comprise software (and hardware) components, the externally visible properties of those components, and the relationships among them.

Asynchronous communication   A form of communication where there is a measurable time interval between the sending and receiving of the content of any *message*. *Message-oriented middleware* is typically implemented based on this concept by introducing message queues that queue (persist) messages sent by a system until they are accepted by the receiving system(s).

Asynchronous communication is a form of *loose coupling* because it avoids the requirement that the sender and receiver of a message must be available at the same time.

Asynchronous request/response   Another name for the *request/callback message exchange pattern*.

Backend   A system that maintains the data and/or business rules of a specific *domain*. Usually, it provides a specific role or has a specific responsibility in a system landscape. In SOA, a backend is usually wrapped by some *basic services*.

Basic service   Common term for *services* that provide basic business functionalities of a single *backend*. These services are usually part of the first set of services that wraps or hides implementation details of a specific backend. Basic services can be data-driven or logic-driven. They are the base for composing higher services such as *composed services* and *process services*.

BPEL   Business Process Execution Language. An *XML*-based language used to *orchestrate* services to *composed services* or *process services*. The resulting services are *Web Services*.

*IDE*s allow you to create BPEL files using graphical user interfaces. Engines allow you to run (and debug) services implemented with BPEL.

BPM   See *business process management* and *business process modeling*.

BPMN   Business Process Modeling Notation. A graphical notation for business processes maintained by the *OMG*.

Bus   An abstract software pattern used to transfer data between multiple systems. In contrast to the *hub and spoke* pattern, it uses a federation of components that all follow a common policy or protocol to send, route, and receive *messages*.

Business process   A structured description of the *activities* or *tasks* that have to be done to fulfill a certain business need. The activities or tasks might be manual steps (human interaction) or automated steps (IT steps).

Business processes might be managed (see *business process management*) and implemented using modeling notations such as *BPMN* or *EPC* or execution languages such as *BPEL*.

Some people differentiate between *workflows* and business processes by stating that business processes describe more generally what has to be done while workflows describe how activities or tasks should be carried out.

Business Process Execution Language   See *BPEL*.

Business process management (BPM)   A general term that refers to all activities carried out to manage (i.e., plan, implement, document, observe, and improve) *business processes*.

Business process modeling (BPM)   According to [BloombergSchmelzer06], "a set of practices or *tasks* that companies can perform to visually depict or describe all the aspects of a *business process*, including its flow, control and decision points, triggers and conditions for *activity* execution, the context in which an activity runs, and associated resources."

Business Process Modeling Notation   See *BPMN*.

Choreography   A way of aggregating *services* to *business processes*. In contrast to *orchestration*, choreography does not compose services to a new service that has central control over the whole process. Instead, it defines rules and policies that enable different services to collaborate to form a business process. Each service involved in the process sees and contributes only a part of it.

CMMI   Capability Maturity Model Integration. An approach to categorize and improve the product and software development processes of organizations. CMMI is an extension of SW-CMM (formerly just called CMM), which deals with the aspects of software development. Part of it is a model to categorize the maturity of an organization by different levels ("initial," "managed," "defined," "quantitatively managed," and "optimizing").

Compensation   An approach for maintaining consistency over multiple systems. In contrast to *2-phase commit*, compensation

doesn't update all the backends synchronously. Instead, it defines compensating activities to be performed in the event that not all corresponding updates of different systems succeed (regardless of whether the updates are performed sequentially or in parallel). As a consequence, this approach leads to *looser coupling* of systems; however, it might require more effort to implement. *BPEL* has direct support for compensation.

Composed service   Common term for *services* that are composed of *basic services* and/ or other composed services.

Consumer   General term for a system that has the role of calling ("consuming") a *service* (which is offered by a service *provider*). Another term used for this role is (service) *requestor*.

Contract   The complete description of a *service* interface between one *consumer* and one *provider*. It includes the technical interface (signature), the semantics, and nonfunctional aspects such as *service-level agreements*.

Sometimes a contract is also called a "well-defined interface."

CORBA   Common Object Request Broker Architecture. An *OMG* standard that allows remote access to objects of different platforms. Although its initial purpose was to provide an infrastructure to access distributed objects, CORBA can be used as a SOA infrastructure by focusing on its concept of Object by Value (OBV).

Domain   A definable (business) area or scope that plays a specific role and/or has a specific responsibility. In SOA this might be a company, a division, a business unit, a department, a team, or a system.

Domain-specific language (DSL)   A specific graphical or textual notation for a *meta model*. It allows you to specify the concrete behavior of a *model* in a precise, condensed, readable, and complete form.

EAI   Enterprise Application Integration (sometimes also just called Enterprise Integration, or EI). An approach to integrate distributed systems such that they use a common infrastructure (middleware and/or protocol). With this approach, for each system it is enough to provide and maintain only one adapter to the infrastructure, instead of a specific adapter for each of the systems with which it communicates.

The infrastructure might use a *bus* or *hub and spoke* approach.

SOA can usually be described as an extension of EAI that provides the technical aspect of *interoperability*. For this reason, the concepts of EAI can be considered as being a major part of or even the same as an *enterprise service bus*.

EDA   See *Event-driven architecture*.

Enterprise Application Integration   See *EAI*.

Enterprise service bus (ESB)   The infrastructure of a SOA landscape that enables the *interoperability* of services. Its core task is to provide connectivity, data transformations, and (intelligent) routing so that systems can communicate via *services*. The ESB might provide additional abilities that deal with security, reliability, service management, and even process composition. However, there are different opinions as to whether a tool to compose services is a part of an ESB or just an additional platform to implement composed and process services outside the ESB.

In addition, while tool vendors tend to define an ESB as something to buy, you might also consider a standard such as *Web Services* to be an ESB because, conceptually, they define all that is necessary to provide interoperability between systems (without the need to buy some specific hardware or software).

An ESB might also be heterogeneous, using various middleware and communication technologies.

You can consider *EAI* solutions as (part of) an ESB.

EPC   See *Event-driven process chain*.

ESB   See *Enterprise service bus*.

Event   A notification sent to a more or less well-known set of receivers (*consumers*). Usually, the receivers of an event have to subscribe for a certain type of event (sent by a certain system or component). Depending on the programming or system model, the systems sending the events (the *providers*) might or might not know and agree to send the events to the subscribing receivers.

You can consider events as part of the *publish/subscribe message exchange pattern*.

Event-driven architecture (EDA)   A software architecture pattern promoting the production, detection, consumption of, and reaction to *events*. Some consider EDA to be an extension of or complement to SOA; others consider EDA to be part of the SOA approach (a special *message exchange pattern* where the service *provider* sends a message to multiple *consumers*).

Event-driven process chain (EPC)   A graphical notation for *business processes*, mainly promoted by SAP.

Fire and forget   Another name for *one-way* messages (a *message exchange pattern* where a service sends a message without expecting a response).

Frontend   A system that initiates and controls business processes by calling the necessary *services*. That is, it acts as a service *consumer*. A frontend might be a system with human interaction or a batch program.

Governance   In general, a term that describes the task of "making sure that people do what's right." In SOA, governance is about architectural decisions, *processes*, tools, and *policies*.

HTTP   HyperText Transfer Protocol. The fundamental protocol of the World Wide Web. In a secure form (using *SSL* transport-layer security), it is called HTTPS.

Hub-and-spoke   An abstract software pattern used to transfer data between multiple systems. In contrast to the *bus* pattern, it uses a central component that coordinates all communication between senders and receivers.

IDE   Integrated development environment. A (usually graphical) project-oriented environment for the development of specific software.

Idempotency   The ability of *services* to deal with *messages* that are delivered more than once so that redeliveries do not have unintended effects.

In an unreliable network, if you don't receive a confirmation, you don't know whether a message was delivered (it is possible that the receiver processed the message and its response was lost). If you send the message again (to be sure the message gets delivered), the receiver should be able to deal with this second message in such a way that it does not produce an effect different from that of receiving the message only once. For example, if the message is a request to add money to a bank account, the receiver should add the money only once even if, for reliability reasons, the message was sent twice.

Interoperability   The ability of different systems to communicate with each other. Interoperability between different platforms and programming languages is a fundamental goal of *SOA*.

Note that standards do not necessarily ensure interoperability. For this reason, in the *Web Services* world a special organization called *WS-I* provides *profiles* to make the standards interoperable.

JMS   Java Message Service. The standard Java API for *message-oriented middleware* (MOM). Because it is only an API standard, it provides portability (allowing you to change the middleware while keeping the interfaces) but not *interoperability* (allowing you to use different MOM implementations).

Loose coupling   The concept of reducing the dependencies between systems.

There are different ways to decrease the tightness of coupling between systems, such as having different object models, using *asynchronous communication*, or using *compensation* instead of *2PC* to maintain consistency. In general, loose coupling leads to more complexity. For this reason, in a specific SOA you have to find the right amount of loose coupling.

Maturity model   A model to categorize the maturity of an organization by different levels. Most famous are the Capability Maturity Model (CMM) and its successor, the Capability Maturity Model Integration (*CMMI*). Following this approach, many organizations have developed SOA maturity models.

MDSD Model-driven software development. An approach where a significant amount of schematic code, which has the same structure but varies depending on the concrete situation, is generated out of an abstract *model*. In the context of SOA and this book, MDSD might also stand for model-driven *service* development.

Message A chunk of data sent around as part of a *service* call. *Message exchange patterns* define typical sequences of messages to perform service calls.

Message exchange pattern (MEP) A definition of the sequence of *messages* in a *service* call or service operation. This sequence includes the order, direction, and cardinality of the messages sent around until a specific service operation is done.

The most important message exchange patterns are *one-way*, *request/response*, and *request/callback* (asynchronous request/response).

For example, the request/response MEP defines that a *consumer* sends a request message and waits for the answer, which is sent by the *provider* as a response message.

Message-oriented middleware (MOM) Middleware that is based on the concept of *asynchronous communication*. Examples are WebSphere MQ (formerly MQ Series) by IBM, MSMQ by Microsoft, Tibco Rendezvous, and SonicMQ.

Meta model A description of a *model*. A meta model refers to the rules that define the structure a model can have. In other words, a meta model defines the formal structure and elements of a model.

Model An abstraction. In SOA, a model is typically used to specify *services*. With the help of *MDSD*, you can generate different code and other artifacts out of it. The structure of a model is typically described with a *meta model*. For the model, there are typically one or more specific graphical or textual notations (sometimes called *domain-specific languages*, or DSLs) that allow you to specify the concrete behavior in a precise, condensed, readable, and complete form.

Model-driven software/service development See *MDSD*.

OASIS Organization for the Advancement of Structured Information Standards. An international not-for-profit computer industry consortium for the development, convergence, and adoption of e-business and *Web Services* standards. See *http://www.oasis-open.org*.

OMG Object Management Group. An international, not-for-profit computer industry consortium for the development of enterprise integration standards. OMG's standards include UML, MDA, and *BPMN*. See *http://www.omg.org*.

One-way A *message exchange pattern* where a service sends a message without expecting a response. Another name for this pattern is *fire and forget*.

Orchestration A way of aggregating services to *business processes*. In contrast to *choreography*, orchestration composes services to a new service that has central control over the whole process.

For *Web Services*, *BPEL* is a standard for orchestration, for which development tools and engines are available.

Participant General term for a *consumer* or *provider*. Alternatively, in *Web Services* terminology, *agent* is used.

Policy A general rule or guideline. In SOA, policies have an impact on the infrastructure (*ESB*), the *provider*(s), and the *consumer*(s). A policy might be a mandatory law (such as a required naming convention) or a goal (such as the maximum number of versions of a service in operation).

Process   A structured set of steps (*activities* or *tasks*) to carry out to fulfill a certain need or reach a certain goal.

Different processes are involved in SOA: the goal is to implement *business processes*. To do this, you must have processes to establish and manage solutions and *services* (solution lifecycles, service lifecycles, and so on). Also, on a meta level, you have the process of establishing SOA and SOA *governance*.

Process service   A *service* that represents a long-term *workflow* or *business process*. From a business point of view, this kind of service represents a *macro flow*, which is a long-running flow of *activities* (services) that is interruptible (by human intervention).

Unlike *basic services* and *composed services*, these services usually have a state that remains stable over multiple service calls.

Profile   In the context of SOA and especially *Web Services*, a profile is a set of standards, each of specific versions, combined with guidelines and conventions for using these standards together in ways that ensure *interoperability*.

Provider   General term for a (part of a) system that has the role of offering ("providing") a *service*, which might then be used/called by different *consumers*.

Publish/subscribe   A *message exchange pattern* where a service *consumer* subscribes to get a notification message from a service *provider* when a certain condition or state occurs or changes.

The subscription might happen at design time or at runtime. If the provider doesn't know the consumer, this pattern is the base of *event-driven architecture*, where the notification is an *event*.

Registry   Registries manage services from a technical point of view, unlike *repositories*, which manage services from a business point of view. Registries manage all the technical details necessary for using services at runtime (signatures, deployment information, and so on). Usually, a registry is considered to be a part of the infrastructure (*ESB*).

Repository   Repositories manage services and their artifacts from a business point of view. That is, they manage interfaces, *contracts, service-level agreements*, dependencies, etc., to help to identify, design, and develop services. Unlike for a *registry*, the service description should be independent of technical details and infrastructure aspects. That is, it should not be necessary to change a repository when a company switches to a new infrastructure (*ESB*).

Request   A *message* that is sent by a *consumer* as an initial message in most *message exchange patterns* (see *request/response* and *request/callback*).

Sometime this term is also used as a synonym for a *service* call.

Requestor   Alternative term for *consumer* (mainly used in the context of *Web Services*).

Request/callback   A *message exchange pattern* where a service *consumer* sends a *request* message but does not block and wait for a reply. Instead, it defines a callback function that is called later, when the *response* message sent by the service *provider* arrives.

Sometimes request/callback is called *asynchronous request/response*.

Request/response   A *message exchange pattern* where a service *consumer* sends a *request* message and expects an answer.

Usually the consumer blocks until the *response* message sent by the service *provider* arrives. Sometimes, however, blocking is not required. In that case, there is a separation between synchronous and *asynchronous request/response*. The latter is also known as the *request/callback* message exchange pattern.

Response   A *message* that is sent by a *provider* as an answer to a service *request* (see *request/response*).

Service   The IT realization of some self-contained business functionality.

Technically, a service is a description of one or more operations that use (multiple) *messages* to exchange data between a *provider* and a *consumer*. The typical effect of a service call is that the consumer obtains some information from and/or modifies the state of the providing system or component.

Services can have different attributes and can fall into different categories. The most famous categorization differentiates between *basic services*, *composed services*, and *process services*.

A service is usually described by an interface. The complete description of a service from a consumer's point of view (signature and semantics) is called a "well-defined interface" or *contract*.

Service-level agreement (SLA)   A formal negotiated agreement between two parties, which in the context of SOA are usually a service *provider* and a service *consumer*. For a specific subject, an SLA usually records the common understanding about priorities, responsibilities, and warranties, with the main purpose of agreeing on the quality of the service. For example, it may specify the levels of availability, serviceability, performance, operation, or other attributes of the service (such as billing and even penalties in the case of violations of the SLA).

Service-oriented architecture (SOA)   There are various definitions for SOA. Some specify only that it is an approach for architectures where the interfaces are *services*. However, in a more specific sense (and according to my understanding), SOA is an architectural paradigm for dealing with *business processes* distributed over a large and heterogeneous landscape of existing and new systems that are under the control of different owners.

The key concepts of SOA are *services*, *interoperability*, and *loose coupling*. The key ingredients of SOA are the infrastructure (*ESB*), *architecture*, and *processes*. The key success factors for SOA are understanding, *governance*, management support, and homework.

Note that *Web Services* is not a synonym for SOA; Web Services are one possible way of realizing the *infrastructure* aspects of SOA.

SOAP   SOAP is the basic protocol of *Web Services*. As an *XML*-based format, it defines the format of the header and body of a Web Services *message*.

Formerly the acronym stood for "Simple Object Access Protocol," but because SOAP was neither simple nor for objects or access, the term now stands for itself.

The protocol still allows different types of message exchange. The most commonly used is the document/literal wrapped pattern.

Software architecture   See *architecture*.

SSL Secure Sockets Layer. A cryptographic protocol that provides secure communication over the Internet protocol *HTTP* (which is often called HTTPS then).

Task Possible term for one step of a *business process*. In the context of SOA, a task is typically implemented by a *service*.

Two-phase commit See *2PC*.

UBR The *UDDI* Business Registry, which was founded in 2000 with the intention of becoming a worldwide *registry* for public *Web Services*. However, the idea didn't work, and the UBR was switched off in 2006.

UDDI Universal Description, Discovery, and Integration. A *Web Services* standard for *registries*. Initially designed for the UDDI Business Registry (*UBR*), it now serves as a standard for the technical management and brokerage of Web Services.

W3C World Wide Web Consortium. An international consortium for the development of standards for the World Wide Web, which also develops SOA standards such as *XML* and *SOAP*. See *http://www.w3.org*.

Web Services A set of standards that serves as one possible way of realizing a SOA infrastructure. Initially started with the core standards *XML, HTTP, WSDL, SOAP*, and *UDDI*, it now contains over 60 standards and *profiles* developed and maintained by different standardization organizations, such as *W3C, OASIS*, and *WS-I*.

Workflow Similar to a *business process*, a description of the *activities* or *tasks* that have to be done to fulfill a certain business need.

Some people differentiate between workflows and business processes by stating that business processes describe more generally what has to be done while workflows describe how activities or tasks should be carried out.

WS General abbreviation for *Web Services*. Also used as common prefix for Web Services standards.

WSDL Web Services Description Language. An *XML*-based language that describes *service* interfaces from a technical point of view. Although it is a *Web Services* standard, WSDL can also be used for other infrastructures.

WS-I Web Services Interoperability Organization. An open industry organization that standardizes *Web Services* standards as *profiles* to make them interoperable. See *http://www.ws-i.org*.

XML eXtensible Markup Language. A human-readable general-purpose notation widely used for the description and exchange of data. Specific XML formats can be defined by and validated against an *XML schema definition*.

XML Schema Definition (XSD) A language used to describe a set of rules to which a corresponding *XML* document must conform in order to be considered valid. It includes a set of basic data types.

K

Kerberos, 174, 183
key success factors of SOA, 282

L

labeling, 250
landscape, 47
large distributed systems, 3
    bottlenecks, 4
    design of, 170
    heterogeneous systems, 3
    imperfections of, 4
    landscape maintenance, 3
    redundancy, 4
    tale of the Magic Bus, 4–6
    types of owners, 4
layers
    abstraction and distributed processes, 175
    binding, 212
    business layer, 179
    description of primary, 212
    ESB, 179
    infrastructure-independent, and Web
      Services standards, 227
    mapping, 55
    MEP (message exchange patterns),
      132–133
    MEPs and, 131
    messages, and constraints, 58, 179
    multiple users, 179
    problems with, 176
    process, 73
    security and, 175
    SOA and, 62
    special, 73
    SSL (Secure Sockets Layer), 177
    transport, 130
    transport-layer
      browsers, 55
      implementation tools, 55
      protocol HTTPs, 55
      security, 179
    validation, multilayers, 117
    workflow layers, 82
    WSDL and, 212
LDAP, 219
leadership, 273
legacy, 3
Liberty Alliance Project (LAP), 181, 187
lifecycles
    establishing, 269
    governance and, 263

    services and, 137
    WSDL and, 223
lifetime of data, 3
limit of SOA, 283
limits
    collaboration, 171
    orchestration and, 168
    signatures, 206
lists
    data types, 206
    meta models, 244
load balancing
    endpoints and, 52
    failover, 51
    statefulness and, 196
local services, 74
logging, 57
logic services, 64
logical architecture models, 109
loose coupling, 16, 30, 297
    2PC (two-phase commit), 44
    asynchronous communication
      advantages of using, 38
      choosing whether to use, 128
      correlation ID, 38
      drawbacks of using, 38
      race conditions, debugging, 38
      reply problems, 37
    binding, 43
    BOM (business object model), 38
    common object models, disabling effect
      of, 56
    compensation, 44
    complexity and, 282
    complexity of, 36
    data types
      advantages of using, 40
      disadvantages of using, 40
      heterogeneous, 38–41
      mappings, 40
      multiple address types, 41
      type checking, 42
      versioning, 45
    deployment, 45, 255
    ESB (enterprise service bus), 42
    fault tolerance, 35
    flexibility, 36
    forms, 36, 46
    mediators, 41
    point-to-point approach, 41
    process logic, 45
    repositories, 232
    scalability, 36

model, 240, 298
model transformation
    consumer-driven, 247
    (see also MDSD, transformation)
model-driven service development
    (MDSD), 237
model-driven software/service
    development, 298
modeling language, 241
modeling services, 81, 239
models
    choice of, 113
    cross-department domains, 111
    domain, 111
    logical, 110
    mixed, 111
    technical models, 112
modification
    versus bug fixes, 147
    of services, 140
MOM (message-oriented middleware), 298
    defined, 127
    MEP (message exchange patterns) and, 127
    message exchange, 124
    one-way messages, 127
    request/response, 127
    service calls, 124
monitoring, 143
    BAM and, 58
    ESB and, 57
    governance and, 265
monolithic systems, 101
MQ, 127
multiapplication support, 119
multichannel support, 119, 195
    stateful services, 197
multiclient capabilities, 177
multiple requests, 198
multiproject management, 268

N

name server, 52
namespaces
    higher data types, 206
    WSDL, 214
    WSDL 2.0 and SOAP 1.2, 216
national services, 74
network (see infrastructure; ESB)
networked SOA (see federated SOA)
new aspects of SOA, 281
nightly builds, 250
NIL, 205
nillable, 205

nonblocking request/response, 136
nonfunctional attributes
    backward compatibility, 148
    BPEL and, 172
    REST and, 228
nontechnical governance tasks, 263
not invented here syndrome, 104
notation
    BPEL and, 89
    services and, 246
notifications
    event-driven architecture, 134
    publish/subscribe and, 129
null semantics (see data types,
    reference semantics)

O

OASIS, 298
Oasis SOA Reference Model
    definition, 20, 31
    distributed systems, 13
    granularity, 30
    loose coupling, 30
oAW (openArchitectureWare), 258
objectives, 263
object-oriented programming (see OOP,
    object-oriented programming)
objects
    distributed, 23
    models, disabling effect of, 56
    OBV (Objects by Value), 23
    versus SOA, 23
    (see also SOAP, Simple Object Access
    Protocol)
observer pattern, 129
OBV (Objects by Value), 23
official process, 264
offline ability, of repositories, 234
OMG, 298
once and only once
    messages, 201
    reliability, 57
one-way, 298
    fire and forget, 125
    MEP (message exchange patterns), 125
    request/response, 125
OOP (object-oriented programming), SOA
    and, 283
open standardization, 220
openArchitectureWare (see oAW,
    openArchitectureWare)
operating system interdependence, 16
operations, in meta model, 245

orchestrated services, 67
orchestration, 298
    choreography
        and SOA, 97
        process chains, 97
        versus, 96–97
    customized service, 168
    design process drawbacks, 96
    EDA versus, 134
    limits of, 167
    REST and, 228
    of services, 67, 88
order management, 120
order of messages, 123, 128
organizational structures
    backends, 65
    profit centers and, 105
organizations
    collaboration, 104
    distribution, 102
    governance, 263
    incident management procedure, 104
    management support, 106
    model funding, 106
    monolithic systems, 102
    SOA and, 101
    solutions for, 103–105, 111
ownership
    different owners, 2
    domains, 13
    service modification and, 140

P

paradigm, 11, 21
parameters, in meta model, 245
participant, 24, 298
passwords, 174
payload, 203
PDP (policy decision point)
    policy enforcement point versus, 118
    security, 180
    validation, 118
PEP (policy enforcement point), 180
perceived process, 264
perfectionism
    expense of, 87
    large systems and, 4
    versioning and, 145
performance, 159
    security and, 181
    service quality and, 164
physical location of a service, 212
pilots
    copy-and-paste, 269
    first, 267

infrastructure, establishing, 268
    project approaches, 274
    second and third, 268
PIMS (platform-independent models), 242
platform dependencies
    fundamental data types, 44
    independence of, 43
    interaction patterns, 43
platform independence, 16, 63
platform-independent models (PIMS), 242
Plug and Play, 88
point-to-point
    connections, 50, 221
    encryption, 179
    security, 177
    Web Services and, 221
policies
    decision points, 118
    enforcement points, 118
    governance and, 263
    law versus guideline, 274
    three strikes pattern, 269
policy, 298
policy decision point (see PDP, policy decision
        point)
policy enforcement point (PEP), 118, 180
policy enforcement point (see PEP, policy
        enforcement point
port type, 212
portal, call center and, 119
portfolio management
    reusability and, 169
    services, 94
    (see also services,
        lifecycles)
post-conditions, 33
practice versus theory, ix
preconditions, 33
presentation of backend data, 114
presentation services, 117
prevalidation, user input, 117
process, 299
process logic control, 45
process services, 299
    business process chain versus, 135
    domains, 111
    human interaction, 114
    orchestration platform, 76
    third stage expansion and SOA, 71
process steps, 82
process-enabled SOA (service-oriented
        architecture), 71
processes
    governance, 263
    governance and, 263
    large systems and, 19

Nicolai M. Josuttis is an experienced systems architect and IT manager who is responsible for the successful realization of several large distributed systems. Recently, he spent three years rolling out a SOA at a major international phone company. He is well known to the IT community as an experienced speaker and is the author of *The C++ Standard Library* and *C++ Templates* (both for Addison-Wesley). He is always interested in the practical and appropriate application of technology and principles.

COLOPHON

The cover image is an original photograph overlaid with artwork by Mike Kohnke. The cover fonts are Akzidenz Grotesk and Orator. The text font is Adobe's Meridien; the heading font is ITC Bailey.

Lightning Source UK Ltd.
Milton Keynes UK
UKOW020357300413

209938UK00004B/126/P